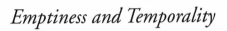

Emptiness and Temporality

Emptiness and Temporality

BUDDHISM AND MEDIEVAL
JAPANESE POETICS

Esperanza Ramirez-Christensen

STANFORD UNIVERSITY PRESS
STANFORD, CALIFORNIA

Stanford University Press
Stanford, California

Printed in the United States of America on acid-free, archival-quality paper

Library of Congress Cataloging-in-Publication Data

Ramirez-Christensen, Esperanza U.
  Emptiness and temporality : Buddhism and medieval Japanese poetics / Esperanza
Ramirez-Christensen.
      p. cm.
  Includes bibliographical references and index.
  ISBN 978-0-8047-4888-9 (cloth : alk. paper)
    1. Renga--History and criticism. 2. Buddhism and literature--Japan. 3. Japanese poetry--
1185-1945--History and criticism. 4. Shinkei, 1406-1475. Sasamegoto. 5. Poetics. I. Title.

PL732.R4R27 2008
895.6'1209382943--dc22   2007041851

Typeset by Bruce Lundquist in 10.5/14 Adobe Garamond

To Steen

Contents

Acknowledgments

This book began modestly as an introduction to the annotated translation of the medieval poetic treatise *Sasamegoto* (Murmured Conversations, 1463–64), one of two translation projects I undertook during a Mellon Foundation faculty fellowship at Harvard back in 1986–87. At the time, I was inspired by the intellectual fellowship of colleagues from the Western humanities to rethink medieval Japanese poetics from a comparative perspective that drew on my sense of the striking affinities between it and some critical concerns raised by Western poststructuralist theory. Since then, I have continued to reflect on these unexpected connections, while continuing work on the *Sasamegoto* translation project and the treatise's philosophical foundation in Buddhism.

Another appointment as faculty fellow in 1999–2000, this time with the Institute for the Humanities at the University of Michigan, provided me with the crucial mental space to disengage from the complexities of administrative and curricular issues, as well as from competing publication commitments, in order to bring to completion both the original translation project and the accompanying theoretical reflection recorded in this volume. I am grateful to all my colleagues and the staff members at the institute for contributing to the genial, intellectually liberating environment that enabled me to write again. Their lively reception of a medieval Japanese poetic form like *renga*, notably their participation in our "Stumbling Moon Renga Sequence," which would be the year's memento, was very heartening. The poet and classics scholar Anne Carson was positively bracing in her acuity and wit, as well as in her pregnant silences, and so were Aamir Mufti and Kathryn Babayan in their shared concern for the global political and humanistic implications of scholarly practices in the academy. I thank the younger scholars, particularly Jocelyn Stitt and Elise Frasier, for bringing the Fellows into dialogue with Michelle Cliff, a wonderfully unfettered

Jamaican novelist of colonial themes. The director of the institute, Tom Trautmann, made sure we had the resources to pursue our researches productively, and Eliza Woodford was unfailingly engaged when coordinating our rich program of seminars, invited lectures, and artistic events.

Thanks are also due my department chair then, Donald Lopez, for recognizing my need for a leave from teaching and administration and for recommending my work to the institute, along with Karen Brazell, Edwin Cranston, and Norma Field. Many other colleagues read drafts of the book and encouraged its publication over the years, and I have regrettably tried their patience by a tendency to be engaged in multiple research projects at once. Linda Chance did me the signal honor of reviewing the manuscript, and the *Sasamegoto* translation and commentary as well, for Stanford University Press. This was surely a time-consuming task; her dauntless alacrity in undertaking it fills me with grateful admiration. The publication of these volumes was subsidized by a grant from the Center for Japanese Studies of the University of Michigan. The completion of this project also owes much to the forbearance and steady moral support of my husband, Steen Norman Christensen, during a specially challenging period of my professional career. To all, including those unmentioned here, who remain strong in their conviction of the critical importance of the humanities in our time, I express my deep gratitude.

ER-C
Ann Arbor, Michigan

List of Abbreviations

The following abbreviations are used in the main text and Notes. For complete citations, see under title in the Bibliography, pp. 191–196.

FGS	*Fūgashū* (seventeenth imperial *waka* anthology)
HF	Ramirez-Christensen, *Heart's Flower*
JCP	Brower and Miner, *Japanese Court Poetry*
Kenkyū	Kidō, *Sasamegoto no kenkyū*
KKS	*Kokinshū* (first imperial *waka* anthology)
NKBT	*Nihon koten bungaku taikei*
NKBZ	*Nihon koten bungaku zenshū*
NKT	*Nihon kagaku taikei*
Oi	Shinkei, *Oi no kurigoto*
RH	*Rengaronshū Haironshū*, *NKBT* 66
RS	*Rengaronshū*, 1 or 2, ed. Ijichi Tetsuo
SKKS	*Shinkokinshū* (eighth imperial *waka* anthology)
SNKBT	*Shin Nihon koten bungaku taikei*
SSG	Shinkei, *Sasamegoto*
Tokoro	Shinkei, *Tokoro-dokoro hentō*

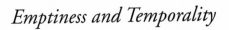

Emptiness and Temporality

Introduction

This is a book of poetic theory, philosophy, and critical practice. It deals primarily with medieval renga 連歌 (linked poetry composed by a group), waka 和歌 (the individual 5-line poem), the Nō 能 drama, and the aesthetic philosophy they all shared. It is intended, first of all, to provide a theoretical framework for understanding linked poetry and the poetic treatise considered most representative from the Japanese medieval period, *Murmured Conversations* (*Sasamegoto* ささめごと, 1463–64) by the poet-priest Shinkei 心敬 (1406–1475). I wrote the book with two general thoughts in mind. One was to uncover the larger philosophical context that generated the numerous Buddhist citations and allusions in the treatise, an analysis that early revealed the crucial importance of the twin concepts of emptiness and temporality for an understanding, not only of poetry, but of other Japanese medieval arts, such as black-ink painting and the Nō theater. My other thought was to draw medieval Japanese poetry and poetics into the contemporary Western discourse of poststructuralism, in particular the Derridean concepts of *différance* and deconstruction that first alerted me to

the structural necessity of the gap or spacing in renga, and in turn the affinity between Buddhist emptiness and deconstruction. The method I follow,
an intertwining of critical citation, explication, and poetic demonstration,
is irreducibly marked by a sense of the inadequacy of discursive language as
such to grasp what most eludes it in poetry. The method inscribes implicitly
my desire to promote the understanding of collective linked poetry and its
particular relevance for our globalizing times as an art that makes room for
every participant of a conversation, as a discursive practice that instead of
evading difference honors it by a strenuously demanding application of the
mind, in terms of dialogical confrontation and accommodation.

For readers coming from a Western literary tradition, the fascination of
renga would undoubtedly lie in its uniqueness as a poetic form, and then
in the way that form demonstrates marked affinities to the contemporary
critical re-discovery (the *re-* inscribes the present situation as a re-marking
of an older practice) of decentered structures, indeterminacy of meaning,
the instability of the notion of autonomous authorship, and the corresponding valorization of the reader's activity in the construction of a text. In the
following pages, I undertake a theoretical description of renga by way of
elucidating these startling affinities between a medieval Japanese poetic
practice and post/modernist critical and philosophical concerns. I insert a
slash here initially to indicate the difficulty of observing a strict distinction
between modernism and postmodernism in intellectual history. The break
with the past signaled by the decentering of the subject, of structure, and of
the West had already happened in the poetry of T. S. Eliot and Ezra Pound
(the *Cantos*, the *Cathay* poems), Yeats's reading of Nō as symbolist drama,
the hybrid renga/sonnet sequence produced in Paris by Octavio Paz and
three other poets; the multi-perspectivalism in the novels of André Gide
and Ford Madox Ford or the paintings of Picasso, and so on. In the field of
literary studies, I regard the distinction between modernism and postmodernism as principally one of sensibility. The modernist poets, closer to both
the classical traditions of Europe and the harsh immediacy of two world
wars, were still susceptible to the nostalgia and the anguish of loss; indeed,
the elegiac lyrical voice seems all they had left against the fragmented shards
from an exploded center. Contemporary postmodernists, on the other hand,
apparently view the end of humanism as a matter of indifference or, more
positively, as the liberation of the humanities into a field of Nietzschean play.
It seems to me that what is called postmodern in literary theory primarily
signifies that the decentering that took place in modernist poetry and the

visual arts became adopted as an approach, a mode of proceeding, in critical discourse itself, which has been in the wilderness for a long time now.

My initial aim here is wholly heuristic; it is to illustrate what a literary "structure" might look like that apparently answers to the contemporary deconstruction of the governing concepts (of author or subject and of organic unity) of orthodox Western criticism. My ultimate aim, however, is to situate medieval Japanese poetic practice and aesthetics within the discourse of Buddhist philosophy and religion, with the central Buddhist concepts of emptiness and temporality as the leading themes, renga and waka as the principal illustrative models for analysis, and the critical writings of Shinkei, Shunzei, Teika, and Shōtetsu as primary references. The book thus has three foci or, more accurately, it is woven of the three strands of medieval Japanese poetry and aesthetics, Western postmodernist theory, and Buddhist philosophy.

If I were to situate my project in the varied history of East-West cultural relations, it would find a resonance with the "Dialogue on Language" between a Japanese and an inquirer that opens Heidegger's 1959 work *On the Way to Language*.[1] There is here a mutual incomprehension between Heidegger and his native Japanese informant attributable to the German philosopher's lack of experience with Japanese cultural forms. In comparison, the Japanese shows a touching familiarity with Heidegger's works and ideas, and it is this, finally, along with a sincere desire for mutual comprehension on the part of each that enables the dialogue. What compels the reader's attention, then, is not what has been comprehended—which is not at all clear—but the event of two minds engaging each other, and the reader's too after them, to open a path toward some unnamed destination. What is notable is Heidegger's eager desire to discover if the vision toward which he was groping would resonate with and perhaps become clarified through dialogue with the Japanese.

This attitude is somewhat distinct from Derrida's more recent skeptical response, in an interview during his 1984 visit, to Karatani Kōjin's suggestion that even before its "discovery" in the West, deconstruction was already prefigured in Japan, given the absence there of a logocentric structure. In effect, Derrida questions "whether Buddhist thought or the Zen of Dōgen was already a kind of deconstruction."[2] That is indeed the question. In a 1987 article, David Loy would seem to answer it positively, when he compares the theoretical basis of Zen practice, Nagarjuna's Madhyamika "antiphilosophy," to Derrida's as "another form of deconstruction that antedates his by some nineteen centuries" and criticizes the latter for not going far enough in deconstructing only one term of an opposition instead of demolishing both and thereby arriving at the Zen sphere beyond logos or language.[3] The dialogue between the modern Western philosophers (especially Heidegger and Derrida) and Buddhist thought continues. In introducing the thought of both into this study, it is not my intention to resolve and clarify the issues on the field of philosophy per se, for that is not within my competence, but to demonstrate rather how these issues (of language and mind) operate in both the practice and critical discourse of medieval poetry. Thus the book, while intertextual in method, is ultimately focused on understanding the cultural products arising from a milieu strongly influenced by Buddhist ways of seeing and speaking.

In fact, the presence of Buddhist ways of understanding in the very structures and aesthetics of classical Japanese poetry has not, I feel, been adequately appreciated or rigorously examined in Western scholarship, and the situation, oddly enough, is little better in Japanese scholarship.[4] The reason, in the former case, is surely the former dominance in Anglo-American literary studies of the New Criticism, with its proscription, particularly in poetic analysis, of what were considered extraliterary factors, such as biography and philosophy. The Japanese case is more difficult to explain, but it is probably related to the anti-intellectual, intuitionalist orientation of Japanese literary critical writing (as distinct from the philological rigor of Japanese textual studies); in general, modern native scholars of classical poetry take the ubiquity of Buddhist themes and attitudes in premodern literature for granted; an obligatory nod to the idea of impermanence and the practice of medieval reclusion is deemed sufficient to confirm it. Common in both Anglo-American and Japanese cases, however, is a concern to mark out a territory for literature per se, to demarcate the boundaries of a discipline in the interest of preserving autonomy in an academy fragmented into various competing fields. Yet there is no need, surely, to belittle the achievements in rigor of the orthodox approaches of philology and New Criticism on both sides of the Pacific, or to ignore the illuminating insights of what in some quarters is dismissed as Japanese "impressionistic" writing. Contemporary critical practice is not likely to produce works equaling them either in philological rigor or literary insight.

Time, however, has moved on. The compartmentalizing of human knowledge attendant upon academic specialization was viable in the chastened period after the conflagration of world war, when the importance of the humanities was unquestioned. But it has proved inimical in our own globalizing times, when we are confronting the emergence of a new totalitarianism in the seemingly irrepressible conjuncture of high technology, economics, and a new world order, a global "empire" laying waste in its wake the farthest remnants of premodernity. The space for the study and reflection on the historical practices of man has dwindled to beggarly proportions within the academy, while outside its walls, "the end of history and the last man" has already been proclaimed. While this is not exactly a case of Nero fiddling while Rome burns, one must nevertheless question our own apparent lack of reflection about the state of our "civilization" while we stage the old quarrels between the ancients and moderns or—what is not even pertinent in medieval studies—studiously observe the borders between poetry and philosophy, literature and religion. This study straddles these disciplines. Shinkei, the principal author of the primary texts it examines, was both poet and Buddhist priest, as were many of his contemporaries in the various arts.

It is also my belief that it is time to restore the ancient vital kinship between poetry, sacred writing, and spirituality that was banished by the relentless secularization of the twentieth century, just as it is time to take a stand with third-world human beings everywhere, whose destinies must perforce remain an abiding concern of the humanities, instead of counting them merely as the objects of a cold discipline. Since, as this book observes, there are also startling congruences between premodern Buddhist philosophy and the deconstructive movement in contemporary Western thought, it becomes a compelling task to reflect on where the links lie, and, further, to suggest how deconstruction might be turned toward the ethical ends pursued by Buddhism as a way of mental liberation.

The book is divided into two parts. The first, "The Poetics of Renga," begins with a consideration of the known rules of renga structure, as demonstrated by the first twelve or so verses of the *Three Poets at Minase* sequence, if only to reject them as the sole or even leading moment in the extemporaneous unfolding of a sequence from verse 1 to 100. I felt, in other words, the necessity of underscoring the unpredictable element of fate or chance, contingency, in the movement of this poetry, which is only one of the several medieval arts that similarly honor the specific time and occasion, temporality as it inscribes itself in the verse continuum always for the first time. Subsequently, I focus on what I deem a central—though heretofore obscure—passage in Shinkei's treatise dealing with a principle of structural progression called *hen-jo-dai-kyoku-ryū* 辺序題曲流. In my analytical reading, this principle turns out to reveal that *tsukeai* 付合, the individual link from one verse to the next, which is also the dialogical process operating between two poets at any point in the sequence, can be described in several ways: first, as apparently a structure of signification, and then as a process of interpretation and displacement, which may also be expressed as figuration or metaphorization. In this section, the leading idea is the process of meaning-production from a gap, what Derrida calls *différance*, whose significance I generalize by association with what Shinkei calls "the *jo-ha-kyū* 序破急 of the myriad arts," wherein *ha* (the break, the breach) is in effect the spacing that enables both continuity and change in renga and Nō drama structure.

The book's second part, "*Kokoro*, or the Emptiness of the Sign," is the principal site for the drawing together of Buddhist and poetic/critical discourses only briefly raised in the affinity revealed in Part One between emptiness and différance. The starting point here is the distinction between the so-called Close Link (*shinku* 親句) and Distant Link (*soku* 疎句) in renga, and Shinkei's apparent valorization of the Distant Link in his equation of it with the formless (*musō* 無相), with emptiness (*kū* 空), and with Zen meditation. Meditation, in particular Tendai *shikan* 止観, "stillness and insight," is then foregrounded in a reconsideration of the *Shinkokinshū* poets' understanding of poetic process, and of the existence of the poem on three levels as provisionally real, simultaneously empty, and ultimately embodying the "truth of the middle."

Such an understanding raises the nature of medieval poetic symbolism and its ground in the Mahayana or Madhyamika way of looking at phenomena. In this view, a poem is neither a representation of meaning nor the expression of an inner feeling, but rather the evocation of the indefinable "aura" of phenomena when understood in three orders of being and projected upon the principle of the interpenetrability of all the dharmas in the Dharma realm (*dharmadhatu*). It is this "aura" that has heretofore been understood principally as connoting aesthetic qualities such as "ineffable depth" (*yūgen* 幽玄) and "overtones" (*yojō* 余情). In this book, the modern, specifically aesthetic construction of medieval poetry is revised in the process of showing the roots of such terminology in the Buddhist apprehension of the universe. In an important sense, therefore, poetry is here understood as the symbolic demonstration of a religious or philosophical system.

Hence, it is not sufficient to describe poetry as the endless play of différance, or the endless displacement and proliferation of signifiers. That would not be adequate to account for the view of poetic process as Zen meditation, and of poetic training as discipline in the mind-ground (*shinji* 心地). Rather than being an apparently perfect model of the dissemination of signs, poetry is viewed here first and foremost as the transformative power of the liberated mind (*kokoro* 心) to breach the predetermined meanings of the linguistic system, which is the same as to show the ultimate emptiness of the sign, and how it is precisely emptiness that enables the play of language, the infinite possibilities of metaphorization.

The book continues with an account of the aesthetic philosophy of distilled reduction (*hieyase*, "the chill and meager"), or the privative, that is considered Shinkei's contribution to a distinctively medieval Japanese aesthetic. At the end, two poems by Teika and Shōtetsu, cited as models of the mode of ambiguity, which is "constituted solely of nuance," and equivalent to the Dharma Body in *Sasamegoto*, are analyzed to show their outwardly serene, yet "inwardly" vertiginous configuration as demonstrations of the permeability of semantic boundaries and oppositions, and, in sum, as *dharani*s (see Glossary) of the tearing apart of the veil of illusion.

Although this book is inevitably limited by its "dependent origination" (*engi* 縁起), that is, its arising from the discourse of Shinkei and other medieval poets, my hope is that it will further the understanding of the past in order that we may grasp the new more clearly; that it may restore in our minds what has been historically forgotten or repressed and so condemns us to unthinking repetition. It is my conviction, as a native of the Philippines, a twice-colonized third-world country, that the knowledge practices of the modern industrialized nations have principally redounded only to the efficient exploitation of the poor of this earth. I believe, too, that the only way that the so-called humanistic sciences can justify themselves is to undertake an overturning of those hierarchically organized dualisms that again and again merely confirm the system of oppression that operates the global society we have constructed.

Surely the winners in the new world order will eventually become bored with such a one-sided game? But will they? Is there an end to the blindness of ignorance or is education, in particular the liberation of the mind from prejudice, an area that must be vigilantly cultivated again and again to avoid easy, mindless collusion with the powers of oppression? How do we teach the thought of différance and emptiness, of being and time, in a way that will make the earth inhabitable again by all of us, and not only by the fortunate few among us?

PART ONE

The Poetics of *Renga*

The Grammar of the *Renga* Sequence

Pragmatically considered, the structural uniqueness—or so to say, the initial impression of the otherness—of a renga poem is a product of two distinct factors; namely, that renga is composed extemporaneously by a collectivity of poets, a circumstance virtually unknown, and perhaps heretofore impossible, in the West; and two, that its poetic structure negates the traditional Western concept of an integral, teleological unity in a literary work and is not oriented to the production of any specific meaning. The hundred-verse renga *hyakuin* 百韻 neither narrates a continuous sequence of events nor delineates the nature of a particular feeling or thought through logical argument and poetic figures. Instead, various scenes, thoughts, and feelings are taken up for a moment only to be discarded in the next, without developing any one of them, so that nothing adds up to a total meaning. Renga progresses by continually frustrating the development of any single plot or thought. Like a pen that erases even as it writes, it takes away as much as it adds with every verse, so that the end is exactly the same as, yet infinitely changed from, the beginning. In contrast, of course, the classic Western structure, which also grounds the conventional Western method of reading, progresses by accumulating information in order to build up a meaningful design that is particular to each work and may be used to describe its integral form or to paraphrase its specific semantic content.

That the one hundred verses of a hyakuin do not add up to a cumulative meaning is clearly evident in the fact that it is not possible to distinguish a particular hyakuin from another by paraphrasing what it is about. In content, they are all the same. Renga is like a miniature waka anthology, in that it presents verses on exactly the same series of themes that the waka tradition had found sufficient through the ages to express human existence in the midst of nature. Even the vocabulary is the same, a poetic lexicon that centuries of monolithic composition on unvarying subjects had rendered so precisely and minutely differentiated that it became possible to distinguish the group of images and quality of feeling that would evoke each theme. Yet a renga hyakuin is clearly not just a shorter version of the waka anthology or even a waka *hyakushu* 百首 (hundred-poem sequence). The crucial difference is that it broke the primarily linear progression of the waka anthology in favor of a circular pattern of thematic recurrence decisive for its development as a distinct genre. In other words, renga adopted waka's poetic lexicon, with its already inscribed differentiations according to theme and emotional content, and fixed these into categories that could be the "parts of speech" of a wholly new grammar, one whose function would be to make the 100-verse continuum intelligible by giving it a coherent shape.

These grammatical rules, called *shikimoku* 式目, or "code," are many and various, but an analysis would show that they are grounded in the twin principles of continuity and change or, put more abstractly, similarity and difference.[1] Themes as well as new lexical categories developed in renga practice were governed principally by two rules. The duration, or seriation, rule ensured that once a particular theme was introduced, it would continue for a minimum number of verses, and the intermission rule ensured that other themes would intervene between occurrences of the same theme. The first prevented fragmentation on the one hand, while the other, which is its converse, prevented deadly monotony. For instance, Spring and Autumn must continue in a series for three to five verses; Love for two to five; and the remaining themes, along with the geographical lexical categories Mountains, Waters, and Dwellings followed behind at one to three verses.[2] The intermission for the same season was set at a minimum of seven verses; for the other themes, five. This means, for instance, that after a passage of three to five successive verses on Spring, that theme may not be repeated until at least seven verses on a different theme or themes have intervened. Further-more, "marked" words that belonged to closely associated pairs of images like tears = wet sleeves/weep, or dream = awakening/reality, were required to be separated by at least two verses, that is, if they did not occur, as would be natural, in immediate succession from one verse to the next.[3]

Thus, on the level of lexical similarity or contrast, while the sequence *aa'b*, or *abb'a'* is acceptable, *aba'* is strictly prohibited, because it produces a monotonous rhythm that is like the beat of metronome between two fixed points and retards the forward movement of the whole. This prohibition rule—called *uchikoshi o kirau* 打越を嫌ふ, "clashing of words across one-verse intervals," or, more expressively, *rinne* 輪廻, "karmic return," which any Buddhist knows is not good—governs the occurrence of similarity on the level of words rather than themes or categories. It also tells us that the functional unit of *yukiyō* 行様, or sequence, the progression of the whole, is not a pair of verses but three. In this basic triad, verse 2 is, of course, ex-pected to look back or link up to verse 1, but verse 3 may not do so, for it would precipitate the beginning of a retrogressive movement. In any series of three verses therefore, the third verse must draw the preceding two for-ward and out. In practice, this would mean that the poet must attend, not only to the immediately preceding verse, or *maeku* 前句, but also to the *mae-maeku* 前々句, the verse before the maeku. Historically, the *uchikoshi* rule must have had the same decisive significance on the level of lexical items that the principle of thematic recurrence had for the formation of the hyakuin as poetic structure. This is because it marks the decisive break with the more primitive *fushimono renga* 賦物連歌, where the 100 verses are literally just fifty paired units, each unit oscillating stiffly between the two fixed points of a binary topic like "Black and White" or "Fish and Fowl," instead of describing more complex movements of continuity and variation across larger blocks of verses, as in the fully developed hyakuin of the late Muromachi period.

Theoretically, the widest functional difference or contrast in the grammar of renga sequence would seem to be between thematic verses and nonthe-matic so-called *zō* 雑, or miscellaneous verses. In practice, however, the sec-ond level of contrast between the season themes (Spring, Summer, Autumn, Winter) and the *jinji* 人事, or what might be called human affairs, themes (Love, Travel, Laments, Shintō Rites, Buddhism) seems to be the domi-nant one. In other words, the movement of the verses within the 100-verse structure oscillates between the two extreme poles of purely seasonal and purely human themes, with the middle range occupied by "polyphonic" verses wherein these two major threads come together, as in the occurrence of compound themes like Spring + Love or Autumn + Travel in the same verse. Miscellaneous verses, when they do occur, apparently provide a transition between themes because of their neutral, "unmarked" character. The primary distinction between the seasonal and the human themes is useful because it parallels the alternation between high and low points in the sequence as a whole. There is a recognizably general pattern by which a passage of emotionally loaded and subjective verses gradually shades off into another that is purely seasonal and objective and has a calm, muted effect.

The brief sketch of the grammar of sequence above, and indeed the numerical character of the shikimoku themselves, indicate that the absence of a paraphrasable content that would serve to define a particular hyakuin simply manifests the fact that the one hundred verses as a whole are not intended to reveal meaning as such but to trace the path of a progression. Meaning in a renga sequence is not a quantity or content but a shape that writes itself always for the first time, as the sequence progresses, and as music that constitutes itself in time, in a process that can only be temporal and directly manifests itself as such. The musical analogy is not an idle one; renga was a discipline whose mastery required long years of training, and a renga session was like a musical performance, except that there was no written score to read from. Like the Nō drama, where the actors and musicians do not rehearse together before the performance, or the art of ikebana, where the flowers seem even more "natural" than in the wild, renga honors the spontaneous and contingent—that is, the coming into appearance of the particular time or occasion—paradoxically, through the strictest calculation embedded in rules and training.

Formally speaking, the succession of specific meanings and emotional colorings borne by the verses themselves are merely being employed as materials to mould or shape the movement of the whole as it evolves. In actually reading the poem, one perceives the movement as formal patterns of progression from simplicity to complexity, from impersonal evocations of scenery to highly charged expressions of personal emotion, from distant perspectives to details in close-up, from slackness to intensity, and so on along various binary axes that are both thematic and aesthetic in character. At its best, which is to say when it is composed with a highly conscious and deliberate eye for aesthetic effect, the art of yukiyō approaches the state of the plastic arts or of painting, which according to Piero della Francesca, "is merely a demonstration of surfaces and bodies becoming ever smaller or larger according to their term."[4] Or, to take an analogy from an art contemporary with renga, it is like calligraphy in the cursive style, where the original shapes and meanings of the successive graphs appear to dissolve into the formal, expressive properties of ink and brushstroke. In that model sequence, the *Minase sangin hyakuin* 水無瀬三吟百韻 (Three Poets at Minase, 1488), the aesthetic shaping of the verse continuum is so finely modulated that it is hard to believe the whole performance was extemporaneous. Let us briefly examine its first fifteen verses.[5]

1 yuki nagara
   yamamoto kasumu
   yūbe kana
      Sōgi

While snows remain,
the foothills are vaguely
hazy   the evening.
      Sōgi

2 yuku mizu tōku
   ume niou sato
      Shōhaku

Distantly the water glides past
a village tinged with plum flowers.
      Shōhaku

3 kawakaze ni
   hitomura yanagi
   haru miete
      Sōchō

A cluster of willows
waving in the river breeze:
   spring is apparent.
      Sōchō

4 fune sasu oto mo
   shiruki akegata
      Sōgi

Sound of a boat pole dipping
distinct in the paling dawn.
      Sōgi

5 tsuki ya nao
   kiri wataru yo ni
   nokoruran
      Shōhaku

The moon—does it
still through the coursing
night mists linger?
      Shōhaku

6 shimo oku nohara
   aki wa kurekeri
      Sōchō

Over fields covered with frost
autumn has drawn to a close.
      Sōchō

7 naku mushi no
   kokoro tomonaku
   kusa karete
      Sōgi

Mutely before
the crying insects,
grasses wither.
      Sōgi

8 kakine o toeba
arawanaru michi
Shōhaku

When I came to call, beyond
the hedge the path lay bare.
Shōhaku

9 yama fukaki
sato ya arashi ni
okururan
Sōchō

Deep in the mountains
is the village buffeted by
tempests all the long day?
Sōchō

10 narenu sumai zo
sabishisa mo uki
Sōgi

Unfamiliar dwelling—even
the loneliness is dismal.
Sōgi

11 ima sara ni
hitori aru mi o
omou na yo
Shōhaku

Every man
is ultimately alone—
stop brooding.
Shōhaku

12 utsurowamu to wa
kanete shirazu ya
Sōchō

Did you not know before
that all things fade?
Sōchō

13 okiwaburu
tsuyu koso hana ni
aware nare
Sōgi

The pathos of
a dewdrop pendent upon
the frail flower!
Sōgi

14 mada nokoru hi no
uchikasumu kage
Shōhaku

Remaining light of the sun
shimmering through haze.
Shōhaku

15 kurenu to ya
nakitsutsu tori no
kaeruran
Sōchō

For the dark gathers,
crying, do the birds fly
back to their nests?
Sōchō

The thematic path taken by the passage may be indicated thus: Spring (1–3)—Miscellaneous (4)—Autumn (5–7)—Miscellaneous (8–9)—Laments (10–12)—Spring (13–15). It starts out with Spring, moves through a single transitional verse (4) into Autumn, crosses another Miscellaneous bridge to emerge into the field of Laments, and from there returns to Spring. In this way thematic progression in renga may be characterized as a going forth and a coming back, but never to the exact same place. The point of return being modified by the "journey" out—which is, it turns out, also a journey back—it is the same yet also altered from the beginning. These wavelike, wide or narrow oscillations, these thematic comings and goings, in sum, the principle of modified recurrence from verse 1 to 100, mark the dynamics of the renga sequence. Again one should note the contrast between the objective seasonal scene evocations in verses 1–8 on the one hand, and the predominance of human affairs from verse 9, which assumes a tonally darker cast in the Laments passage 10–12, then tapers off in 13 to return to a generally impersonal mode in 14–15.

Within the predominantly seasonal verses of the first page of the renga manuscript (1–8), there is also a symmetrical juxtaposition of two opposed motions: the coming-into-appearance of spring in 1–3 and the disappearance of autumn in 5–7, which is punctuated in 8 by the finality of the image of *arawanaru michi*, a path wholly exposed and bare of growth. Within 1–3, spring's appearance is introduced by the rising haze upon the foothills of the *hokku* 発句 (opening verse); the remaining snow, understood to be on the peak, in turn comes to resonate with the gliding water of 2 through the unspoken suggestion that the snow on the foothills has melted into this water; we understand, furthermore, that the village of 2 is nestled among those foothills. The third verse initiates a movement toward specificity and particularization. The visual perspective, distant in the first two scenes, is nearer. We have drawn close enough to get a vivid view of tender green willows waving in the river breeze ("river" specifying the "gliding water" in verse 2). Thematically unmarked as such, verse 4 takes specificity further, reducing it to a point, so to speak, as the sound of a boat being poled along the river is isolated from the rest of the scenery. This sound accentuates the stillness as the night begins to grow pale; aesthetically, it is an aural counterpoint to the visuality of 3. *Shiruki* (distinct), a zeugma modifying both the sound and the whitening dawn in the verse as such, echoes *miete* (apparent) in 3. This conjunction in sense, however, simultaneously underscores a disjunction of reference (the subject of "apparent" in 3 is "spring"), and takes us away from spring into the Autumn passage beginning in 5.

The link between 4 and 5 is both temporal—the same moment is seen as the beginning of dawn in 4 and the lingering of the night in 5—and inflexional in that the adverbial *nao* (still, yet) is made to resound dialectically with the "distinct" dawning of 4. The functional value of *nao* as a semantic marker of temporal suspension in turn gives way to the definitive perfective inflexion of *kurekeri* (has already drawn to a close) in 6. The celestial image of the moon in 5 also yields to the contrasting terrestrial images of frost-covered fields, withering grasses, and bare path from 6 to 8 in a motion of exhaustion (of autumn) that seems somehow quite rapid compared to the measured slowness of spring's appearance in the beginning.

Viewed as a whole, this prelude passage from 1–8 progresses quite smoothly from 1 to 3, takes a slightly more complex turn in the transition from 3 to 5 (Spring to Autumn) through the bridging intervention of 4, and thereafter proceeds again smoothly from 5 to 8. In other words, from the perspective of tensility as the major aesthetic parameter in renga's linking progression, we may locate the greatest aesthetic tension in this passage in verses 3–5. By tensility, I refer to the continuity and difference from one individual verse to the next, as well as across larger passages, in terms of a perceptible aesthetic quality that one senses as one reads, as demonstrated by the verse analysis above. I use the term to designate the concrete aesthetic effect or actualization of the grammar of sequence.

The dialogue transpiring on the thematic field of Laments in 10–12 is prepared by 8–9. Verse 8, with its image of a visitor standing by the hedge, introduces the human world, which becomes geographically specified in 9 as a village deep in the mountains. The conversation between friends that subsequently transpires in 10–12 turns, appropriately, upon the loneliness of dwelling in such a remote location. It acquires a philosophical character with the construction of the immanent aloneness of each individual in 11, and the unspoken allusion to the inevitable fading of human relationships in 12; both are conventional sentiments belonging to the topos of Laments. The run from 9 to 12 is generally plain compared to the carefully minute design of the prelude. As before, it falls to Sōgi in 13 to effect a major shift, back to the Spring theme as it happens, and to the objective, impersonal mode that opened the sequence. This verse has the effect of compressing the meanings of the preceding prosaic statements into a tiny, concrete image that is simultaneously the ultimate symbol of evanescence: a single dewdrop upon the equally transient flower. In turn, Shōhaku maintains the thread of objective spring imagery in 14, even while evoking a similar pathos (*aware*) in the dying sunlight. There is a marvelous aesthetic juxtaposition here between the tiny, focused image of 13 and the sudden widening of perspective in 14. Shōhaku's verse generates a montage-like effect in which 13 instantly becomes animated as the brief glimmer of a dewdrop, quickly succeeded by waves of shimmering haze as the poetic camera pans back to encompass a wide, hazily gloaming scene. In the ensuing dark, Sōchō then points up the crying of the birds as they fly back (*kaeru*, to return) to their roosts. This verb, "to return," effects an opening into the Travel theme that Sōgi will introduce in 16, where he interprets the word to mean that the birds migrate back north at spring's end, a fine example of the semantic doubling, commonly effected by homonyms, which enables the silent transitions in renga movement, the gaps in language by which one verse slips seamlessly, as it were, from one topos into another.

The generation of such a shapely sequence as *Minase* required participants of uniformly high skill and experience, artists who would not only follow the rules but apply them in subtle, expressive ways.[6] The sequences produced by the innumerable amateurs who practiced renga no doubt remained at the level of "grammaticality," which is to say they merely followed the rules to ensure the movement of the whole and seldom rose to the purified realm of art. For the majority, no doubt, what was most fascinating about renga was less its aesthetic than its gamelike aspect, the generation of links between individual verses that is called *tsukeai* 付合. Renga was, needless to say, first and foremost a social gathering; a study of its history will quickly reveal its considerable social and ritual uses to celebrate or to mourn, to petition the gods and buddhas (for success in an endeavor, whether an impending battle or the inauguration of a shrine), or simply to enjoy the company of literary friends. But what made this poetic form of sociality enormously popular, apart from the varied occasions, was its aspect as performance, the excitement or sense of expectation attending each moment as everyone waited to hear how the poet whose turn it was responded to the preceding verse composed by someone else; in other words, the excitement lay in the dynamic intrusion of chance in an activity otherwise so highly circumscribed by rules. To put it precisely, this act of linking up to a verse composed by someone else, the specific words and syntax of the response, is not predictable wholly by the grammar of sequence, no more than is a play in a game by the rules of the game. In sum, the popularity of renga arose from its temporality.

The Link as a Structure
of Signification

If meaning on the level of sequence has the purely functional value of shaping the movement of the whole, what then of its status in the minimal verse-pair unit, which is precisely where the meanings may be expected to connect, where the signifying event of renga as a literary performance, a thing of words, finds its special place? Among the renga masters of the Muromachi period, it was Shinkei who delved most deeply into the question of the link and who may rightly be said to have thought through a general and structural theory of tsukeai, not only as poetic rhetoric, but also within the framework of Buddhist intellectual philosophy. His most concrete explanation and illustration of it may be found in his adaptation of the *hen-jo-dai-kyoku-ryū* 辺序題曲流 structural concept of waka to renga. The concept, whose very name is obscure, has not previously been examined by Japanese scholars, since the main orientation of Shinkei research has hitherto been on his aesthetics and philosophy as the utmost development of medieval critical thought. I find, however, that *hen-jo-dai-kyoku-ryū* provides a key, within the field of formal rhetorical analysis, not only to the structure of tsukeai itself, but to the whole question of medieval critical thought. This is to say that his theory of tsukeai constitutes the field where poetry and philosophy become, if not fused, at least directly correlated. Moreover, it will be seen in the course of this presentation that Shinkei's understanding of tsukeai has close affinities with contemporary Western theories of structuralism and deconstruction, specifically as these bear upon the questions of meaning, "truth," difference, and the metaphor.

A technical term referring to the structural sequence of the five-line waka, *hen-jo-dai-kyoku-ryū* is described in Shinkei's most likely source, the treatise *Sangoki* 三五記, thus:

> *Hen* 辺 is at the margin where you signify that you are about to begin, *jo* 序 is when you have actually begun, and *dai* 題 is the poem's topic; you should directly manifest the topic in this line. In *kyoku* 曲, you express a graceful sentiment in an interesting way, and with *ryū* 流, you let the whole flow away, like a five-foot length of vine undulating in the water.[1]

With no further explanation in the *Sangoki,* this passage is not necessarily easy to grasp. The gist of it is that the progression of a five-line waka may be described as a slow buildup toward a central point, line 4, or *kyoku,* followed by a graceful fade-out. *Hen-jo-dai-kyoku-ryū* may therefore be translated as "prelude-beginning-topic-statement-dissolve." Shinkei gives a plainer illustrative analogy in *Sasamegoto*:

> *Hen* [Prelude] is the point when, having come to visit someone, you are still standing outside the door;
> *Jo* [Beginning] is the stage when you inquire whether he is home and so on;
> *Dai* [Topic] is the part when you state the purpose of your visit;
> *Kyoku* [Statement] is when you reveal the matter of it; and
> *Ryū* [Dissolve] is when you bid him farewell and leave.
>
> (SSG 40: 173-74)[2]

It would obviously be improper to apply this pattern literally to a line-by-line analysis of a waka poem. Shinkei's analogical reading—clearly an attempt to elucidate the *Sangoki's* description—also traces a progression, a way of proceeding from the preliminaries to the principal matter, from the "nonessential" to the "essential," in any human activity. (The reason for the scare quotes will become clear later on.) What is important is that in applying the principle to renga, he converts it into a bipartite structure, namely, *hen-jo-dai / kyoku*, which is supposed to correspond to the two verses and illumine the relationship between them.[3] Below, I quote from the main passage in *Sasamegoto* to help us determine exactly what *hen-jo-dai* and *kyoku* verses mean from the standpoint of tsukeai.

> For example, if the short verse contains *kyoku*—that is to say, intends to make a statement, then the long verse should adopt the *hen-jo-dai* posture and leave something unsaid [*iinokosu*].[4] Or again, if the long verse intends a statement [*kyoku no kokoro arite*] and is emphatically saying so [*momitaraba*], then the short verse should take the *hen-jo-dai* stance and let it flow through [*iinagasu*].

tsumi mo mukui mo sa mo araba are	As for sin and retribution, if it be so, so be it!
tsuki nokoru kariba no yuki no asaborake Gusai	The moon lingers over snowy hunting fields in a glimmering dawn. Gusai

---

kaeshitaru ta o mata kaesu nari	The field already plowed lies plowed again.
ashihiki no yama ni fusu i no yoru wa kite Zen'a	The wild boar that lurks in the foot-dragging mountain comes in the night to call. Zen'a

---

kōri tokete mo yuki wa te ni ari	Though the ice has melted, snow alights on the palm.
chirikakaru nozawa no hana no shitawarabi Junkaku	Fronds of fern under scattering flowers on the meadow marsh. Junkaku

In each of the three verse-pairs above, since the preceding short verse intends to make a statement and is straining hard to do so (*momikudokitaru*), the following long verse consequently takes the *hen-jo-dai* stance, leaving something unsaid and giving it over to the maeku (*maeku ni yuzurihaberi*).

<table>
<tr><td>

omokage no
tōku naru koso
   kanashikere

hana mishi yama no
yūgure no kumo
     Ryōa

</td><td>

The image of a face
growing distant in the memory,
   brings sadness.

Over hills where I saw flowers,
the dimming clouds of twilight.
     Ryōa

</td></tr>
</table>

———

<table>
<tr><td>

mae ushiro
to wa futatsu aru
   shiba no io

idete iru made
tsuki o koso mire
    Shinshō

</td><td>

In front, in back,
two doors does it have,
   the brushwood hut.

From its rising till its falling,
he gazes at the moon!
    Shinshō

</td></tr>
</table>

In the two pairs above, since the preceding long verse intends a statement and is openly saying so, the lower verse falls into the *hen-jo-dai* stance, merely acknowledging the maeku and allowing it to flow through. In renga, therefore, it is the rule that the upper verse leaves something unsaid, entrusting it to the lower verse, while the lower verse expresses itself incompletely (*iihatezu shite*), so that it may be completed (*iwasehatsu*) by the upper verse. This means that excellence, that quality of moving the heart and mind, is not to be found in a sequence wherein each successive verse is wholly complete in itself (*ono'ono ni iihatetaru*) (*SSG* 34: 156-57).

In these examples, if we separate each verse from its corresponding partner and consider it in isolation, all that can be said is that each makes literal sense. In addition, however, the maeku in each case is said to have an emphatic aspect that calls attention to itself. It is not only saying something, but implying that it has a reason or intention in doing so. This illocutionary aspect that marks a *kyoku* verse is not particularly apparent in the maeku to the second, third, and fifth examples. They sound like riddles. Yet it is precisely there that they betray an intention. For all riddles compel attention through their paradoxical character, which emphatically demands a solution. Why should a field be plowed twice, snow fall when the ice has receded, and why assert the trivial fact that a hut has two doors? The first and fourth examples are not couched as riddling questions, but they clearly mean something, in the sense that a desperate or sad face is emphatically the expression of something.

In contrast to the maeku, the *tsukeku* 付け句 here are generally unemphatic, apparently innocent of purpose and intention. The first, third, and fourth tsukeku in particular are probably representative examples of what Shinkei means by the *hen-jo-dai* verse. They neither express an emotion nor shape a thought, as attested by their flat and uncomplicated diction. A string of nominatives strung together by the genitive particle *no*, the whole statement is syntactically undifferentiated, like a subject without a predication. They merely present things as they are, without a trace of emotion or assertion in them. This is no doubt what Shinkei means by a verse that "leaves something unsaid" (*iinokosu* 言ひ残す) or "expresses itself incompletely" (*iihatezu* 言ひはてず); the meaning or significance behind their surface has been left out, or rather they are pure surface.

What, then, is Shinkei saying about tsukeai by means of the *hen-jo-dai-kyoku-ryū* concept? First, that in renga, the single verse whether or not marked by intentionality is, strictly speaking, ambiguous and characterized by a lack. The so-called *kyoku* verse by its emphatic inflexion inscribes an unspoken intention, while the *hen-jo-dai* verse in all its unperturbed blandness of expression has left something out. Second, that the verses in each pair are in a contrastive relationship, in that they fulfill opposite functions relative to each other. It might be helpful to characterize the relation between the *kyoku* and *hen-jo-dai* verses as corresponding to Frege's sense and reference (*Sinn/Bedeutung*) distinction, where the sense refers to the thought expressed by a sentence and the reference to that which it designates, its object or, in the case of an assertion, its truth value.[5] The correspondence, while useful in theorizing the distinction between maeku and tsukeku in renga, has to be applied with some qualification, however, since Frege, like most positivist philosophers, is concerned with the truth and falsity of statements, that is, with the issue of judgment entailed in objective knowledge, and expressly denies that poetry or fiction has a *Bedeutung*, a "real" referential object or truth value. Needless to say, such an assertion is far from unassailable, but I shall bracket the issue for now and merely observe that in principle, the maeku may be said to have a "sense" for which the tsukeku provides a "reference"; the one gives the other a cognitive value by providing the referential context that reveals its "truth."

Here it is crucial to note, moreover, that Shinkei converts the five-line waka structure into a reversible dyad—that is, it becomes immaterial whether the maeku is the long or the short verse—but he retains the functional difference between the two as the index of a connection. That is, he collapses the difference between *kyoku* and *hen-jo-dai* in the final statement: "In renga therefore, it is the rule that the upper verse leaves something unsaid, entrusting it to the lower verse, while the lower verse expresses itself incompletely, so that it may be completed by the upper verse." And thus he effectively empties out the names as signifiers for immanent characteristics of the verses themselves and implicitly reveals them to be primarily functional designations. In other words, if the maeku clearly indicates an unspoken intention, then the tsukeku should privilege it (whatever *it* may be), give way to it (*maeku ni yuzuri*) by desisting from coming up with a new and additional intention, in order to effect a connection. What is important is that between any two verses in renga, there should only be one single statement, whose meaning, intention, or, in the Fregean sense, "reference," the other should "fathom" and acknowledge by adopting the *hen-jo-dai* posture. But what exactly is entailed in this posture?

Judging from the examples above, the *hen-jo-dai* verse is supposed to provide the context, or concrete set of circumstances, in which the *kyoku* statement becomes true, in that its purpose becomes revealed. That is to say, it functions as a topic (the same *dai* 題 in the term *hen-jo-dai*) would in waka composition, and we owe to Shinkei this particular insight into the close affinity between renga tsukeai and the standard waka practice of *daiei* 題詠, composing on fixed, given subjects. In his commentary to verses by the "seven sages" and Gusai, *Oi no susami* 老いのすさみ, Sōgi reads the link in the first example thus: "This manifests the feel of morning in the mountain where the speaker is lodging. The scenery is so tremendously absorbing that he has forgotten all about the retribution of sins. The poet linked up to the maeku by adopting the persona of a hunter."[6] One could go further and say that the point of the link is that the persona has been suddenly liberated, uplifted as it were, from the vicious karmic cycle of "sin and retribution" and into the realm of Suchness (*jizai* 自在) by the tremendous beauty of the pale, silent landscape. In Gusai's amazing tsukeku, what seemed initially to be a mood of desperation ("If it be so, so be it!" in the maeku) turns out to be an ecstatic contemplation. The link has the starkly powerful quality of an instantaneous illumination and particularly appealed to Shinkei, who quotes it more than once in his writings. In example 2, the rice field plowed by the farmer during the day has been "plowed again" (*mata kaesu nari*) by a boar who came foraging for food during the night. In example 3, the falling cherry flowers are the "snow" and the "fern fronds" the "hand" upon which they alight; the scene suggested is of picking young ferns in spring. In 4, the *omokage* 面影, or "image" receding into the distance,[7] is made specific as the memory of hills alight with flowering cherry trees, where now only the darkening evening clouds remain as traces (also *omokage*) of a former splendor. And, finally, example 5 securely resolves the riddle of the two doors by imagining a hermit moon-gazing all night ("from its rising to its falling"), first from the front door, then the back.

It should be observed that all these examples date from renga's initial efflorescence in the Kamakura-Nambokuchō period, more than a century before Shinkei's own time in the fifteenth century. The "riddle" verses especially have an archaic flavor and lack perhaps the poetic "aura" of Muromachi-period renga. But what Shinkei is illustrating here is the original, bare-bones structure of the renga link, and it was precisely Zen'a, Gusai, Junkaku and the other early masters of the noncourtly popular milieu who brought the art of linking, in the sense of the tension of opposition between the two verses, to such a pitch that, to borrow the words of Kidō Saizō in another context, "if you hit it, it would resound," presumably like the skin stretched taut over a drum.[8]

In all these cases, the tsukeku, itself empty of explicit meaning or intention, functions as a mirror reflecting the maeku's meaning. If we take the maeku to represent a figure, then the tsukeku is the "empty" space that makes its outlines visible. But the converse is also true: as space is not really apprehensible until defined by a figure, the words of the tsukeku itself also fall into a meaningful configuration by virtue of the maeku's statement. The two verses are therefore in a mutually defining contrastive relationship; each is what it is only through the other. Each lacks something that is filled in by the other, and together they fall into an underlying unity, which is not, however, the sum of one added to the other but rather an unknown quantity that registers itself in the reader's mind the moment he comprehends the link; in the terminology of modern renga scholarship, it is called a "tension" (*kinchō*) running between the two verses. The perception of a lack or absence in each verse as such, moreover, has nothing to do with syntax; syntactically, each is a complete statement in itself. Nor is it a semantic lack, since both verses obviously make literal sense. Rather, this very "incompleteness" or, as we would now say, "indeterminacy," which Shinkei declares is a sign of excellence in renga, is the aspect of a verse that is tautly linked to its maeku, such that it is meaningless without it, just as, one may add, the answer to a riddle is not apparent as such apart from the riddle itself, and vice versa. This is as much as to say that meaning in tsukeai is not a semantic "content" present in either verse as such; it is rather a third and invisible field in which the two verses, each insignificant as such, suddenly come together, and in the process illuminate each other, in the sense of filling each other with momentary significance.

What implications does Shinkei's adaptation of the *hen-jo-dai-kyoku-ryū* concept to renga linking have for *yukiyō* 行様, the movement of the sequence as a whole, as distinct from the individual link between any two verses? Taken literally to its logical conclusion, it would cause the sequence to fall into a rather monotonous alternation between verses with explicit intentionality and verses lacking it, between what we might call "strong" verses and "weak" ones. But this would clearly be a mistaken application for two reasons. First, every verse in renga is, strictly speaking, ambiguous or Janus-faced, so to speak. Open on two sides, it combines with its maeku on the one hand and with its tsukeku on the other; the same verse provides a context for the preceding and reads as a statement for the following verse. Second, a verse's degree of explicit intentionality will inevitably be governed by the yukiyō factor, in that human affairs themes—Love, Buddhism, Laments, and so on, will tend to be explicit, while wholly seasonal themes will be much less so. It is crucial to remember that *hen-jo-dai* and *kyoku* are functional designations indicating the mutually defining relation of opposition, or difference, between any two verses, not immanent characteristics of the verses as such. Shinkei's choice of the extreme examples above indicates that he wished to illustrate the operation of tsukeai in the specific cases where it is most clearly perceptible and where the tension is greatest—namely, in the interaction of an explicit or strong verse with a nonexplicit or weak verse. In practice, one would expect the tense opposition between the verses in a hyakuin to span a whole range from weak to strong, but the tension must always be there to a certain degree, for it is the mark that an authentic connection has taken place. No matter how apparently flat or empty of intention the maeku might be, the poet must always compose as if it were a statement containing a meaning and intention in order to effect a connection; he must find the referential context that validates its truth. Since that same maeku was composed primarily as a *hen-jo-dai*, or context verse, in response to the statement of the mae-maeku, or verse preceding the maeku, it is, in fact, initially like a riddle with its back turned to the poet, whose job is to turn it around to face him; to make it speak to him by recontextualizing it. And it is precisely in the sense of yukiyō as a dynamic, rotating process of continuing reinterpretation, rather than as a Fregean referral of sense to a notion of objective truth, that Shinkei's adaptation of the *hen-jo-dai-kyoku-ryū* concept finds its greatest application in renga. And it is also here where the link between renga, deconstruction, and Buddhist philosophy becomes manifest.

THREE

Emptiness, or Linking as *Différance*

One of the central concepts of Mahayana philosophy is undeniably that of emptiness (J. *kū* 空; Skt. *śūnyatā*), since it is crucial to establishing Buddhism's two most important observations about dharmas, or phenomena: namely, that they have no self-nature (J. *shohō mujishō* 諸法無自性, Skt. *anātman*) and that they come into existence wholly from circumstance (J. *engi* 縁起; Skt. *pratītya-samutpāda*). Therefore they are at base "empty"; their identity is constituted wholly in relation to other phenomena. The same is true, as demonstrated in the foregoing analytical presentation, of the isolated renga verse; it is "empty" in the sense Shinkei indicates when he describes it as "incomplete," or in the sense we mean by "indeterminate," because subject to various interpretations, depending upon circumstances— here, the verse's position in the ongoing sequence and the specificity introduced by the next poet's mind. While the verse makes perfect literal sense, it does not become meaningful until the tsukeku provides it with a context. Thus tsukeai, the signifying event in renga, can be seen as a dynamic instance of dependent origination, or engi, the coming into appearance of phenomena, or meaning, through correlation.

Tsukeai may also be described, in terms of contemporary structuralist and poststructuralist theory, as the generation of meaning through the mutual opposition, or difference, between two terms, or among the units of a system. The idea that meaning inheres neither in a fixed correspondence between word and thing nor in the single linguistic unit (whether phoneme, word, sentence, etc.), but is rather a product of the term's differential relation with other units of the linguistic system of which it is a part, originated with the linguist Ferdinand de Saussure (1857–1913) and has since become axiomatic in the modern understanding of how language operates. Saussure analyzed language as a system of mutual oppositions or differences; what constitutes a phoneme, for instance, is not the sound in itself but its difference from the other phonemes in the system. That /r/ and /l/, for example, mutually define each other is obvious from minimal contrastive pairs like rye/lye, red/led, and so on, where the distinction between the two terms is the sole signifying mark of meaning. The same may be said of the series thread/tread/dread, or in Japanese grammar, of the terms of the demonstrative pronoun paradigm *kore/sore/are*. To grasp the sense of *kore* ("this" object by me) requires at the same time an understanding of *sore* ("that" object by you) and *are* ("that" object over there, away from both of us) because its identity is constituted by its difference from the other two terms. This illustrates, though in a trivial way, that languages are constituted of mutually defining units within a closed system, and the formal impossibility of translating from one language system to another. The value of *kore* is not equivalent to "this" in English, which is defined only by a binary opposition to "that," while Japanese recognizes three loci in the usage of the deictic pronoun. A more notorious example, for students of Japanese, is a whole extensive lexicon of politeness, whereby "give" and "receive" assume different morphemes according to the social rank of the agent vis-à-vis the patient, as well as the third party in the case of an indirect quotation. Whole social identities pass unremarked when Japanese dialogue is transposed into a language system that does not allow for the inscription of the superior/inferior difference in its morpho-syntactic system.

"In language," according to Saussure, "there are only differences without positive terms." The isolated unit has no intrinsic value apart from its relative position within the systemic structure. This postulate may be dubbed the engi, or "dependent origination," of linguistic value. Saussure also said that "everywhere and always there is the same complex equilibrium of terms that mutually condition each other. Putting it in another way, language is a form and not a substance."[1] The significance of this statement, in turn, may be construed as the *kū*, or "emptiness," of language. Meaning does not adhere to words as the "substance" of their correspondence with "reality." As a product of the mutual internal differences among terms, meaning is a purely formal value or convention. Beyond the simplest names of things—and even there the correspondence with reality is complicated by the fact, for instance, that *gohan* (rice) has a far more extensive semantic field than "rice" in English—what words signify is the structure of a synthetic, man-made culture, not "reality" as such. Indeed, it is language that by structuring our very way of thinking constitutes our reality and not, as had been assumed all along, the other way around. If meaning lies neither in reality as given nor in words as such but only in relation, then like the dharmas or phenomena in Buddhist philosophy, they are at base empty.

The extent to which contemporary Western thinking on language and meaning has come to resemble the basic concepts of Buddhist philosophy is undoubtedly one of the more remarkable intellectual developments of our time. The so-called linguistic turn by which thought was liberated from metaphysics and meaning from the illusion of the "transcendental signified" has obvious affinities, in its implications, with the Mahayana concepts of dependent origination and emptiness. The modern undoing of metaphysics, understood as the assumption of an ideal essence, form, presence, or substance that lies at the core of physical reality and language, invisibly grounding their truth and ultimate reality, has a long and complex history in European philosophy from Kant and Hegel through Kierkegaard, Nietzsche, Husserl, and Heidegger, to name only the most influential names, down to Derrida.[2] Logocentrism is the belief in the universal validity of reason to explain the world, and of the power of rational logic to represent it in language, including the languages of disciplinary knowledge. This logocentrism, which is such a striking characteristic of Western thought and culture, and may be said to underwrite the science and technology that are the all-encompassing ideological engine of the new world order, is perhaps the most powerful application of the Western metaphysics of presence and substance. Despite the deconstruction of metaphysics undertaken by modern Western philosophers, it still governs mundane affairs, albeit mostly divested of any conviction of idealism, divinity, and ethics, and shown up as bare calculation, the instrumental use of reason for profit.

In the field of philosophy, however, the dismantling of metaphysical certitude has been in process since Nietzsche's assertion that meaning is relative and truth "a movable host of metaphors."[3] The Sausurrean postulate of the wholly formal or "arbitrary" nature of the sign, and its consequent uncoupling of the signifier from the signified, inaugurated the so-called linguistic turn in the humanities and the reign of textuality in poststructuralist criticism. Saussure's concept of meaning as a differential function of terms was appropriated by Jacques Derrida, in his governing notion of *différance*, to challenge the metaphysics of presence and its allied concepts of *archē*, absolute origin or founding principle, and *telos*, the final end—concepts constituting the principle of causation, which logically requires a fixed linear chain of progression from the prior to the subsequent in order to prevent an infinite regress at both ends of the chain.

In Western philosophy, language, or the sign, has always been seen as secondary or provisional, that is, as a substitute for the so-called thing in itself in the fullness of its presence. In other words, "the sign, which defers presence, is conceivable only on the basis of the presence that it defers and moving toward the deferred presence that it aims to reappropriate."[4] In the Sausurrean demystification of the sign, however, this "presence" or meaning that is signified by the sign can no longer be referred to a fixed origin or end outside of language, no longer finds its cause in a subject or a substance, but is merely the "effect" of the play of differences, that is, the movement of différance, as both spacing, the becoming-space of time, and temporization, the becoming-time of space. Derrida says, and here I quote the passage that I found most relevant to Shinkei's analysis of renga structure and my pursuit of the initial question of meaning in renga as a literary event:

It is because of *différance* that the movement of signification is possible only if each so-called "present" element, each element appearing on the scene of presence, is related to something other than itself, thereby keeping within itself the mark of the past element, and already letting itself be vitiated by the mark of its relation to the future element, this *trace* [emphasis mine] being related no less to what is called the future than what is called the past, and constituting what is called the present by means of this very relation to what it is not: what it absolutely is not, not even a past or a future as a modified present. An interval must separate the present from what it is not in order for the present to be itself, but this interval that constitutes it as present must, by the same token, divide the present in and of itself, thereby also dividing, along with the present, everything that is thought on the basis of the present, that is, in our metaphysical language, every being, and singularly substance or the subject. In constituting itself, in dividing itself dynamically, this interval is what might be called spacing, the becoming-space of time or the becoming-time of space (*temporization*). And it is this constitution of the present, as an "originary" and irreducibly nonsimple (and therefore, *stricto sensu* nonoriginary) synthesis of marks, or traces of retentions and protentions . . . that I propose to call archi-writing, archi-trace, or *différance*. Which (is) (simultaneously) spacing (and) temporization.[5]

And at this point, before going further with Derrida, I should like to pause and circle back to the renga that initiated my own movement of temporization, this detour into différance. To make short shrift of the matter, what begs to be said first of all is that in renga, tsukeai, or the link between any two verses, can also be characterized by the concept of différance. Which is, in one sense, merely a resounding way of confirming Shinkei's analysis that in renga, the single verse signifies only by a relation of opposition, or difference, from the verse preceding or following it. But the Derridean concept also reveals it as an art of spacing and temporization; of "spacing" in that it is the gap from one verse to the next, though silent, that enables each to signify. And here we should recall the Muromachi poets' critical underscoring of the syntactic/semantic autonomy of the single verse, which is the same as to clarify the intervening gaps between the verses, and appreciate how definitive the stricture was for the development of the art of linking. Linking is also an art of "temporization" in that it is first when it is "read" or "articulated" by the following verse that the preceding verse comes to be charged with significance. Each verse in this chain is never simply present, but is always already marked by the preceding, always already infecting the following. This is the same as to say that the single verse is no more than a *trace* of everything that preceded it; it is also a "synthesis of marks," a conjuncture of "retentions and protentions."

A crucial word that traces the path from renga to différance is *iinokosu*, "to leave unsaid," in the *Sasamegoto* passage quoted earlier: "In renga therefore, it is the rule that the upper verse leaves something unsaid [*iinokosu*], entrusting it to the lower verse, while the lower verse expresses itself incompletely [*iihatezu*], so that it may be completed [*iwasehatsu*] by the upper verse. This means that excellence, that quality of moving the heart/mind, is not to be found in a sequence wherein each successive verse is wholly complete in itself" (*SSG* 156–57). *Iinokoshi* in the one, *iihatezu* in the other, each verse, in other words, is marked by an absence, which becomes presence by force of the other in a relation of alterity marked by the double identity of the single verse. As noted earlier, "what is left unsaid" is not a semantic content; rather, it is the enabling gap of différance, a term that may in fact be productively associated with the Japanese concept of *ma* 間, which is both space between, as in *kumoma* 雲間, "between the clouds," or *ōsetsuma* 応接間, "drawing room," and temporal interval, as in *hiruma* 昼間, "daytime," or *ma ga nukeru* 間が抜ける, "miss the beat" in music. The single word *ma* names both space and time—which in English are considered two separate dimensions—in the same nexus, signaling that one is unthinkable without the other. *Ma*, which we may render "space-time," constitutes, I believe, a major aesthetic-philosophical dimension in medieval Japanese arts like black-ink painting that privilege empty space as much as figure, or poetry with its valorization of what is left unsaid, over and above the words as such.

Between Buddhism and the linguistic turn, however, there is a crucial distinction. As a religion, the former's ultimate aim is soteriological; the purpose of knowledge is not the establishment of objective truth through predetermined laws of logic. It is to see through the fact that our mundane reality is a linguistically constituted entity, through the deconstructive practice of Zen meditation, for instance, and thereby liberate the mind from the oppressive fixations that generate suffering. In other words, the aim is to go beyond the very dualisms and oppositions inscribed by language itself and reified by everyday usage until they have become the very stuff of rational common sense.

As the first offshoot of the linguistic turn, structuralism uses precisely the concept of binary opposition to describe and explain phenomena as various as kinship relations, food and fashion, and the literary text—if only to say, in the last case, that it is no different from nonliterary discourse except in being self-referential, and thereby inadvertently confirming Frege's exclusion of literature from truth-value.[6] Subsequently, poststructuralism exposed the error inherent in dualistic thinking by turning its logic against itself, that is, by privileging the opposite term whose suppression enabled the claim to validity to begin with. In disabling this hierarchical opposition in which one term is always favored over the other, the deconstructive movement asserts that every fixed position is untenable, because as a sheer product of difference, it is always already divided within itself; its very identity is assured by the term it opposes, as we saw in the preceding structural analysis of the renga link. Such a movement is exemplary in exposing the unreflective dogmatism that lies hidden in every positive assertion and thus promoting an attitude of impartiality upon logical grounds.

While such impartiality has a liberating influence upon the use of language as an endless proliferation of signs, none more privileged than the next, since all are wholly interdependent, it is not clear what the value of this deconstructive practice would be, apart from revealing the solipsistic hall of mirrors that is language. Buddhism, on the other hand, would point to something beyond language and the thought-categories it inscribes. But this aim, too, seems incoherent or self-contradictory, to say the least. How can language, the vehicle of thought, be employed to show something that is commonly characterized as "beyond words" and hence "beyond thought"? This is the same as to ask, what is the status of language in a philosophy that negates its ultimate adequacy? Both as artist and as priest, Shinkei would not be satisfied with a wholly defensible view of renga as a mere play of signifiers, the solipsistic reflection that what its poetry reveals is merely its own structure as a special linguistic system constituted by a mutually defining network of thematic and lexical differentiations. In a sense, indeed, the tenor of his critical writing, and that of his predecessors, who similarly drew upon Buddhist thought to articulate their understanding of poetry, is oriented precisely against this misunderstanding, as will become clear in a later discussion.

Liberated from its assumed ground in reality, language is now seen as a system of signs, a sign being further analyzed as an "arbitrary" correlation between the signifier, the utterance as a phonological object, and the signified, what the sound means. Now it is certainly possible to see the maeku in renga, whose indeterminacy Shinkei noted, as a signifier whose signified the tsukeku reveals. But it is more accurate to say, since the two verses are in a mutually defining relation, that each verse signifies, while simultaneously being signified by, the other. In other words, each partakes in the paradoxically dual nature of the sign, that of being most itself there where it is inhabited by the other in a relationship of alterity. This implies that reading the links in linked poetry is not a matter of adding one verse to the next and forcing them to yield a single discursive statement. Reading the links is a matter rather of projecting or filtering the one against the screen of the other, that is, of locating precisely where the two verses are most similar and different at the same time. For instance, in Shinkei's examples, there is a differential equation between "plowed again" in the maeku and "comes in the night" in the tsukeku; these two terms constitute the node of the connection. The same relation obtains between "snow . . . on the hand" and "flowers [on] fronds of fern," "image of a face growing distant" and "dimming clouds of twilight," and so on. Example 1, however, is quite special; the correspondence between "sin and retribution" and "hunting fields," it is true, yields a context where the scenery is seen through the persona of a hunter. Apart from this, however, there is nothing else on the verbal surface to clue us in on the relation. This is an instance of the Distant Link that depends wholly on a labor of the imagination, which is also the mind of meditation, the focus of Part Two of this book.

FOUR

Linking as Hermeneutical Process

INTERPRETATION, COMMUNICATION, AND
THE TRANSMISSION FROM MIND TO MIND

Perhaps the most interesting facet of renga's uniqueness as a poetic genre
is the centrality in it of the act of interpretation. Here, poetic composition
is an interpretive act before it is a creative one; its creativity is specifically
judged on the basis of the quality of its interpretation of the previous verse.
And it is this hermeneusis that resists a reductive description of renga as
only an endless play of signifiers. This is because each link represents the
crucial intervention of a reading/speaking subject in the chain of supple-
mentarity generated by the movement of infinite deferral that is différance.
So much is this true that Shinkei would go so far as to declare that

> To discern the particular quality of another's verse is said to be far more dif-
> ficult than to compose an interesting verse oneself. This means that the Way
> [of renga] lies less in the making of verses than in the discipline of illuminat-
> ing the intelligence of another [*hito no saichi o akiramemu koto* 人の才智を
> 明らめむ事]. (*SSG* 40: 173)

Such a statement clearly underlines the nature of tsukeai as a semiosis, a production of meaning that is simultaneously a hermeneutic labor of keenly discerning the maeku's expression and then engaging it as a prior text. At once a reading and a writing, tsukeai inscribes the verse and its exegesis in the very fabric of the poem itself; intertextuality is woven into its very structure, since lack of connection, no matter how impressive the verse, will result in a breakdown of meaning and in turn "cramp" the flow of the sequence.

> In renga you should be able to sense this structure [*hen-jo-dai-kyoku-ryu*] by reciting the upper and lower verses together as one. Lack of attention to this matter frequently results in absurd compositions where the hat has somehow ended up on the foot and the shoes on the head. Those practitioners who do not grasp its significance do not care how twisted, bulky, and cramped [*kudakechijimi futomitaredo*] the sequence itself appears, since they are interested only in their own artificially contrived verses. They apparently have little sense for the expansive, smoothly flowing rhythm [*ōyō ni iinagashitaru tokoro*] of the whole. What this means is that between any two verses, there must always be something left unsaid in the one that flows through in the other. It means to make the maeku your own and compose and recite your verse together with it. (*SSG* 40: 174)

In this case, Shinkei is focusing on *hen-jo-dai-kyoku-ryū* as the structure of a clear reception, the proper working of the channel of communication between two minds. A "twisted, bulky and cramped" sequence indicates that either the poet does not understand how the channel works and the signals have gotten crossed (hat on the foot, shoes on the head), or he is more interested in displaying his own ingenuity than in reading and interpreting the maeku. In that case, his verse will assume a "bulkiness" (*futomi*), a kind of obtrusive materiality, like that of a foreign object that does not belong, and it will "cramp" the ideally expansive flow of sequence. Either way, the channel reception becomes disturbed and the sequence unintelligible; nothing is "going through"; no link has taken place because the maeku has not been understood.

Here it is significant to note that in Japanese there is one common verb, *tsūjiru* 通じる, which refers to the process of understanding, of making contact or connection, as an unobstructed passage between two points. Thus, "I don't understand it" could be expressed simply as *tsūjinai*, said, for example, by someone who hears but does not comprehend a foreign language, and where *tsūjinai* means literally, "it is not coming through." When a message does not reach its addressee, or a phone line breaks down, the same verb is used, as in *Tokyo ni tsūjinakatta*, "I didn't get through to Tokyo." Again, an interpreter, one who mediates by translating between two languages, opening up a passage between them, is called a *tsūyaku* 通訳, where the first syllable uses the same ideograph.

We are now in a better position to see that what is "left unsaid" in renga linking and sequence is what I have previously referred to as the third field or territory—"dimension" is perhaps a better word, in which every two verses make contact, achieve connection. It is the channel of communication that Shinkei everywhere in his writings identifies as the elemental "mind-ground" (*shinji* 心地), the locus of discipline and training in the Way of poetry, which is also the way of Zen meditation, the subject that can "read" or see through the maeku's words and "rewrite" his understanding in a linked verse that keeps open the channel of communication. Thus what is apparently absent on the verbal surface of the sequence as such, that which is "left unsaid in the one that flows through in the other" (*iinokoshi iinagashitaru tokoro* 言ひ残し言ひ流したる所) is the flow of mind, that is, of understanding, from one verse to the next, from poet to poet, in the ideally *ishin denshin* 以心伝心 (literally, by means of mind transmit the mind) transaction that is the "passage" denoted by the verb *tsūjiru*. This passage, the "smoothly flowing rhythm" of the whole, is invisible, but it is what animates the movement of the sequence from one poet to the next. Like the flight of an arrow, as Jonathan Culler explains in his reading of Zeno's paradox, "motion is never present at any moment of presence. The presence of motion is conceivable, it turns out, only insofar as every instant is already marked with the traces of the past and the future."[1] In renga poetics, therefore, the mind is the engine that generates the impression of fluid motion, of something being passed on from hand to hand, a runners' relay. It is a peculiar poetic speaking that pits the powers of the mind against the sheer contingency of the moment that brings the utterance of the other, demanding recognition and a response. Given renga's nature as extemporaneous performance, not even the grammar of sequence can ultimately predetermine how the poet understands the maeku; it can tell him whether to continue the previous theme or move to a new one, but not how to respond with understanding to the maeku's specificity, even its brilliance. And so each verse is, strictly speaking, unpredictable; it is a hazard, an irruption of chance that is barely governable by grammar. But understanding remains, as it were, the condition of possibility for linking; it is easier to compose a verse without the preconditions set by the maeku, easier to speak one's piece without addressing the other.

THE PHENOMENOLOGICAL THEORY OF
MEANING-FULFILLMENT, THE PHENOMENAL
OBJECT'S HORIZON, AND THE RENGA WORLD

What might it mean exactly to say that the renga verse is at every point a "reading" or "interpretation" of a prior text? Earlier, we characterized the link as a "signifying process" involving the "contextualization" of the maeku. But what is entailed in this process? We could fetch a hint from the investigations of Edmund Husserl (1859–1938) and his phenomenological theory of meaning and meaning apprehension. For Husserl, things are not simply given out there as fixed objects of perception or empirical observation. Rather, they are entities encountered by the subject in an "intentional act" of consciousness, which constitutes them and endows them with meaning. Furthermore, since this meaning grows out of lived experience, the object exists within consciousness, not as an isolated, atomic entity, but within a complex network of prior contexts that form its "world."

An "expression" is commonly understood to consist of (1) the written sign or sound-complex, and (2) a sequence of mental states, called the sense or meaning, associatively linked with the expression. But for a phenomenological theory of meaning, this dual structure is not adequate to describe the signifying process. An expression functions as such by virtue of the fact that its sense indicates something more, an "objective correlate" intended by the speaker. This is a reflection of the dual acts involved in signification, as explained below:

> We shall have to distinguish between two acts or sets of acts. We shall, on the one hand, have acts essential to the expression if it is to be an expression at all, i.e., a verbal sound infused with sense. These acts we shall call the *meaning-conferring acts* or the *meaning-intentions*. But we shall, on the other hand, have acts, not essential to the expression as such, which stand to it in the logically basic relation of *fulfilling* (confirming, illustrating) it more or less adequately, and so actualizing its relation to its object. These acts, which become fused with the meaning-conferring acts in the unity of knowledge or fulfillment, we call *meaning-fulfilling* acts. . . . In the realized relation of the expression to its objective correlate, the sense-informed expression becomes one with the act of meaning-fulfillment.[2]

To understand what is indicated here by "meaning-fulfillment," it is necessary to recognize a distinction, in the case of a name, between what it "shows forth" (a mental state) and what it means, and again between what it means (the sense or "content" of its naming presentation) and what it names (the object of that presentation). "Meaning-fulfillment" refers to grasping the thought or the intended object, such that the expression acquires an intuitive fullness. Without it, the meaning-intention remains unrealized, empty, which is, we could theorize, the state of the maeku in renga, when the tsukeku fails to achieve connection with it.

I find Husserl's analysis of the signifying act into two components somewhat more useful than Frege's in explaining the relation between maeku and tsukeku in renga, because it entails the act of interpretation. It could be said that from the vantage point of the tsukeku, the maeku is an initially empty "meaning-intending" expression, which it then endows with the fullness of "meaning-fulfillment" in the act of *construing* it, that is, interpreting it, which is also an act of concretizing it into an "objective correlate." Here "empty" indicates that the maeku itself is meant for, "intended" or directed to, the verse immediately preceding it and thus presents itself to the tsukeku poet initially as a kind of "virtual" expression needing to be "real-ized," actualized, in his encounter with it. Whether or not the tsukeku's realization coincides with the maeku's "intended" meaning is a fascinating philosophical question, one that in the Husserlian perspective would have an affirmative answer. However, because of the doubling whereby the same verse means one thing in relation to its maeku and another in relation to its tsukeku, as entailed by the renga structure of signification, the issue of whether the semantic intention of the tsukeku coincides univocally with that of the maeku is not, I believe, crucial to determining the success of its "fulfilling" performance in the virtual, or poetic, discursive process that is renga.

Still, it is significant that tsukeai seems to coincide with Husserl's description of the grounding of scientific truth by the finding of evidence, which is also the act of cognition. The tsukeku's meaning-fulfilling act seems, oddly enough, to be an adjudicating process of presenting evidence to support and confirm a claim of the meaning or truth of a state of affairs. It is the evidence that "justifies" the maeku. "In explicating more precisely the sense of a grounding or that of a cognition, we come forthwith to the idea of *evidence*. In a genuine grounding, judgments show themselves as 'correct', as 'agreeing'; that is to say, the grounding is an *agreement* of the judgment with the judged state of affairs . . . '*itself*'."[3]

kaeshitaru ta o   The field already plowed
mata kaesu nari   lies plowed again.

ashihiki no   The wild boar that lurks
yama ni fusu i no   in the foot-dragging mountain
yoru wa kite   comes in the night to call.
Zen'a   Zen'a

In the pair above, Zen'a's judgment regarding the state of affairs given in
the maeku is in the form of an evidence that agrees with "the judged state of
affairs" itself. Of course, the act of judging, being an act of thinking, is itself
never present in the words as such; there is only the *evidence* of the tsukeku
that a judging has taken place, that is, that the second plowing of the field
(this assumes the first plowing to have been done by the farmer during
the day) was caused by a wild boar who came foraging for food during the
night. In turn, the renga reader must judge for herself if the evidence fits.

Another of Husserl's ideas that is suggestive for describing the process
of understanding and signifying in renga (where the two moments are the
same) is that of "horizon." The notion springs from his finding that every
actual act of consciousness contains within itself potential others that can
be actualized later; that when consciousness grasps the object, there are aspects of it that are not directly grasped at the time.[4] These aspects constitute
the intentional object's horizon and, while not given in the perception, are
nevertheless "predelineated" as references to or anticipations of possibilities
that can be actualized in further acts of perception or reflection.[5] "There
belongs to every genuine perception its reference from the 'genuinely perceived' sides of the object of perception to the sides 'also meant'—not yet
perceived but anticipated."[6]

This is a theory of the phenomenological object as a non-simple entity
located, as it were, against a background or "horizon" of components that
belong to it, and are "also meant" by it in a relation of "reference" from
the perceived side to the other sides, but that reference is unfulfilled in the
specific temporal instance of perception. Such dormant horizonal aspects
of the object, the accumulated layers of experiencing the object, may be
viewed as its varied contexts, a horizon of anticipations or "protentions"
whose components may be activated at a later time.

Now it seems to me that transposed into the world of poetic practice,
Husserl's concept of the phenomenal object's "horizon" allows us to con-
ceptualize the particular word, image, or expression as similarly perceived

within a horizon of references and associations to other entities to which it is bound by the seasonal or human affairs themes and by verbal correlations culled from the waka, narrative, and other canonical textual traditions that constitute the renga language, its world. Each time a renga poet composes a verse, he is activating a particular reference within this poetic system of mutual differences. Consider, for instance, the aspects of the Spring "horizon" in the renga world laid out in table I, whose components are further differentiated according to their occurrence in the First, Second, or Third Month (of the old lunar calendar).[7]

The items in this list are marked by their belonging to the thematic horizon of Spring, and each item is further marked by its phenomenal

TABLE I

The World of Spring, or, Marked Images for the Three Months of the Spring Season

Things of the First Month		Things of the Second Month		Things of the Third Month	
plum blossoms	remaining snow	pheasant	plowing the field	peach blossoms (limited to the Third Month)	long day (over the three months)
ice melting	returning cold	waiting for the flowers	haze upon the meadow	azalea	flowers
new herbs (this is limited to the seventh day of the First Month)	fields sprouting	cherry blossoms	departing wild geese (may also be in the Third Month)	wistaria	Purification on the Day of the Snake
charred fields of grass	Hymn to the Star (this is an event of the first day of the First Month)	charred miscanthus stubs (this is miscanthus in charred fields)	young grass	mountain kerria	
haze	willows	east wind (over the three months)			
tranquil	warbler				
skylark					

SOURCE: Table created from entries in *Shogaku yōshashō* 初学用捨抄 (Do's and Don'ts for the Beginner), a Muromachi-period renga instruction manual.

occurrence in countless thousands of waka in the official and informal anthologies collected by the court and disseminated by the renga masters as the model and archive for their own pedagogy and practice. In the *Minase* sequence opening passage analyzed in Chapter 1, Sōgi's hokku focuses on the "remaining snow" on the mountain peak and the haze rising from below, but the other items under the First Month in the table may be said to be "meant," implied, by it also, as a horizon of predelineated potentialities. And sure enough, Shōhaku's tsukeku shifts the focus to the "plum blossoms" and even wordlessly suggests "ice melting" in the image of flowing water; in turn, Sōchō in verse 3 activates, makes explicit, "willow" as another sign of spring's arrival, thus completing the theme that opens the sequence.

What is illustrated here is the preexistence of a shared horizon among the participants. Taking a turn means shifting the focus of conscious awareness from one object to another that exists only implicitly, in the silent margins of the first, but available within the same horizon. In effect, any turn in renga enacts what Gadamer calls "a fusion of horizons," a term that describes the act of understanding in the present a text that belongs to the past and conceives of understanding as a hermeneutical situation.[8] A "fusion of horizons" happens only on the premise of an initial separation between the two that are subsequently fused, which in renga is inscribed in the gap of difference that marks the intervention of another speaking subject, and marks itself by the perceived tension required to bridge it. While the existence of a recognizable poetic language system ensures a general sequential continuity, it does not guarantee that every maeku's "meaning-intending act" will achieve "meaning fulfillment," that is, will be "understood" by the tsukeku in the narrow sense of being faithful to its specific syntax. This is particularly so at moments when the sequence shifts from one theme to another in rapid order, as in a later *Minase* passage below:

43	kono kishi o	This shore is
	morokoshibune no	for the ship bound for Cathay
	kagiri nite	the final port of call.
	-chō	Sōchō

44	mata mumarekonu	Would that I may learn the Dharma
	nori o kikaba ya	and not be born here once more!
	-haku	Shōhaku

45	au made to omoi no tsuyu no kiekaeri -gi	Till we meet again, my yearning like the dew fading, returning. Sōgi

The passage features a radical shift from Travel to Buddhism and then Love, all in the space of three verses. As distinct from Season verses, in the case of Human Affairs themes like these, which feature content-laden discursive statements with specific modalities, it is more difficult to achieve a "fusion of horizons," and so the skill of the three poets at Minase is all the more apparent.[9] Each move in the passage is wholly unpredictable, though by hindsight understandable: Shōhaku construes the "ship bound for China" as one carrying priests on a mission to study with eminent Buddhist monks there, while also activating "final" in the fervent modality of the speaker's desire for release from the mundane world. Sōgi in turn elaborates on the maeku persona's state of mind as caught in the vicious circles of passion ("fading, returning") that occasion his desperate wish for Buddhist liberation. Where thematic horizons shift so rapidly, their fusion requires a more radical, and strenuous, overcoming of borders.

THE FUSION OF HORIZONS, OR, THE HERMENEUTICAL CIRCLE OF UNDERSTANDING

If understanding of another's meaning refers to a fusion of distinct horizons, they must already contain that immanent possibility to begin with, which suggests the existence of what in hermeneutics is called a "pre-understanding," the antecedent conditions of possibility enabling the grasp of the object, preparing for it in such a way that when the moment of fusion occurs, it does so as a "re-cognition" of something "foreknown." The existence of the circular movement of understanding known as the hermeneutic circle is particularly evident in renga, whose reading requires at every point a forward motion (to the tsukeku) and a doubling back to the maeku in order to "comprehend" the link. In effect, each verse is double, and read twice; it is the looping back and around, as in a chain, that paradoxically moves the sequence forward.

If we now return to the question of whether the tsukeku may be said to fulfill the maeku's "intended" meaning, the answer must be yes, bearing in mind, however, that the maeku poet is not always aware of all the horizonal structures implied in his utterance, particularly as his verse was directed at its own maeku. In certain instances, particularly when the gap is quite wide on the surface, as in the three-verse passage above, the other's response would surely have taken him by surprise, but this shock of recognition or instantaneous understanding, the something clicking in his brain, is precisely the mark that the other has fulfilled his meaning-intention. "There is more to what is given than it gives itself out to be."[10] And understanding, and the hermeneutic circle it enacts, is possible only on the basis of the preparatory or anticipatory foreknowledge hidden in the margins of an object's horizon, remaining mute but operating to move the sequence along. In effect, the verse is both what is given and what is apparently absent from its surface; its nature is always double.

Since the instance of understanding is itself silent and can only be indicated, in renga, the verses themselves are only signs, traces of an invisible flow of relations, which is, however, perceptible only through them or, more precisely, through the gaps that open up in the transition from one verse to the next. Once more, Derrida might as well be describing renga in this passage from his *Positions*:

> Whether in written or in spoken discourse, no element can function as a sign without relating to another element which itself is not simply present. The linkage means that each "element"—phoneme or morpheme—is constituted with reference to the trace in it of other elements of the sequence or system. *This linkage, this weaving is the text, which is produced only through transformation of another text* [emphasis added]. Nothing, either in the elements or in the system, is anywhere simply present or absent. There are only, everywhere, differences and traces of traces.[11]

The renga text is also this network of linkages, which registers itself as a progressive transformation as the sequence moves from verse 1 to 100. Hence the philosophy of language, aiming as it does to ground the possibility of an unassailable objective knowledge, whether in the Fregean or the Husserlian model, though the latter is more nuanced, cannot finally account for the operation of meaning in renga. "Text," as Derrida is showing through an appeal to the etymology of the word, is a "weaving," and what I have earlier called "contextualization" is therefore a weaving together to make designs. "Design," or pattern, it is revealing to note, is *aya* in classical Japanese, and it is designated with the graph for "letter" or "writing" (*mon, bun* 文), in turn primordially understood as the pattern on oracle bones given over to be read—interpreted—in ancient divination practices. The same graph stands for *mon*, the raised figure or pattern in fabric, and also the impressive poems that emerge against a background (*ji* 地) of plain, ordinary ones in a poetic sequence. In the compound *ayame* 文目, finally, the two senses of "design" and "logic, reasoning" come together; here meaning is understood topologically as a thing's placement within a coherent design. And it is striking to note that the aesthetics of sequence required restraint in the use of "design" verses, the better to enhance their effect among the "background" verses and so preserve the aesthetic coherence of the whole. Thus writing, weaving, patterning or figuration, *and* signifying (or divination) are all linked together in the Japanese language. Within this renga fabric, every verse, except for the very first, the hokku that was required to trace the time of composition itself (the season, the occasion), bears the trace structure of its maeku and its tsukeku, which are in turn traces of their maeku and tsukeku, and so on in an oscillating process of exchange, which poststructuralist criticism might call an "endless play of signifiers." But in Shinkei's Mahayana-inspired poetics, this process is identified as the transparent transmission of mind *through and despite* language, a description that places the most weight on the quality of mind that a poet brings to the session, a point that will be elucidated later.

What is of greater interest in the Derrida passage above is less that it easily lends itself to the construction of renga as a *text*, a fabric of originary differences that is an "archi-writing" (though strictly speaking "nonoriginary" when *archē*, origin, is newly understood as but a synthesis of marks in the absence of the transcendental signified), but that the text is "produced only through transformation of another text," which is itself not simply present but in turn the trace of another text, and so on. This implies that the renga link, which inscribes the act of hermeneutic understanding from one poet to the next, involves a transformation, and that is where we must now turn, since it constitutes a central theme in the classical Japanese understanding of structure and further develops the pertinence of différance in this poetics.

FIVE

The Link as Figuration and Metaphorical Shift

That on the level of formal poetic rhetoric, the economy of the renga link requires transformation, and that this is a process of figuration emerges in Shinkei's analysis when he further equates the *hen-jo-dai-kyoku-ryū* structure with waka poems employing *jo no kotoba* 序の言葉, an introduction or Preface to the main Statement, and so-called *yasumetaru kotoba* 休めたる言葉, pause words, essentially a short preface or "pillow-word" placed in the medial instead of the usual initial position. Both rhetorical figures have the same properties: they usually end in *kakekotoba* 掛詞, or puns, the hinge or joint of a double meaning that breaks the linear continuity of the poem, while effecting a metaphorical transfer of meaning from one part to the other. Some of Shinkei's examples are quoted below (from *SSG* 34: 158). As should be obvious by now, he is seeking to find in the history of rhetorical structures in Japanese poetry, which could be none other than waka history, the origins of tsukeai in renga; at the same time he is considering the nature of poetic rhetoric itself in a synchronic fashion by drawing these comparisons.

Some Poems with a Preface

hototogisu	*Is the cuckoo singing—*
naku ya satsuki no	*'midst the sweet flag, lissome*
ayamegusa	*blossoms of summer,*
ayame mo shiranu	I know not *reason* or *flower*,
koi mo suru kana	why yearningly turns my heart.[1]

shikishima no	*Not to be had in*
yamato ni wa aranu	*all of Yamato's myriad isles,*
karagoromo	*this robe of Cathay;*
koro mo hezu shite	Ah, for a way to meet her
au yoshi mogana	without *a moment's* delay.[2]

yoshinogawa	*Yoshino River:*
iwanami takaku	*spraying high among the rocks*
yukumizu no	*the current flows*
hayaku zo hito o	*Swiftly*, a yearning for her
omoisometeshi	did suffuse my heart.[3]

The most obvious similarity between the Preface / Main Statement structure of these waka and the *hen-jo-dai / kyoku* alternation of the renga verse pair is that in neither case is there is any direct syntactic and/or semantic continuity from one part to the other. An interruption occurs that signals a shift in meaning, an alteration of semantic fields, and forces us to draw an analogy between the two discontinuous parts in order to make sense of the whole. Thus in poem 1, the cuckoo singing among the sweet-flag iris flowers (*ayame* 菖蒲) may be read as an image of the speaker who is in love without "reason" (*ayame* 文目) or without an object, a case of the Aristotelian analogy by a ratio among four terms, A/B = C/D, (cuckoo/sweet flag = persona/x), where the absence of the fourth term is expressly stated in a punning statement, *ayame mo shiranu* (I know no sweet flag / I know no reason), which would then be one reading of the poem. And perhaps this irrational situation of loving without an object, of being in love with love as the potential stage of that peculiar condition, was responsible for the *Kokinshū* editors' decision to place this poem at the very head of the anthology's love section.[4] In poem 2, the three-line preface also ends with a word, *Karagoromo* 唐衣 (Chinese robe), partially homophonous with the initial morphemes in the Statement, *koro* (time) and the emphatic-emotive *mo*, and the whole makes sense only if the rare Chinese robe is seen as an allusive metaphorical substitute or, alternatively, a metonym for the woman whom the speaker is eager to meet. In poem 3, *hayaku* (swiftly) provides a smooth juncture between Preface and Statement; it means specifically "at once, instantaneously" in the context of the Statement, and the action of the surging waters in the Preface comes to stand for the hidden force and violence of love at first sight.

In all these waka with preface, the *kakekotoba* or pun and homophonous repetition may be said to mediate between the two discontinuous parts, in that similarity in sound has the mysterious effect of implying, indeed of enforcing and enabling, a similarity in sense. As concrete image, the Preface clearly has the function of *prefiguring*, embodying beforehand, the feeling or thought expressed by the Statement. It is, if we pursue Shinkei's analogy of the waka poem as a visit, the preliminary "diversion" that smooths the way for the visitor's statement of *purpose*, and in that sense ties in with the nature of tsukeai as an instance of interpretation, of rendering "intentions" visible by reference to a context, of confirming the "correctness" of a judgment by means of evidence.

For waka employing pause words, I shall merely choose two of Shinkei's examples (*SSG* 34: 158). The first is *KKS* 995: Miscellaneous, Anonymous, here given in a literal translation:

Ta ga misogi	For whom the Lustration?
yūtsukedori zo	Tied with sacred cord the cock—
karagoromo	*a robe of Cathay*
*tatsu*ta no yama ni	*rending*—in Mount Tatsuta
orihaete naku	stretching out the moment, cries.

The pause words occur in line 3, *Karagoromo* (Chinese robe), linked to the first morpheme in the following word, Tatsutayama 龍田山 (Tatsuta Mountain) through a pun on *tatsu* 断つ・裁つ, "to tear apart, rend, cut." This intervention, located between the subject and predicate of the Statement, makes it assume a multilayered character; the image and sound of a silken fabric being ripped along its length is superimposed upon the piercing calls of the bird, so that we vividly experience the way these cries tear through the stillness of the sacred mountain precincts. Furthermore, by means of the same intervening image, the seemingly innocent modifier *orihaete* 折延へて in the predication is suddenly animated to assume its concrete and literal sense of something being stretched or pulled across (the verb *hafu* 延ふ), and we seem to feel the very tension of the air vibrating in the sound. Such are the dynamic effects of the pause word, the interval that takes us on a detour to prefigure the moment before its arrival. The following revised translation is only partially successful in rendering these effects, but demonstrates how an innocuous pause word, when taken seriously, can transform the whole configuration of the poem in translation.

ta ga misogi
yūtsukedori zo
karagoromo
*tatsu*ta no yama ni
ori haete naku

For whom the Lustration?
Tied with sacred cord the cock
rends the mountain air,
stretching *sheer* down Tatsuta
its long, bright *train* of sound.

The problem with such a translation, however, is that it lays everything out in a display of rhetorical flourish, so that what is merely suggested in the text, what is given—"Chinese robe / rend"—as the initial clues for a hermeneutic process that transpires in the mind, being directly stated, might indeed hold the interest for a moment, but has lost the power to compel the reader to interpret and himself unravel the problem it poses.

ukaibune
aware to zo omou
mononofu no
yaso ujigawa no
yūyami no sora
Jichin-oshō

Cormorant fishing boats—
it is a sight to break the heart:
a myriad men of arms
flickering lost on the Uji River,
as darkly looms the evening sky.[5]
Priest Jichin

Shinkei's choice of an example from the *Shinkokinshū* period is doubtless an unspoken directive that we should note its utter structural similarity to the foregoing anonymous *Kokinshū* poem written at least three centuries earlier. The pause words *mononofu no* 武士の / *yaso* 八十 link to the main Statement through a double pun on *uji* 氏・宇治 to yield two intervening thoughts, "warriors of the eighty clans" and a more suggestive inference that would turn around the morphemes *yaso ushi*. In the latter case, the numeral "eighty" (*yaso* 八十) becomes a metaphorical intensifier for *ushi* 憂し, "gloomy."[6] As in the previous example, the stock epithet acts like a catalyst complicating the poem's tonal and semantic texture. Much amplitude is gained by the overlap between the present scene of fishing boats' torches glimmering on the water and the thought of warriors who fought to the death in the same Uji River in the Gempei Wars (1180–85). In effect, fishermen and warriors, and ultimately all men, are implicated in the tragic sin of killing for survival in this world, and existence is imaged as a wandering in the darkness of ignorance (*yūyami no sora* 夕闇の空). Yet that would spell out things much too clearly; what is important is that this chilling thought is threaded through with the sense of *aware* あはれ, which is here a compassionate identification.

In *Yakumo mishō* 八雲御抄 (The Sovereign's Eightfold Cloud Treatise), the retired emperor Juntoku (1197–1242; r. 1210–21) deplores pause words as utterly meaningless and undesirable when employed, as no doubt happened, to cover up a poet's inadequacy with words.[7] A more positive view, however, is expressed by Kamo no Chōmei's teacher Shun'e in the *Mumyōshō* 無名抄:

> It is usual to preface the word "moon" by "long and enduring" [*hisakata*], and the word "mountain" by "foot-dragging" [*ashihiki*], but such epithets have no noticeable effect when placed in the first line. It is rather when they are inserted in the third line as a pause, but without breaking the continuity of the whole, that they give the poem an admirably elevated feeling [*shina* 品], while serving also as a pleasing ornament. . . . In compressing the utmost reaches of a thought to the all-too-meager thirty-one syllables of a waka poem, one should not, it is true, waste even a single syllable. But this *hampi* 半臂 unfailingly evokes a refined quality and ornaments the poem's total design [*sugata* 姿]. And it is when this design is as beautiful as possible that it spontaneously evokes the quality of ambiance [*yojō* 余情].[8]

We are accustomed to thinking of ornament as a subsidiary element that is added or grafted on to an entity that is itself complete and self-sufficient. Yet as shown in these poems, the rhetorical figure, in particular the Preface, is precisely what reveals the meaning of the Statement in embodying it; it is the necessary "supplement" without which the Statement remains a mere prosaic utterance or a kind of riddling question demanding an "elaboration." As for the pause word, Shun'e sees its function as "ornamenting the poem's total design" or configuration, that is to say, the poem's inwoven texture, its intertextuality, and thereby promoting "ambiance" (*yojō*). If there is any one single quality that runs through Japanese poetry from the *Kokinshū* to Bashō-style haiku, it is none other than that represented by the term *yojō*, "ambiance," "overtones." Becoming the central principle of *Shinkokinshū* aesthetics, it further influenced renga and *haikai* and made symbolism the characteristic mode of the highest poetry. It is thus no accident that the *Shinkokinshū* poets evinced a great interest in questions of rhetorical technique and figuration, for these devices of intertextuality are intimately linked with the production of the symbolist poetry they aspired to.

Shinkei's privileging of the *hen-jo-dai* mode in turn effectively affirms the centrality of the figure, recognizing that making apparent a hidden intention without directly stating it is what enables the process of signification in a symbolist poetry. In drawing a structural analogy between a type of waka, both from the ancient and early medieval periods, using preface and pause words, on the one hand, and the renga verse pair, on the other, Shinkei was engaged in showing that discontinuity, the difference between two terms that separates and joins them at the same time, as a hinge or joint, is of the essence in renga structure. The two units are not linked in the direct, linear continuity of a single discursive statement, a single waka poem in the orthodox mode, but across a palpable gap, in a relation of parataxis, or trans-formation.

In other words, where Shinkei had earlier seemed to define *kyoku* 曲 as the illocutionary aspect, or intentionality, characterizing the main Statement (see Chapter 2 on linking as a structure of signification), this time he is actually bringing out its original etymological sense of "shift" or "turn" (*magaru* 曲がる), a bend or detour taken by the signifier on its roundabout path to the signified, in a deferral of meaning that is also a prefiguration of it. This parallels the path taken by the reader when he goes from one verse to the next and then back again in order to "comprehend" the link, which may be expressed as an analogical similarity superimposed upon a logical or semantic difference; in other words, we are dealing here with a view of the link as a metaphorical turn. A reexamination, from this new perspective, of the set of verses cited in the earlier *hen-jo-dai-kyoku-ryū* discussion (pp. 22–23 above) will reveal that there tsukeai does operate in a metaphorical mode. Examples 2 to 3 in that set may be said to transpose the relationship between images in the maeku into other terms, while in example 1, the transposition consists in investing the maeku with a new context.

The acuity, and also the breadth, of Shinkei's understanding of the place of the "shift" or *différance* in the renga process of signification is easily appreciated in the *Sasamegoto* passage that precedes the foregoing examples of waka with preface and pause words.

> In waka when one does not wish to express the Statement in two places in the same poem, one frequently resorts to the use of preface and pause words. Without a clear awareness of these things, I should think that you would inevitably end up with a shallow interpretation of even the most excellent poems. The Buddhist sutras likewise possess a pattern called "introduction-proper teaching-propagation" [*jo-shō-ruzū* 序正流通]. To begin with, the introduction preaches various parables [*hiyu* 譬喩] and instances of karmic

connection [*innen* 因縁]; then the proper teaching section expresses the very principle [*manako* 眼, literally, eye] of the sutra itself; and finally the propagation section enumerates the various merits accruing in its transmission. Everyone knows about these parts without realizing that they correspond to the *hen-jo-dai-kyoku-ryū* structure of poetry. Furthermore, the "beginning-amplification-turn-summation" [*ki-shō-ten-gō* 起承転合] sequence of the four-line Chinese poem comes to the same thing. (*SSG* 34: 157)

In part 2 of *Sasamegoto*, which significantly opens by returning to the *hen-jo-dai-kyoku-ryū* question (the interlocutor in the dialogue professing to be still puzzled by it), this list of equivalences comes to include "the prelude-break-climax [*jo-ha-kyū* 序破急] structure of the myriad arts" and repeats the analogy with the design of the Buddhist sutras and treatises, adding immediately thereafter "the concept of cause and condition, and of allegory [*innen • hiyu*]" (*SSG* 40: 174).

The concept that runs through these disparate literatures is none other than *kyoku* 曲 as "turn," called *ten* 転 in the Chinese poem, *ha* 破 or "break" in the Nō theatre, and in the structure of the sutras the difference between speaking in "figures" or allegorical parables in the introduction, and in plain speech in the "proper teaching" section. When in Part II, Shinkei ends his explanation with "cause and condition" (*innen* 因縁, also, karmic connection) and "allegory" (*hiyu* 譬喩, also, analogy), we have an indication that the metaphorical turn was indeed foremost in his mind. In the case of the Chinese four-line *jueju* 絶句 (J. *zekku*), which most approximates the waka in its formal economy, it is almost inevitable that structurally, the shift in direction, that is, the Statement, should occur in the third line, as it is set into the contextual framework of a natural scene in the first two lines, the so-called "beginning-amplification" section. Below I quote two examples that fit this structure; Shinkei does not give any. The first is Wang Wei's "Song of Wei Cheng" 渭城曲, and the second is a piece by Du Fu simply called "Jueju." Both writers were famous Chinese poets in Muromachi Japan.

> At morning in Wei Cheng rain moistens the light earth,
> And at the inn the greening willows are fresh;
> Come, drink deep of another cup of wine—
> When you come out west of the Yang Barrier, old friends will be gone.[9]

> Birds recede whitely along the jade river,
> Upon the green hills the flowers seem to burn;
> In a while this spring too will come to pass,
> What day shall see the year of my return?[10]

In the latter piece, by Du Fu, the first two lines, themselves, set in paratactic relation to each other, constitute a minutely subtle prefiguration of the Statement in the last two: the remote whiteness of the birds fleeting along the vivid green of the spring river (an implicit contrast with their stark outlines against a bare winter landscape) and the "burning" flowers concretely image the persona's yearning homesickness in two modalities, as it were, first as an immeasurable extension, and then as an intensity. It is a parataxis repeated in reverse in the Statement itself; the urgency or pain of spring's passing is countered by the unspoken remoteness of the possibility of the persona's returning home. The play on *gui nian* (returning year) in the last line paradoxically underlines the reality of time itself for the persona: this year, "this spring" that passes will ineluctably return, but his is a different destiny. In a sense, the pain of passing time is also the underlying theme of Wang Wei's poem, for within the imagistic frame of its statement, the present moment in the company of old friends is full with the fullness and vitality of time (the life-giving rain on the loosened spring soil, the greening of the willows), and is clearly set in contrast with another time that impends, when the departing friend has been cut off from the others, and time has moved on. In the "turn" of the third line therefore, "drink deep" (*jin yi bei* 盡一盃) becomes invested with spring's fullness, and "old friends will be gone" (*wu gu ren* 無故人) with its utter exhaustion. Perhaps there is also a suggestion of a pun in the juxtaposition of "morning" in line 1 and coming "out west of the Yang [literally, light, sun] Barrier" in line 4, when this is read as the coming into appearance of the dying sun.

Différance and "the *Jo-ha-kyū* of the Myriad Arts"

By "the *jo-ha-kyū* 序破急 of the myriad arts," Shinkei no doubt had in mind both the structure of the renga sequence itself and Nō drama, the performing art with which it is historically closely allied. Renga is, of course, not only a performative art in that each verse is the poet's response to the preceding one composed by someone else; it was also literally a public performance held on various occasions, be it of celebration, prayer, or commemoration. In the treatise *Tsukuba mondō* 筑波問答 (Tsukuba Dialogues), Nijō Yoshimoto 二条良基 (1320–88), an older contemporary of the great Nō actor and theorist Zeami 世阿弥 (1363–1443), determined that the *jo*, or Prelude in renga corresponds to the first fold, the *ha* or Break section to the second fold, and the *kyū* or Climax, to the third and fourth folds.[1] The Prelude, according to him, should be in a "tranquil" (*shitoyaka*) mode, the Break begin to "rustle and whisper" (*sasameki ku o shi*), and the Climax should be in "a specially spirited mode" (*koto ni ikkyō aru yō ni*), which means featuring arresting and complex connections.[2]

While the qualities so described by Yoshimoto remained generally accepted, by the mid-Muromachi period, the location of the division boundaries had changed radically, the Prelude now ending in verse 10, the Break comprehending the remaining verses in the back of fold 1, plus folds 2, 3, and the front of fold 4; and the Climax, the back of fold 4, or the last eight verses. Yoshimoto's grandson Ichijō Kanera 一条兼良 (1402–1481), for instance, notes this change: "In modern times, just as in the front (of the first fold), one does not, in the first two verses of the back, employ verses on Love, Laments, famous places, and so on."[3] Interestingly, this confirms what was theorized earlier, that one of the governing oppositions in renga sequential structure (*yukiyō*) is between the seasons and the human themes, or that "tranquility" is associated with the "objectivity" of natural scenes, as against the complicated human destiny of desire expressed in the Love theme, and of suffering inscribed in the theme of Laments. The proscription of famous places (*meisho*, *nadokoro*)—that is, named places with specific connotations, similarly ties in with the avoidance of "content" in favor of generality in the prelude. Senjun 専順 (1411–1476), one of the "seven sages" and Sōgi's first teacher, observes similar divisions in his *Katahashi* 片端 (A Fragment): "Until the beginning of the back of the first fold, the pace should be quick; the second and third folds require more strenuous reflection, then by the back of the fourth fold, the verses should again be simple."[4] It appears then that Yoshimoto's "spirited" climactic third and fourth folds were incorporated into the Break section, and the new Climax was conceived as a quiet short passage paralleling the Prelude. The general pattern was therefore from simplicity to complexity and back.

Here it is important to point out that what is indicated when one reads the texts of actual sequences is that *jo-ha-kyū* obtained not only across the whole but also within each of the three large divisions. Within the Break or Development section, in particular, one will mark the pattern recurring at least twice. Thus taken with Shinkei's analogy of *jo-ha-kyū* to *hen-jo-dai-kyoku-ryū*, the conclusion to be drawn is that the principle of difference applies to the minimal verse-pair unit, the larger blocks of verses marked off by the folds and sides of the manuscript itself, as well as to the sequence in toto.

That *jo-ha-kyū* is a principle of dynamic progression operating from the smallest to the largest units is confirmed in Nō by Zeami's statements on it in his various treatises. The *jo-ha-kyū* section of the *Kakyō* 花鏡 (The Mirror of the Flower, 1424), which applies the principle to a whole day's program of six plays, is the clearest exposition of what these three terms signify in Nō. For our purposes, what is important to point out about the Prelude in Nō is that the plays (the first two in the program) must be simple and straightforward. "Such a play should have a simple source, be constructed without any complex detail, be felicitous in nature, and have a plot that is easy to follow." And further, "song and dance should be the main elements in such a play."[5] In other words, this is no different from the Prelude section in renga, with its tranquil simplicity and avoidance of the human themes in favor of the wholly seasonal. Indeed, Zeami's term, *shitoyakanaru fūtei*, recalls Yoshimoto's own words as quoted above. In Nō, this opposition corresponds to the emphasis on the basic arts of song and dance (viz., *kabu wa kono michi no hontaifū nari* 歌舞は此道の本態風なり) in the Prelude, as against the importance of role-playing (*monomane*) in the Break or Development section, which is defined by Zeami thus:

> The Break begins from the third play. This is a form that manifests a shift in the direction of rendering in detail the basic, straightforward and orthodox form of the Prelude [*Kore wa, jo no hompū no, sugu ni tadashiki tei o, komakanaru kata e utsushiarawasu tei nari* これは、序の本風の、直ぐに正しき體を細かなる方へ移しあらはす體なり]. The term "Prelude" refers to the original configuration, and "Break" means a commentary that in turn annotates and renders it comprehensible [*Jo to mōsu wa onozukara no sugata, ha wa mata, sore o washite chūsuru shaku no gi nari* 序と申すはをのづからの姿、破は又、それを和して注する釋の義なり]. Therefore, from the third play onward, the performance becomes more detailed and elaborate, and should include role-playing. This constitutes the substance of the day's program. Since the fourth and fifth plays are also included within this Break section, it should be performed with the greatest possible variety of artistic means.[6]

Zeami's definition of *ha* in terms of a hermeneutic or exegetical process performed upon the "original configuration" of the *jo* is quite unexpected, yet it also fits in well with Shinkei's statement about the universal applicability of *hen-jo-dai-kyoku-ryū*, renga's process of linking, to the various arts.

Zeami's understanding of the "break" as a laying out in detail (*komakanaru kata e*)—in effect, an elaboration or "analysis" of the Prelude, a hermeneutical "annotation" (*chūsuru shaku* 注する釋) in the process of adapting the "original figure" to (Japanese) understanding (*washite* 和して)—is like Shinkei's analogy of renga linking to the device of parable and allegory as *figurative* elaborations of the teachings in the Buddhist sutras. In both cases, we have the key to the Japanese way of making the foreign object, whether Chinese or, later, Western, signify by translating it into the local context. Thus, in Shinkei's terms, linking is also *innen* 因縁, the signifying transformation resulting from the interaction of the subject or residual "cause" (*in*) with the object or external "condition" (*en*). As in renga, contextualization in the sense of the bodying forth of meaning occurs in Nō when its two formal elements of song or chant and dance (*kabu* 歌舞) interact with the "content" of role-playing. Chant and dance, the formal gestures of the voice and of the body, acquire meaning by being translated, elaborated, in short, contextualized, within the framework of a role, of a character and his/her story. Like statement and figurative elaboration in poetry, these two—chanting and dancing on the one hand, and role-playing on the other, are in a mutually signifying relationship in Nō. The formal, abstract gesture becomes filled with significance through the role, and the role acquires a formal external body through the gesture.

This is not, of course, a matter of a naturalistic imitation of action as in the conventional Western theater; it is no more "realistic" or mimetic than is the figurative image in relation to the thought or feeling of the statement in poetry. Rather, the relation between formal gesture (the grammar of Nō dance) and story is wholly allusive and symbolic, like the relation between maeku and tsukeku in renga, which requires a reading based on knowledge of the formal language of poetry in the anthologies.[7] Similarly, Nō is less a visual than a hermeneutic theater; "reading" it entails knowledge of the formal grammar of the dance and literacy in the stories of major characters and personages from the literary tradition, including their famous poems. For Nō aims to conjure up and embody these phantoms—the dead and even those who never existed, except in literary imagination—and these famous words through the crucial signifiers of song and dance. This signifying relation constitutes the actor's fundamental training, called by Zeami "the two basic arts and the three role types" (*nikyoku santai* 二曲三體, i.e., old person, woman, and warrior) in the *Shikadō* 至花道 (The Path to the Flower, 1420).

Returning now to the dimension of *jo-ha-kyū* as a sequential progression understood as différance, the importance of role-playing in combination with chanting and dance in the Break section parallels the introduction of the human themes and their combination with the seasons in the corresponding section in renga. The character of the correspondence seems to break down, however, when it comes to the *kyū*, or Climax, the sixth and final play, even though Zeami adopts renga terminology in the passage defining it.

"Climax" means the final verse [*Kyū to mōsu wa ageku no gi nari* 急と申すは、揚句の義なり]. As the "remaining trace" [*nagori* 名残] of the day, it is performed with a sense of reaching the limits. The Break is a configuration that breaks up [*yaburite* 破りて] the Prelude, rendering it minutely and exhausting a manifold artistry.[8] The Climax in turn is the form of a remaining trace that takes the Break to its utmost limits [*Kyū to mōsu wa, mata sono ha o tsukusu tokoro no, nagori no ittei nari* 急と申すは、又その破を尽くす所の一體なり]. In the process, the performance rises to an intense pitch, with wildly inspired dancing and violent movements to amaze the eyes of the beholders [*Saru hodo ni, kyū wa, momiyosete, rambu. hataraki, me o odorokasu keshiki nari* さる程に、急は、揉み寄せて、乱舞・はたらき、目を驚かす気色なり]. Intensity is the mode of this final stage [*Momu to mōsu wa, kono jibun no tei nari* 揉むと申すは、この時分の體なり].[9]

Zeami's characterization of *kyū* is similar to that of his contemporary Nijō Yoshimoto in renga, who says that this stage should be "especially spirited in mode." But by the time of Shinkei, Senjun, and Sōgi, this final passage was interpreted as a winding down, a muted reminiscence of the lively activity in the preceding lengthy *ha* section, like the barely discernible ripples in the wake of a boat that has passed off the scene. Zeami's reading of *kyū* is like Yoshimoto's, more faithful to the sense of crisis and rapid movement denoted by its ideogram, and in a sense, it confirms that *jo-ha-kyū* had its origins in music and dance. Renga, though it might attain to the music of sequence in its finest moments, is still an art of the word, and words have meanings. The intense ending of a Nō program would seem inappropriate to a literary sequence, whereas in musical performance, the heightened pitch of the grand finale of a ballet or concert is familiar and seems fitting. Be that as it may, if we pursue Zeami's terminology of *tsukusu* (i.e., "the form of a remaining trace that *takes* the Break *to its utmost limits*"), *kyū* in Nō might be represented as the most extreme tension of a fullness, while in renga, it is the gradual process of *emptying out* (*tsukiru*); the two endings are but the dual manifestations of the same process; both signify the sense of an ending.

As a universal principle, Zeami conceived of *jo-ha-kyū* as structuring, not only a day's sequence of plays, but also the single play itself,[10] a single dance or section of chant, or indeed even the single gesture and the one breath. Thus when an actor is about to start chanting, the moment when he draws in his breath to align with the pitch of the accompanying flute is the *jo* stage; the instant he begins to discharge his breath in consonance with that pitch is the *ha*, and the actual eruption of his voice is the *kyū*.[11] Thus pitch, breath, and voice, the elements crucial to the event, are all in perfect accord, and the same goes for every action that is grounded in the ineluctable order of *jo-ha-kyū*. The seed of *kyū*, the "end" that is both "trace" and fruit, is sown in *jo* and nurtured in *ha*; once the two have been established, *kyū* will burst into flower of itself. In other words, *jo-ha-kyū* is the principle of a successful, well-prepared, and thus fully realized action. Nō is at base the perfect mastery of a fundamental function, the inhalation and exhalation of the breath. Linking is essentially the controlled art of making words actually speak, the process of *charging* the maeku with significance. Nō, renga, sumi-e, ikebana, the landscape garden—Muromachi art is everywhere informed by the principle of *symbolic* animation that is *jo-ha-kyū*, the ability to infuse life into the simplest gesture, the briefest word, the brushstroke, through a control of formal elements grounded on an understanding of the life process itself, or founded rather on the knowledge that life *is* process.

PART TWO

Kokoro, or
the Emptiness of the Sign

SEVEN

The Close Link and the Distant Link

Distance, the space-time, or différance, between any two verses in renga, may be said to constitute its poetic nexus, for this is where the link, renga's signifying event, takes place. The concept of distance as an intervening space to be bridged, a gap to be filled, was originally the basis for describing the structural continuity or discontinuity of the five lines of a waka poem. Thus *shinku* 親句 (the Close Link) refers to a poem whose lines, being closely connected phonologically, syntactically, and semantically, constitute an immediately apprehensible unity, while *soku* 疎句 (the Distant Link) is a poem with a caesura that divides it into two disparate parts, giving the impression of a fragmented or discontinuous surface structure. Although earlier waka treatises had dealt with the issue of continuous and discontinuous structures, it was the *Chikuenshō* 竹園抄 (ca. 1275–88), attributed to Fujiwara Tameie's son Tameaki, that first employed the terminology of *shinku* and *soku* to refer to these two types of structure. The *Chikuenshō* distinguished two kinds of *shinku*, namely, *hibiki no shinku* 響の親句 (echoing), the phonologically close link in which the final vowel or consonant of one line is "echoed" or repeated in the initial syllable of the next line; and *sei no shinku*

正の親句 (the close link proper), the semantically close link in which the sense of each line logically continues into the next. This includes the use, in close proximity to each other, of words linked through association (*engo* 縁語), such as "cherry blossoms" and "scatter," "mountain" and "peak," or "bow" and "shoot." *Soku*, on the other hand, was described here as a poem lacking in phonological, syntactic, and associative fluidity, but nevertheless producing a unified feeling or thought (*kokoro*).[1]

Fluidity in diction was already an important consideration in the works of Gusai and the other early renga masters. Nijō Yoshimoto, who was Gusai's renga student, dealt with the assonantal techniques of vocalic and consonantal matching in his treatise *Chirenshō* 知連抄 (1374) whose influence, along with that of *Chikuenshō*, is reflected in turn in his disciple Bontō's *Chōtanshō* 長短抄 (1390). It is this work that deals for the first time with *shinku-soku* in the field of renga. It does not, however, depart significantly from the explanation already set forth in the preceding waka treatises, and it applies the principle only to the single verse and not to the verse pair. Bontō illustrates "echoing," the phonologically close link, with the following verse examples. Vocalic matching: *Sora ni naki/hikage no yama ya/ame no uchi. Consonantal Matching: Yama tōki/kasumi ni ukabu/hi no sashite.* And he gives this example for the semantically close link, *Azusa yumi/ikeru o hanatsu/yahatayama,* wherein the sequence of closely associated words, namely, "bow—pierce—shoot—arrow," effects an immediately apprehensible coherence.[2]

In both the *Chikuenshō* and the *Chōtanshō*, the discussion deals mainly with the Close Link and only peripherally with the Distant Link, which is dismissed in a sentence or two at the end. The authors' primary concern was to delineate the principle of integral unity in a waka poem or single renga verse, and this was obviously best manifested by the Close Link. In fact, as Tanaka Yutaka has demonstrated, among renga poets and critics, it was Shinkei who first understood the far-reaching significance of the *shinku-soku* concept and its proper application in renga.[3] As distinct from Bontō, he rightly saw that it could be more fruitfully employed to describe the relationship between two contiguous renga verses rather than among the lines of an individual verse. That is to say that he saw *shinku* and *soku* as a function of renga's unique nature as a poetry of the link between two separate entities. Although in consonance with his overarching principle of non-discrimination, Shinkei advised against an obsessive partiality for either one of these two modes in actual practice, as distinct from the aforementioned treatises, he clearly set the highest value on the Distant Link, seeing in it the most challenging and potentially the most creative space for generating renga's distinct poetry.

"It is because most people do not discern this distinction [between Close and Distant] that they are often bewildered by the precise nature of the link between verses," Shinkei writes in *Sasamegoto* (*SSG*, 33: 154). Basically, his concept of the Distant Link applies to verse pairs that are apparently incoherent on the verbal surface but linked on a deeper level of meaning through the dynamic operation of *kokoro*, or the "mind." Drawing, as always, upon his knowledge of waka, he says: "A Distant Link poem is said to be one wherein it does not matter that the upper and lower parts are put together in a seemingly unnatural and arbitrary way, as long as they cohere in the mind [*kokoro dani tsūjihabereba* 心だに通じ侍れば]."[4] After giving two examples from renga, he comments: "In each of these verse pairs the poet, discarding the maeku's words [*kotoba*] and configuration [*sugata* 姿], has made the link solely through the mind [*kokoro*]" (*SSG*, 33: 154).

Shinkei is clearly drawing a distinction between the verse as such, a formal entity constituted of words (*kotoba*) arranged into an integral shape or configuration (*sugata*), and some underlying deep level of meaning (*kokoro*). That is, "discarding the maeku's words and configuration" is equivalent to going beyond its overt literal sense in favor of some deep and universal significance that includes and simultaneously transcends it. In *soku*, then, the connection between the two verses seems "unnatural and arbitrary" on the surface, but "coherent" at a deeper level. And this apparent discontinuity or incoherence is precisely due to the fact that the tsukeku does not relate directly to the words and specific sense of the maeku, but rather to a deeper significance suggested by it as registered in the poet's mind. Let us examine Shinkei's two examples in turn (*SSG* 33: 154):

Verses in the Distant Link Mode

hajime mo hate mo	Unknown the beginning, or yet
shiranu yo no naka	the ending, of this our world.
wada no hara	The vast sea-plain:
yosete wa kaeru	from the offing the waves roll in
okitsunami	but to roll back again.

In this first example, "discarding the maeku's words" undoubtedly consists first of all in avoiding a discursive elaboration of its sense in favor of a concrete image that illustrates it, and here the "sense" must initially be construed (since we lack the mae-maeku and must justify Shinkei's characterization of the link as Distant), as a statement about the unfathomable character of love, reading *yo no naka* (literally, in the world) in the thematic field of love as the ties that bind two persons in a relationship that constitutes their world. In juxtaposing the dynamic image of distant waves rolling in upon the shore and pulling back again in a never-ending round, the tsukeku "discards" the initial sense of *yo no naka* 世の中, animates the maeku's inert and somewhat prosaic statement, and simultaneously broadens its horizon to include the unfathomable origins and final end of the universe, turning love, so to say, into philosophy. At the same time, however, it subtly shifts the focus to the related idea of ceaseless flux and, ultimately, timelessness. The unknown temporal "beginning and ending" of love is translated into the circularity of the waves' motion, which significantly confounds point of origin and destination. In short, the link here is achieved wholly through the mind's imaginative contextualization, or reinterpretation, of the maeku; it is the allegorical illustration to the maeku's abstract proposition, and the whole structure recalls the Preface / Main Statement of a waka poem, but in inverted order. Significantly, the tsukeku ignores the conventional placement of the word "world" (*yo*) as such within the thematic frame of laments, and uses none of the expected verbal correlates for that word as indicated in the renga dictionary *Renju gappekishū* 連珠合璧集.[5] The reason could be that the maximum duration value of three consecutive verses for Laments (or of five for Love, if *yo no naka* is the significant phrase) had been reached at this point, and so the poet of the tsukeku had to introduce a new theme or, as here, create a transition by an unmarked miscellaneous verse. This observation suggests that the Distant Link, which does not rely on the expected word associations evoking the maeku's theme, but must nevertheless relate to the verse itself, tends to occur at the especially challenging moments of thematic shift within the sequence, such as we examined earlier in a three-verse passage from *Minase*.

The second Distant Link example given in *Sasamegoto* is not comprehensible without some prior knowledge of the significance of its main image, the broom tree. This was a legendary tree that was said to grow by a lowly hut in Sonohara, Shinano Province (modern Nagano) and to appear from a distance but mysteriously vanish or turn into plain evergreens when approached. In classical waka, the fabulous broom tree was often used as a metaphor for a woman seen from afar but impossible to actually meet and possess. The poem below, by Sakanoe Korenori (fl. ca. 908–24), is one of the earliest and most representative on the theme.

> Sonohara ya
> fuseya ni ouru
> hahakigi no
> ari to wa miete
> awanu kimi kana

> As the broom tree
> that grows by the lowly hut
> on Sonohara Plain,
> manifest to the eye, but beyond
> arms' reach are you, my love.[6]

Korenori's waka in turn provided the inspiration for the famous title poems in the "Broom Tree" chapter of the *Tale of Genji*. They occur in the scene where the lovesick Genji attempts to spend another night with the Lady of the Locust Shell but is met by her adamant resistance—caused, as she hints in her poem, by a consciousness of her inferior station. Genji's sense of deflated expectations when she flees from his approach is evident in the apparent tone of self-rebuke, which is also implicitly a complaint and a veiled request for sympathy.[7]

> hahakigi no
> kokoro o shirade
> sonohara no
> michi ni ayanaku
> madoinuru kana

> Ignorant of
> the broom tree's heart,
> to no purpose
> have I lost my way, clueless
> on the road on Sonohara Plain.
> [Genji]

> kazu naranu
> fuseya ni ouru
> na no usa ni
> aru ni mo arazu
> kiyuru hahakigi

> Crushed by a name
> lowly as the hut by which
> it grows,
> here, and yet not here,
> vanishes the broom tree.
> [The Lady of the Locust Shell]

As in the quoted poems above, the broom-tree image is central in the second verse-pair example for the Distant Link in *Sasamegoto*:

> kore ya fuseya ni
> ouru hahakigi

> Is this then the broom tree
> that grows by the lowly hut?

> inazuma no
> hikari no uchi no
> matsu no iro

> In a flash
> of lightning, the color
> of the pines!

But in a brilliant departure from the love or travel thematic context in which it has traditionally been embedded, the broom tree emerges here as a highly charged symbol for the enigmatic and elusive character of phenomenon, or form. *Iro* 色 (color) in line 3 of the tsukeku is apprehended in the Mahayana Buddhist sense of phenomenal reality: it is empty in that its existence depends upon external circumstance—here the lightning flash—yet it is also vividly and wholly real within those conditions. Though earlier waka had not focused upon this philosophical implication in the broom-tree image, the poet of the tsukeku was doubtless inspired by the line *aru ni mo arazu* (here, and yet not here) in the Locust Shell Lady's poem, which he has nevertheless brilliantly reinterpreted to mean "real, and yet unreal." On a rhetorical level, he has also skillfully animated the precise inflection of the phrase *kore ya* (Is this it?) in the maeku, bringing out its latent implication of surprise and focusing, through the vision of vivid green pines suddenly emerging from the surrounding dark in a lightning flash, while yet implicitly rejecting the self-identity of the "this." There is also wit in the inversion of the reader's conventional expectations: whereas the broom tree is supposed to disappear or turn into a prosaic evergreen, here the magic is in the sudden, startling apparition of that same common evergreen pine in a new light.

The impression of a radical disjunction between the two verses in a Distant Link necessarily entails knowledge of the Muromachi reader's horizon of expectations. That this horizon is, as implied above, grounded in familiarity with the *Genji* poems and the one by Sakanoe Korenori is evident from the entries under *hahakigi* (broom tree) in the *Renju gappekishū* dictionary of conventional word associations (*yoriaishū*) cited earlier. There, under entry 293, "broom tree," the following associated words or correlates are listed: *sonohara* (Sonohara Plain), *fuseya* (lowly hut), *ari to wa miete awanu* (manifest to the eye but not to be met), *nakagawa no yado* (the mid-river abode),[8] *momijishinikeri* (turned into crimson leaves), *kokoro o shirade* (ignorant of the [broom tree's] heart), *aru ni mo arade* (here and yet not here). With the exception of *momijishinikeri*, which is from a *Kin'yōshū* poem on the broom tree, all the correlates are from the two sources quoted above. It would seem, therefore, that what Shinkei means by "discarding the maeku's words" is breaking free of the conventional associations (*yoriai* 寄合) ringing the word and, in so doing, discovering and revealing some new, unexpected significance latent in them. In short, he means to go beyond the slavish practice of verbal quotation, which would have been the case had the author of the tsukeku merely included the words *aru ni mo arazu* in his verse. In this sense, *soku*, the Distant Link, may be seen as a procedure that renews, lends a fresh vigor to, received language; it is a means of breaching the dictionary of word associations and extending the margins of poetic language through the imaginative exercise of the mind. If renga is at every point a negotiation between freedom and necessity (the rules of the grammar of sequence, the dictionary of word usage), then the Distant Link is where freedom finds its place and generates new significance.

That this new significance, however, does not mean mere reinterpretation is evident from the examples Shinkei cites for the Close Link (*SSG* 33: 155).

Verses in the Close Link Mode
The manner of linking is commonplace.

| kōri no ue ni | Over the icy surface, |
| nami zo tachinuru | waves have risen! |

sayuru yo no	In the chill night
tsuki no kageno no	across fields of moonlight,
hana susuki	miscanthus in flower.
Ryōa	Ryōa

———————

| aruru yakata o | They are restoring now |
| ima tsukuru nari | the ruined manor. |

kataoka no	Turning the area
sato no atari o	round the village of Kataoka
ta ni shite	into rice fields.
Ryōa	Ryōa

In the first example, the manner of linking is similar to the riddle/answer structure seen earlier in the discussion of *henjodaikyokuryū*. Closely following the syntactic configuration of the maeku, the tsukeku essentially sets up a verbal correspondence with it, such that the pale moonlit fields are the "ice," and the ripening tasseled miscanthus grasses undulating in the wind are the "waves" of the maeku. Moreover, "waves" of plumed miscanthus in the passing wind is, as readers of waka will recognize, a common autumnal image. In the second example, the link turns on the reinterpretation of the word *tsukuru* (build, repair) in the maeku to its homonym meaning "cultivate, plow," so that together the pair comes to mean: "They are restoring the ruined manor in Kataoka village, and the adjoining land, long overgrown, has been brought under cultivation." There is an associative correspondence between "manor" and "village," and "build" (in the second sense of "cultivate") and "rice fields."

Thus, although Shinkei refrains from defining the Close Link, except to note that "the manner of linking is commonplace," it is clear from these examples that what distinguishes it from the Distant Link is a comparatively predictable conception and an emphasis on verbal correspondence, whether discursive or figurative, as a means of connection. In the first, the imagery is rather lovely and Ryōa evinces much imaginative wit, but the connection lacks the "deep" implications of the *soku* verses quoted earlier. The same may be said of the second, which features a plotlike, metonymic elaboration of setting and action, an incipient narrativity that is also a common procedure in renga. It is important to note again, however, that in renga, narration is always arrested, never allowed to develop into a continuous story, by the intermission rule of the grammar.

In *shinku* as in *soku*, one experiences the same pleasurable surprise generated by any renga link, that of a riddle successfully solved, the faculty of wit employed to break through an indeterminacy, but in *soku*, the shock of recognition, when it does come, is far more powerful due to the absence of the expected verbal associative clues, or, if present, their inadequacy in enabling an immediate comprehension of the link. Ultimately, however, the question of distance in Shinkei's renga poetics is connected with his valorization of a symbolic poetry where the "meaning" generated by a Distant Link is strictly speaking beyond verbal formulation and can only be suggested in the open space between the two verses. As distinct from the boundedness and closure of the witty thought, the beautiful image, or the discursive explanation produced in the Close Link, the poetry of the Distant Link employs language in such a way as to evoke the "metaphysical" openness of the Real as understood in Buddhist philosophy, and in classical poetry in the *Shinkokinshū* ideals of *yojō* (overtones) and *yūgen* (ineffable depth). These conjunctions will become clearer in a later discussion of *Sasamegoto*'s equation of the Distant Link with Zen.

THE LEGACY OF THE SHINKOKINSHŪ
AESTHETICS OF DISCONTINUITY

Shinkei's critical foregrounding of discontinuous structures reveals the central importance of the intervening space between verses as the definitive element of renga as a unique genre. There is no doubt that such an emphasis stems from his reading of Teika and *Shinkokinshū* poetry, in particular, the syntactic fragmentation and frequent use of a third-line caesura there. There is obviously a vital link between the *Shinkokinshū* aesthetics of discontinuity and ambiguity and Shinkei's full appreciation of the value of "spacing" in renga, as manifested in the fullest degree in the Distant Link. It is no surprise then that the examples he cites for *soku* in waka (*SSG* 33: 155) are all by Teika and Jichin, except for one by his waka mentor Shōtetsu. And Shōtetsu *is*, of course, the poet who stalked Teika, dissected his mind, and brought his stylistic tendencies to such a radical pitch in his own poetry that it can be called a "mannerist," or brilliantly exaggerated version of the other.

Poems in the Distant Link Mode

sato tōki
yakoe no tori no
  hatsukoe ni
hana no ka okuru
haru no yamakaze
        Teika-kyō

With the first calls
of the oft-calling morning fowl
  in a distant village,
the breezes send from the hills
a breath of spring flowers.[9]
        Lord Teika

sagi no iru
ike no migiwa ni
  matsu furite
miyako no hoka no
kokochi koso sure
        Onaji

A heron stands in
the pond by whose bank years
  deepen on the pines—
How remote from the capital
is the feel of this scene![10]
        Lord Teika

omou koto
nado tou hito no
  nakaruran
aogeba sora ni
tsuki zo sayakeki
        Jichin

Of the sorrow
in my heart, why comes no one
  to inquire?
I gaze up at the sky, and oh,
how keen and clear the moon![11]
        Jichin

makomo karu
mitsu no mimaki no
  yūmagure
nenu ni mezamasu
hototogisu kana
        Onaji

A shadowy dusk
across the pastures of Mitsu where
  men reap the wild rice:
Half-lidded eyes flicker wide
at the cry—*hototogisu*![12]
        Jichin

shii no ha no	In the wind gusts
ura fukikaesu	blowing back the undersides
kogarashi ni	of the oak leaves,
yūzukuyo miru	apparition of moonrise
ariake no koro	in the dark predawn hour.
Shōtetsu	Shōtetsu

All these poems have in common a caesura at the end of the third line, which marks varying degrees of syntactic closure. They range from the partial suspension of the particle *ni* in the first example by Teika and the last by Shōtetsu, as well as the *-te*-suffix ending in the second, to the full closure in the two poems by Jichin. What is crucial to note is that in all of them, the syntactic break coincides with the end of one statement and the beginning of another that has no direct logical continuity with the first, and is unpredictable from it. This break has the effect of setting off a juxtaposition or superimposition of images instead of following a linear continuity with a single image.

In the first poem by Teika, the clear structural division between upper and lower sections marks an unexpected shift from an aural to an olfactory emphasis, and makes it seem *as if* the delicate fragrance in the spring dawn air was summoned by the cock's calls, a fine example indeed of the novel and marvelous effects of the Distant Link technique. In example two, the superposition of an objective image in one section against the statement of subjective feeling in the other section underlines the country-city, solitude-society, time-timelessness dichotomy implicit in the poetic message. This dyadic Statement/Image juxtaposition comprises a classic *Shinkokinshū* structure featured in such famous poems as Saigyō's *SKKS* 362, *Kokoro naki mi ni mo aware wa shirarekeri / / shigi tatsu sawa no aki no yūgure* (Even to a self empty at heart is revealed a moving power / / From the marsh a snipe rising in the dimming autumn dusk) and Teika's own *SKKS* 363, *Miwataseba hana mo momiji mo nakarikeri / / ura no tomaya no aki no yūgure* (Gazing out, I see neither crimson leaves nor flowers / / The straw-thatched huts along the bay in the dimming autumn dusk).

The ironic and paradoxical effects of discontinuous structures is most radically demonstrated in Jichin's two poems; here the gulf between upper and lower part is very deep indeed and defies any facile explanation. Nevertheless, the first comes into focus when the reader recalls that the moon, and specifically its pure, transparent rays, is a metaphor for the all-penetrating mind of the Buddha. The poetic structure plays upon the paradox that although no person comes to visit with whom the persona can share his thoughts, he finds deep consolation in the very transparency of moonlight, before which all thought and sorrow must vanish into emptiness. In other words, the poem is, among other things, about the self-effacement of desire. In Jichin's second poem, the reader will no doubt register the startling paradox in the line *nenu ni mezamasu* 寝ぬに目覚ます (literally, not asleep yet startled awake) which may be said to be its rhetorical node. The upper half sketches a wide, brooding, and shadowy landscape, which is so to say an image of the speaker's vague, abstracted mood, suspended between waking and sleeping. It thus provides an effective foil for the instantaneous, piercing clarity of the cuckoo's call that startles him wide awake in the poem's lower half. Both diction and syntax closely mimic the experience of a powerful shock of awakening, but within what context are we to interpret it? To say that such a poem uses the strategy later clarified and made popular by Bashō in such haiku as *Furuike ya / kawazu tobikomu / mizu no oto* (Old pond: / a frog leaps in—/ the sound of water) is perhaps to beg the question, but what else can one say of poetry that in both cases is wholly trained on making existence perceptible? In fact, this particular poem by Jichin was the subject of superlative praise from Shōtetsu, who noted in particular the inspired quality of the upper half.

Among the "Waka in the Three Modes," the one by Jichin that goes "not asleep yet startled awake" [*nenu ni mezamuru*] is truly a poem of ineffable profundity [*gemmyō naru mono*]. First, with regard to "not asleep yet startled awake," this means that in that vague hour before evening, say, when one is not really asleep, suddenly one hears the *hototogisu* crying and becomes wide awake. Someone who does not grasp this might say, with reason, "Why should one wake up when one was not asleep," but such considerations are beside the point. Ineffably deep as this line is, could the merely skilled poet have conceived of it? Even if he had arrived at the same words, for the upper verse he would have said something like "Gazing at the distant edge of the clouds as evening falls," or "Seeing the moon in the vague hour before evening." But it is precisely this "Nebulous twilight across the pastures of Mitsu, where men reap the wild rice" that confounds ordinary understanding [*bonryo mo oyobazu* 凡慮も及ばず], and whose ineffable profundity goes beyond rational sense [*kotowari no hoka naru gemmyō* 理の外なる玄妙] and wholly resists description. To thus take and combine things wholly divergent from each other is the work of a master who composes spontaneously from the realm of suchness [*Kayō ni kakehanaretaru tokoro o toriawasuru koto, jizai no kurai to noriite no shiwaza nari* か様にかけはなれたる所を取り合はする事、自在の位と乗りゐてのしわざ也].[13]

Shōtetsu's high valuation of the poetic strategy of bringing disparate things together—the basic dynamic of the metaphor, we might note, was no doubt instrumental in Shinkei's own reading of the *Shinkokinshū* and his application of its principles of difference and discontinuous structures in renga. Indeed, it is quite possible that what Shinkei perceived to be the *Shinkokinshū* style's specific relevance to renga was originally brought into waka by those poets' practice of renga itself. It is also noteworthy that a similar partiality for discontinuity is expressed in the putative Teika manuscripts, the *Guhishō* 愚秘抄 and *Sangoki* 三五記, which influenced both Shōtetsu and Shinkei and definitively favored the Distant Link, in contrast to the *Chikuenshō* indifference to it. In the *Guhishō*, we find the following illuminating passage.

> There are no outstanding poems among those using the Close Link. Even if there were, they would be quite rare. No matter how you look at it, in the Close Link the words succeed one another in a manner too predictable, moving as it were from roots to branches to leaves, and thus invariably producing the merely ordinary and rarely the unusual. In the Distant Link, you interrupt the poem at any line and thereby generate something marvelous.[14]

"Marvelous," "ineffably deep," "beyond rational sense"—how are we to interpret what lies behind the panegyric of the *Guhishō* and of Shōtetsu? At this point, we shall have to return to *Sasamegoto* for the philosophical context of such remarks—the quasi-religious background of their valorization of discontinuous structures, or *soku*.

EIGHT

Emptiness and Enlightenment in Poetry

Shinkei initially equates the *shinku-soku* contrast with the Buddhist dialectic in the following series of oppositions:

> The Close Link is based on form [*usō* 有相]; the Distant Link on the formless [*musō* 無相].

> The Close Link is teachings [transmitted in words]; the Distant Link is [the direct insight of] Zen.

> The sutras of complete meaning [using words directly]; the sutras of incomplete meaning [using figuration as means].

> Conventional truth; the ultimate truth.

> The gate of doctrine; the gate of emptiness.

> If you did not set your mind upon enlightenment, how could you free yourself from the delusions in the way of poetry? (*SSG* 49: 187)

That renga's poetry does not lie in the individual verses but in the relations between them is the central tenet of Shinkei's poetics. This means that renga's poetry is always in an absolute sense invisible in, and has to be extrapolated from, the linguistic surface of the verses themselves. In practice, however, there are varying degrees of visibility. The relation between the words and sense of any two verses might be so close as to be wholly apparent on the surface; or then again it could be so distant as to disappear altogether. It must be noted that this impression of closeness and distance is merely an apparent one; the Distant Link does not refer to a verse that is only slackly or tenuously connected to its maeku. The verses connect in both cases, but Shinkei's concern is with the character of that connection. The Close Link operates primarily on the verbal level of word association and rhetoric (i.e., the realm of *kotoba* and *usō*, or form) and is therefore easily apprehensible. The Distant Link, employing a symbolic mode of discourse, may be difficult to grasp at once, but once it has been grasped, it sets off an implosion of meaning in which the two verses, apparently so disparate, dissolve together in a deeper and larger unity. In other words, it is in the *soku* link as Shinkei conceived it that the generic "invisibility" of renga is at its most extreme and most powerful. For it is here, where the link is most apparently absent, that its presence is most wholly palpable.

Meaning in renga tsukeai is not, as previously stated, a semantic content present in either verse as such. It is rather a third and invisible field in which the two verses, each insignificant as such, suddenly come together, and in the process illuminate each other, in the sense of filling each other with momentary significance. This third field in which the two verses find their significance through connection may be nothing more than that of language itself. This is certainly what Shinkei means by identifying the Close Link with "conventional truth" (*setai* 世諦), a meaning that is fully accountable through the logic of common linguistic usage, including the formal, conventional language of poetry. In the case of the Distant Link, however, this third realm is identified as that of "the ultimate truth" (*dai'ichigitai* 第一義諦), based on formlessness (*musō*), Zen, and "emptiness" (*kū*). This series of equations is fairly consistent with Shinkei's earlier drawing of a distinction between a verse's "words and configuration," on the one hand, and its "mind-heart" (*kokoro*), on the other; the Distant Link goes beyond the former's endless mirroring play of signifiers, what Shinkei calls poetry's "delusions" (*shōji* 生死, literally, life-and-death, arising-and-ceasing) to reveal the truth at the heart of phenomena as apprehended in the operation of the poet's mind. In this Buddhist-inspired poetics, the realm of the poet's mind at its highest stage is that of *shinji* 心地, the "mind-ground" or "original mind" as understood in Zen literature. It is, as noted in the passage quoted above, further identified with the realm of *kū*, or emptiness. Itself "formless" or beyond form, this realm gives birth to all the dharmas in the universe through the dynamic operation of *innen*, the principle that phenomena mutually cause and condition each other into existence and nonexistence. In renga, this principle of dependent arising points to the fact that the tsukeku is, in a quite literal sense, conditioned by the maeku, since it is composed in response to it. Conversely, the maeku itself is conditioned by the tsukeku, since it comes to life through the tsukeku's interpretation of it. The whole dialectical process is, moreover, at once the manifestation and extinguishing of a world, in that at the very moment at which the maeku *cum* riddle is answered, it at once disappears or collapses, its materiality "dissolved" at the very instant of understanding. At the very moment when the maeku becomes filled with significance, it is emptied. The solution, so to speak, is its own dissolution.

> In a flash
> of lightning, the color
> of the pines!

If one is permitted to quote this verse as a metaphor for tsukeai, the lightning flash is the dynamic interplay that momentarily illumines—in the sense of giving significance to, the maeku before it falls back again into the indistinguishable formlessness of *śūnyatā*, the unbounded openness of ultimate reality.[1]

Because the realm of emptiness is the field of the dynamic interplay of which the two verses are but the mere external signs or manifestations, as may be expected, Shinkei's idea of poetic training is the same as the Way of mental discipline by which one arrives at this ultimate realm of enlightenment (*satori*), or of the direct insight of "Zen."

WISDOM AND COMPASSION:
GROUNDING AESTHETICS IN MORAL KNOWLEDGE

> Someone once asked a great master of former days, "Tell me exactly, how should one compose poetry?" To which the master replied, "Miscanthus reeds on a withered moor, the pale moon at dawn."

This means to train your mind upon that which remains unsaid in the poem until you awaken to its chill and stilled aspect [*hiesabitaru kata* 冷え寂びたるかた]. The verses of those who have arrived at the ultimate realm are in a mode none other than this. Thus to a verse that suggests "miscanthus reeds on a withered moor," they respond wholly with the mind of "the pale moon at dawn." Those who have no discipline in such matters will without doubt fail to grasp the import of such a link.

Again, when teaching poetry, the old masters would tell their students to keep the following poem in mind while mulling over their own.

honobono to	Dimly, dimly,
ariake no tsuki no	in the faint pool of moonlight
tsukikage ni	shadowing the dawn,
momiji fukiorosu	red leaves come fluttering down
yamaoroshi no kaze	in a gust of wind from the hills.[2]
Minamoto Saneakira	Minamoto Saneakira

This too means to compose your poem gracefully, in a measure long-drawn out and tranquil, while setting your mind upon its aura and overtones [*omokage yosei* 面影・余情]. It means that those who would enter the Way must put the ideal of grace [*en* 艶] at the core of their training. Grace, however, is by no means simply a matter of a charming refinement in the diction and configuration [*kotoba. sugata*] of a verse. Rather, it has its source in the heart of a man with but meager worldly desires, one who is keenly aware of the trackless passing of all phenomena, and values human feeling [*hito no nasake* 人の情け] so well, he would not begrudge even his own life in return for another's kindness. The verses of those whose hearts are "adorned" [*kazaritaru*], though refined in style and diction, would ring but falsely to the true ear. This is because the mind in such verses lacks spiritual clarity [*kokoro kiyokarubekarazu*]. Among the famous old poems and verses esteemed by their own authors, not even rarely do we find any that employ style as a mere adornment. (*SSG* 41: 175–76)

This passage, one of the most central in *Sasamegoto*, raises the crucial philosophical and critical issues dealt with throughout the treatise and Shinkei's other essays; it presents a good opportunity for discussing these points and their resonances in the other places. We have already encountered his characteristic foregrounding of kokoro, the heart-mind, over and above diction and configuration in the concept of the Distant Link. Here the primacy of mind is invoked within the context of a definition of en, "grace," or what in Western aesthetic philosophy goes by the name of "beauty." Simply put, for Shinkei, beauty has its ground in existential knowledge. This knowledge, which is more properly called wisdom, springs from a keen experience of the mutability of all phenomena and ideally results, if not in the renunciation, at least in the tempering of desire. Clearly, if one truly knew oneself as mortal and the objects of one's desire as equally ephemeral, it would be the height of ignorance to cling to anything at all. Such was apparently Shinkei's conviction when he delivered an impassioned diatribe against some fairly universal illusions in reply to the question of how one should "train the mind to reach the highest realm" in poetry.

> Someone has said that whether in undergoing Buddhist training to discover the ultimate source of the mind [*kokoro no minamoto* 心の源], or in studying the way of poetry to gain insight into the profoundly moving character of things [*aware fukaki koto o satoramu* 哀れ深きことを悟らん], the highest realm is quite beyond the reach of those who put their trust in an enduring life, who are wholly absorbed in the objects of the senses, value worldly goods, and being complacent, have neither anxieties nor fears. . . . One need not go so far as to lead a solitary life remote from the world, but still, not to constantly clarify the mind [*kokoro o sumashi* 心を澄まし] and reflect . . . that this world of ours comes and goes in a dream, that for the high as for the low, the wise and the foolish, this thread of life that bides not till the close of day is frailer even than a filament of hair—to remain unaware of all these things while relying solely on oneself, believing that it will go on for a hundred and a thousand years, to be wholly absorbed in the objects of the senses, cherish one's name, and be led astray by the myriad illusions of existence—that indeed is the height of foolishness! When the body turns to dust and ashes, whither goes its vital spark of life? And not only this body but all the myriad phenomena of the universe, whence do they come, whither disappear—we must pursue this question to the utmost! (*SSG* 20: 145–46)

As is well known, the parallelism between two pursuits, that of Buddhism and of poetry—later to become fused in Part II of *Sasamegoto*—is the most essential characteristic of Shinkei's thought and gives the treatise its reputation as the most representative expression of medieval Japanese poetic criticism. Here, too, we are presented with two variants or stages of the same activity, in that to "clarify the mind" (*kokoro o sumashi*) is to free it from the illusions that the mind itself engenders in a deluded state, and "to pursue to the utmost" the origins and end of all phenomena is in fact the same as Buddhism's aim, here expressed as "to discover the ultimate source of the mind," that is, "the mind-ground" of absolute emptiness, where phenomena arise and cease in the dynamic process of interaction of internal cause and external circumstance (*innen*). All this is what is entailed in the moral knowledge that constitutes one of the grounds of poetic grace or beauty, which necessarily reflects an achieved state of "insight into the profoundly moving character of things [*aware fukaki koto*]."

The other half of Shinkei's definition of grace is its radical valorization of "human feeling" (*hito no nasake*), radical because it is "appreciated" at the cost of life itself and thus represents the primary value of human existence. Significantly, "feeling" here is not the expression of individual subjective emotion; it is invoked rather in the context of an interpersonal, or dialogical, reciprocal relation—of a kindness extended by the one eliciting a profound response in the other. To be sure, the affect and response nexus as defined by Tsurayuki in the *Kokinshū* Preface had been at the very core of courtly Heian aesthetics and sensibility; what is specifically "medieval" about Shinkei's formulation is that he invariably couples it with the existential knowledge described above, and specifically with *mujōkan* 無常観, the "awareness of mutability," the conviction of the temporality of being. Another of his statements about the root and function of poetry is illuminating in this regard:

> The mind and language of poetry are rooted in a sense of mutability and sorrow for the human condition [*mujō jukkai* 無常述懐]. It is through poetry that people convey to one another their emotion about things that have moved them deeply [*aware fukaki koto o iikawashi*]; its influence should soften even the hearts of barbarous demons and stern warriors, leading them to a realization of the truth about this transient world. (*SSG* 13: 139)

In other words, since temporality is the ineluctable common condition, a keen awareness of it should ideally bind all in a universal human sympathy, that is, compassion. This forms the basis of Shinkei's valorization of "human feeling," it constitutes the node of a poetic sensibility, an authentic "grace" (*en*) or true refinement that is not merely of verbal surface but of the mind-heart itself. Also expressed as "the profoundly moving character of things" (*aware fukaki koto*), it is the sole common truth about self and other whose realization might recall men from the barbaric and anarchic workings of blind ego and into the gentle light of a truly civilized human community. In sum, Shinkei's concept of beauty is a composite of the wisdom gained from a rejection of illusion and of the human compassion that can only arise from such a renunciation. It possesses, like all ideas born of religious conviction, an ironic and dialectical character for it is an affirmation of pure value that entails a wholly essential negation.

"Miscanthus reeds on a withered moor, the pale moon at dawn": in *Sasamegoto*, renga poetry at its highest pitch is not (or not only) the transmission of meaning, the play of language, but the perfect working of the channel of communication, when the mind or spirit of the one is directly transmitted to the other through and despite language. This mind, however, is of the special kind signified by the two concrete images of phenomena at their most reduced and attenuated, that moment just one step from nothingness when things take on a "chill and stilled aspect" (*hiesabitaru kata*). *Sabi* 寂 is a quality discernible in Shunzei and Teika, but it is in the poetry and critical work of Shinkei that it emerges as the central aspect of a symbolist aesthetics grounded in a moral philosophy of renunciation. The ultimate stage of *mujōkan*, it is indicative of the final end of a dynamic process, when the miscanthus seed, having exhausted its fertile potentiality through summer and autumn, reveals itself as wholly the patient of an impersonal process; the seeping out of a vernal vitality, the shrinking and shriveling of colorless leaves, a lonely and empty page upon which time actively inscribes itself, rust on metal, moss on stone, wrinkles on an aged face, the sparse blossoms on an ancient, gnarled plum tree. To compose poetry "with the mind of the pale dawn moon" is therefore to ground all—self, phenomena, and language, in emptiness and temporality. It is to understand the paradox that reality is a mere appearance, literally an "image" or "face," a "shadow" or "reflection" (*omokage* 面影) behind which there is nothing more solid or more real to grasp as a hypostatized, eternal object of desire; but also that this apparently fragile, "transparent" appearance is simultaneously the ineluctable manifestation of a cosmic process of interrelation involving one and all in the fullness and exhaustion of time. The moving quality of things, which is no less than their simultaneous fullness and emptiness, is also called by Shinkei "the deeply fascinating Principle" of existence, as in this passage from the Epilogue to *Iwahashi* 岩橋:

> A man who is ignorant of the Way is blind to the shifting of the four seasons, unaware of the deeply fascinating Principle [*en fukaki kotowari* 艶深 き理] coursing through the forms and colors of the ten thousand realms. He spends his whole life before a blank wall with a jar pulled over his head. (*Iwahashi batsubun*, p. 327)

A poetry grounded in the dialectical principle of emptiness and temporality can only be a symbolic and impersonal one. If reality is a dynamic process of interrelation, the word is necessarily, in an absolute sense, nonreferential and nonrepresentational. The object is never merely and wholly what it seems to be; to see it so is to stare at "a blank wall with a jar pulled over one's head," that is, a self-inflicted blindness. Rather, the object is part of a network of circumstance whose boundaries are shifting and ultimately immeasurable, since there is no such thing as a final cause, or in the language of deconstruction, a "transcendental signified," in Buddhist cosmology. It is a part that mirrors the whole in being generated by and in turn generating it. In other words, the object, or the word used to represent it, both is and is not itself; its nature is intrinsically ambiguous and double. This is what Shinkei means by training the mind "upon that which remains unsaid" (*iwanu tokoro*) in the poem, the "aura and overtones" (*omokage yojō*) that can only be evoked because it is beyond the power of conventional language to directly express; he means to understand the poem as a symbolic construct and a heuristic device for revealing the true nature of reality.

Springing from his acute reading of the *Shinkokinshū* poets, as well as from a deeply felt personal need to define and promote poetry as an activity of the highest religious and universal human value, Shinkei's work is in a sense a retracing of the beginnings of a symbolism founded on a Buddhist apprehension of reality back to Teika, Shunzei, Jichin, Saigyō, and the other major poets of that anthology. It is a deliberate project to ground future renga practice upon a similar symbolist poetics based on the primacy of mind, or *kokoro*, and registered as the "aesthetic" qualities of aura and overtones. In the following sections, I shall trace the Buddhist philosophical grounding of waka practice in the poetry and criticism of these *Shinkokinshū* poets and thereby clarify how the principles of emptiness and temporality found both medieval aesthetics and poetic process.

NINE

Medieval Symbolic Poetry
and Buddhist Discourse

LYRIC SUBJECTIVITY AND IMPERSONAL SYMBOLISM

Kokoro 心 has, of course, been a central concept in Japanese poetics since Tsurayuki's (868?-945) pioneering manifesto in the *Kokinshū* Preface, where it is seen as the source of poetry, the "seed" (*tane* 種) that sprouts into "leaves of words" (*koto no ha* 言の葉), that is, the poem. In contemporary critical terms, this is a view of poetic expression in which the signifier is seminally linked to the signified, as foliage to seed, as the outside and inside of an indivisible whole. In practice, Tsurayuki apparently required these two elements to be in a relation of balanced symmetry, such that neither one outweighs the other. Thus, "Bishop Henjō achieves the form of poetry, but it is deficient in truth. It is, so to speak, like looking at a woman in a painting and being uselessly moved by her." Here the poem's rhetoric is not justified by the paucity of its content. The opposite case is Ariwara Narihira, whose poetry "has an excess of heart and insufficiency of words [*kokoro amarite kotoba tarazu* 心余りて詞足らず]; it is like a shriveled flower whose color is gone but whose fragrance remains." Tsurayuki's criticism of Narihira's excessive *kokoro* and inadequate words is quite noteworthy in view of the fact that in Shinkei, it will be precisely the "wordless fragrance of the mind" (*iwanu kokoro no nioi* 言はぬ心の匂ひ) that is singled out as the mark of a masterly verse, one, moreover, whose "words are few, chill and reduced" (*kotoba sukunaku hieyasetaru* 言葉少なく冷え痩せたる). These two views of poetry mark the difference between a lyricism understood as an effluence of the heart, an expression of subjective feeling/thought, and a symbolism whose object is to reveal ultimate reality, the Real, as a manifestation of an impersonal, open-ended process. The difference is between a confident belief in the ideal congruence—or adequation—of mind-heart and language, on the one hand, and a sense of the inadequacy of language to *contain*—in both senses of the word—the mind and reality, on the other, and it leads to a poetic practice in which language is deliberately used to evoke the openness of the Real. In this sense, the symbolism of *yojō* 余情 (also pronounced *yosei*) is distinct from what Tsurayuki calls *kokoro amarite* in Narihira, a surplus or excess of feeling/thought whose observation is founded on the postulate of a normative relation of equivalence between mind and language. *Yojō* is, rather, what may be rendered as "uncontained feeling," an awareness of the indefinite extension of objects and events, their dimension of openness, in sum their epistemological indeterminacy.

Historically, the shift in the Japanese understanding of poetry from an expressive lyricism to an impersonal symbolism may be traced back to Shunzei's (1114–1204) redaction of Tsurayuki in the opening passage of his single extant treatise, *Korai fūteishō* 古来風体抄 (Poetic Styles from Antiquity to the Present, 1197, rev. 1201).

> How far Japanese poetry has come from its beginnings. Arising in the age of the mighty flourishing gods, it became the speech act of our myriad-isled country, and its heart-mind has since spontaneously spread through the Six Types, its words flowed copiously through untold ages. Since, as stated in the *Kokinshū* Preface, "it has its seed in the human heart, which springs into numerous leaves of words," in inquiring after the spring flowers and gazing at the crimson leaves of autumn, were there no such thing as poetry, no man would know their color and fragrance, and what then could we take to be the heart of things [*nani o ka wa moto no kokoro tomo subeki* なにをかは本の心ともすべき]?[1]

Tsurayuki sees poetry as a universal human (and animal) response to experience expressed through the medium of the figurative image (viz., "what [man] feels in his heart he expresses through what he sees and what he hears"). For Shunzei, it is the mediating link between man and external reality, the means by which we come to *know* (*shiru*) not only Tsurayuki's originating source, the human heart (*hito no kokoro*), but also "the color and fragrance" (*iro o mo ka o mo* 色をも香をも) of things. The intervention of external phenomena between Tsurayuki's organic human-heart-as-seed metaphor and "the heart of things" (*moto no kokoro*, literally, the original or essential heart) at the end of the passage is wholly crucial, since it turns the *Kokinshū* Preface's expressive theory into a symbolic one.[2] This grounding heart-mind is not a lyrical subjectivity mediated through the language of natural phenomena, but an impersonal *contemplation* of objective reality. Poetry is here seen primarily as a form of knowledge and understanding; existing in the middle ground between subject and object, it ideally manifests "the heart of things." In modern Japanese scholarship, *moto no kokoro* has been equated with the critical concept of the "essential nature," or *hon'i* 本意, of phenomena.[3] And it is true that there is a suggestive affinity between the two terms as such: the first graph is identical, the second synonymous. I suggest, however, that if *moto no kokoro* is indeed to be equated with *hon'i*, then *hon'i* in the present context would not, as commonly understood, primarily and wholly refer to the accepted handling of particular phenomena in the poetic tradition, but rather to their essential nature as seen in Buddhist philosophy. Or to put the matter differently, I am suggesting that the established conventions of how particular images (the moon, the cherry blossoms, pines) are handled are based on an earlier "primordial," historically prior, determination of the nature of reality as a whole rather than of isolated features of it. The issue revolves around Shunzei's reading of the term *kokoro* and his situating of it within the larger question of poetic value.

SHUNZEI'S MEDITATION: THE THREE TRUTHS, TENDAI SHIKAN, AND THE DEEP MIND OF POETRY

Continuing from the passage above, Shunzei observes that because poetry manifests "the heart of things," its practice has continued unbroken through the ages, and books on the subject of poetic diction, famous poetic places, pillow words, and the so-called *shiki* 式 (rules of composition) have proliferated. Yet none of these formalistic studies, he avers, really touches the crucial issue of what precisely makes a poem good or bad, "a question extraordinarily difficult to explain and convey," as he admits, and then immediately proceeds to make the attempt, thus:

> In this regard, in the opening passage of the work called *Tendai shikan*, there are these words written by Shōan Daishi: "The luminous tranquility of stillness and insight [*shikan no myōjōnaru koto* 止観の明静なること] was yet unheard of in ages past."[4] The very sound of these words, evoking limitless depths, fathoming a remotely inward significance, awesome and splendid, is like the good and bad in poetry, the endeavor to know its deep mind [*fukaki kokoro* 深き心], difficult to convey in words; and yet it is precisely this analogy that enables us to comprehend it in the same way. . . . [5]
>
> It is true that the one are golden words of Buddhist scripture, full of a deep truth, while the other seems to be but an idle game of empty words and fine phrases [*fugen kigyo no tawabure* 浮言綺語の戯れ]. And yet it manifests a profound significance in things [*koto no fukaki mune* ことの深き旨] and can be the circumstance that leads one to the Buddhist way. Moreover, because delusion is of itself wisdom, the *Lotus Sutra* says, "Properly explained, the secular classics . . . and the actions of mundane existence are all following the True Dharma." And the *Fugenkan* teaches, "What is the thing that is designated sinful, what designated fortunate? Neither sin nor fortune possesses a subject; the mind is of itself empty." Consequently, here also in speaking of the deep way of poetry, I draw upon its similarity to the three truths of the empty, the contingent, and the middle [*kū.ke.chū no sandai* 空・仮・中の三諦] and write of it in the same terms. (pp. 274–75)

In a move even more startling than his first one of revising Tsurayuki, Shunzei sets out the determination that what constitutes poetry is its "deep mind" (*fukaki kokoro*), which is like the contemplative state of *shikan* (stillness and insight) impossible to describe in words. In the chapter on the signification of the word itself, the *Makashikan* 魔訶止観 explains that from the relative viewpoint, *shi* 止 means cessation from evil views and delusive thoughts, unmoving concentration on the principle of prajna wisdom, and the stillness of prajna as opposed to the incessant motion of the phenomenal dharmas; while *kan* 観 means penetrating and destroying the roots of suffering, achieving the vision of suchness, and the luminosity of the dharma nature. "Stillness is a cutting off; this cutting off leads to liberation. Insight is a keen intelligence; this intelligence leads to wisdom."[6] The first term *shi* (literally, stopping, ceasing) refers to the uprooting of desire, the object fixation of the ego, as well as the partial discriminations of the intellect. The second term, *kan*, refers to the liberated way of "seeing" with absolute impartiality, beyond the dualism of subject and object, or objectification of self and other; it is a trancelike state of tranquility in which things register themselves with absolute unmediated clarity. The operative concept here is nonduality. Again, the *Makashikan*: "All is the Real [*jissō* 実相], and apart from it there are no separate dharmas. When the Buddha-nature has settled quietly over all, that is called 'stillness.' This quietness that is always illumined is called 'insight.' One speaks of before and after, but they are not two, not separate."[7] The affinity between what Shinkei calls "the chill and stilled" (*hiesabitaru* 冷え寂びたる) aspect of the poem, its sparse words, its "chill and reduced" (*hieyasetaru* 冷え痩せたる) quality, and the state of *shikan* speaks for itself. It speaks, in other words, of poetry as a contemplative state of mind, and *sabi* as the state of "spiritual clarity" (*kokoro kiyoshi* or *kokoro o sumashi*) referred to earlier.

From one perspective, the passage from *Korai fūteishō* quoted above may be seen as an apologia for or justification of poetry against the common suspicion that it is no more than "an idle game of empty words and fine phrases." Being nonreferential, it does not represent mundane reality as we know it. Shunzei would have remembered that even Bai Juyi was moved to assign a heuristic function to his works when he dedicated them to a temple late in life, declaring: "I pray that the action of my worldly writings in this life, the error in my 'wild words and fine phrases,' may turn round and become a cause for praising the Buddha's teachings, a circumstance for turning the wheel of the Dharma in the worlds to come."[8]

In effect, Bai's dedication suggests that salvation from the "error" of dealing in empty words is only possible by means of a reading of them that would promote Buddhist belief and convert others. In Japan, there is a whole body of religious poetry called "Buddhist poems" (*shakkyōka* 釈教歌) which are often composed on famous lines from the scriptures. Translating the meaning of sometimes arcane doctrine into the graceful language of poetry and embodying it in concrete imagery, these poems are often moving testaments to the fact that literature is indeed a powerful means (*hōben* 方便) of promoting belief. But Shunzei's subject in the *Korai fūteishō* is like Bai Juyi's in his dedication of his "worldly writings," not overtly religious but wholly secular poetry, and what is implied there is that the poetic experience is essentially similar to the religious state of meditation, and that the ontological existence of the poem is best conceived in terms of Tendai's three-dimensional view of reality as expressed in the truths of the empty, the contingent or provisional, and the middle.

This is not, it seems to me, a matter of using poetry to promote Buddhism overtly, but, on the contrary, using Buddhism to illuminate the nature of poetry, and so ultimately implying what Shinkei openly argues throughout *Sasamegoto*, that the two are one.

THE DOCTRINES OF EMPTINESS
AND THE MIDDLE WAY

The doctrines of emptiness and the Middle Way that undergird the Tendai "three truths" (*sandai*) concept have their source in the Indian philosopher Nagarjuna's *Chūron* 中論 (Skt. *Madhyamaka-śāstra*, "The Philosophy of the Middle Way"). Nagarjuna's project here was to illumine the core of the Buddha's teachings, which had been obscured by centuries of philosophical speculation. To this end he used the famous fourfold logical method (is, is not, both is and is not, neither is nor is not) to demolish the mistaken assertion that there is a substantial inner self (*jishō* 自性; Skt. *ātman*) in humans and phenomena, and thus to demonstrate that reality is empty at the core. The negative method of baffling the permanent validity of any positive assertion was necessary to demonstrate the truth of Buddhism's central observation about the mutability of all dharmas. Such is the gist of the verse or *gatha* that the *Makashikan* quotes from the *Chūron*: "The dharmas that arise out of causes and conditions—/we say that they are empty,/and further, that this is a provisional designation,/and that is itself the Middle Way."[9]

In other words, the true meaning of impermanence is comprehensible only based on the ontological "ground" of emptiness, for if things did have an eternal self—what we understand by unchanging "essence" or "substance"—they could not be said to change at all, and that would nullify the whole Buddhist salvific project of liberating the mind from the false (i.e., mundane, worldly, conventional) view of reality that is the root of suffering. Reality is at every moment contingent upon a conglomeration of cause and circumstance (*innen*), and is thus always relative and provisional. It is wholly real at that moment, yet, lacking an inner core, it is also empty, "and that is itself the Middle Way." What this must mean, ultimately, is that emptiness is the necessary ground for a thing's coming into and passing out of existence; the sheer reality of becoming—both the clinging to and the liberation from desire, is possible only upon this yawning abyss, as is the true meaning of freedom and moral responsibility in human existence.

In this way, Shunzei's appeal to the "three truths" concept may be said to represent a statement about the wholly ambivalent, multidimensional nature of poetry. Poetry is not a faithful representation of the mundane reality that is present to common consciousness; it is a verbal construct and is in that sense "empty." Nevertheless, it necessarily uses the objects of the mundane world—"the spring flowers and the crimson leaves," for instance—as its materials, for otherwise it would not be comprehensible at all; its existence is thus "provisional" or "contingent" upon everyday reality. From a linguistic perspective, a poem is a configuration of signs that signify by force of the words' syntactic relations as undergirded by the special vocabulary and grammar of a whole traditional poetic language, which is superimposed upon ordinary language and reality. As a specific instance, moreover, a single poem is already several removes from mundane reality; its ultimate referent is "reality," but that reality is a supramundane one; it is not simply given beforehand but is constituted by the very fabric and tissue of the poem itself. In this sense, it is a wholly self-referential artificial entity. Being self-referential, it is "empty," but it is precisely this emptiness, mistakenly interpreted as falsehood (as in "empty words and fine phrases"), that enables or empowers it to signify anything and everything. In short, it is the very emptiness of the poem as a sign that enables it to reveal what Shunzei calls "the deep significance of things" (*koto no fukaki mune*), perceiving which, one can be "led to the Buddhist way."

NONDUALITY: THE DEFENSE OF WRITING IN THE MAKASHIKAN

There is a passage from the *Makashikan* Preface that illuminates what Shunzei had in mind when he spoke of poetry in terms of the three truths of the "empty, provisional, and middle." It is the defense of writing, *mon*, literally, "the letter, literature," as a means of illuminating the Buddha's teachings. And it is a defense based on a view of the sign as a nonduality of signifier and signified. Remarkably, two lines from it are quoted in the *Wakan rōeishū* 和漢朗詠集 immediately preceding Bai Juyi's own apologia for his "wild words and fancy phrases," an editorial juxtaposition that must surely indicate a tsukeai-like relation between the two.

> Were you to set explanation and silence [*setsumoku* 説黙] against each other, you would not unravel the intention of the teachings [*kyōi* 教意], and would in time wander far from the principle [*ri* 理]. There is no principle

outside of the explanation, no explanation outside of the principle. The unexplained [*musetsu* 無説] inheres in the explanation, the explanation inheres in the unexplained. These things are not two, not separate; they are, in and of themselves, the Real.[10] Great compassion truly feels for all who do not hear. It is like holding up a fan to exemplify the moon when it is hidden behind layers of mountains, like shaking a tree to illustrate the wind when it is at rest in the great void [*taikyo* 太虚].[11] People nowadays are dull of mind; it is consequently difficult for them to see in the profound darkness. It is through forms [*iro*, literally, color] that the eye penetrates it, through the mediation of the sign [*mon* 文] that vision becomes easy. Were you to suffer harm by being imprisoned within the sign,[12] then you must come to know the sign from the non-sign [*himon* 非文], then you must arrive there where all is at once sign, non-sign, and not non-sign [*hi-fumon* 非不文], and from a single sign achieve release from all and for all. It is for this reason that the three kinds of texts constitute the gate by which one arrives at the one.[13] And here I end the abbreviated explanation of [the *Makashikan's*] dependent origination [*engi*].[14]

In Guanding's introduction, it is possible to read in the *Makashikan's* view of language (*mon*, the sign, the text) a recognizable semiotics, or theory of the sign, in the distinction it initially draws between sign and non-sign, or what would now be called the signifier and the signified. The signifier, brushstrokes on a page, a string of verbal utterances, are merely the empty form of what is signified by them, as intended by the author or read by the viewer or auditor. In this case, it is the invisible principle (*ri*) or truth behind them that makes them meaningful, that constitutes their very nature as a sign to be read, a text to be interpreted and understood. A fan may stand for a hidden moon, a shaking tree for an invisible wind; in that case, they are both "signs" of something else, which is itself a "non-sign," a principle or a truth. The two are distinct, as example is from principle, and not to understand this difference is to become imprisoned by the sign, the letter of the text instead of its significance or intention: the fan instead of the moon, the shaking tree instead of the wind. In other words, the *Makashikan* is taking a standpoint on the emptiness or metaphorical nature of language; the letter itself is void of self-nature. Crucially, however, this does not generate a nihilistic skepticism but only a warning not to take the word literally. The word signifies because it can be read and understood. Like the dharmas, words are both empty and real at the same time, and ultimately, they just are. Such would be the sense of the progressive negations of the anterior term in the statement, "then you must arrive there where all is at once sign, non-sign, and not non-sign." The sheer ambivalence of the last term is the

Middle Way that, by establishing the first two, also enables the signifying function of the innately empty sign. Signification is therefore a process of *engi*, "dependent arising," that is, the birth of dharma or of significant content through contextual circumstance. Signifier and signified, explanation and silence, example and principle mutually depend upon or determine each other. ("There is no principle outside of the explanation, no explanation outside of the principle. The unexplained [*musetsu*] inheres in the explanation, the explanation inheres in the unexplained.") Each would be meaningless without the other and, as we have seen, this is also what Shinkei meant by equating the *hen-jo-dai/kyoku* or tsukeai structure with *innen*, the mutually determining operation of cause and condition, and with *hiyu*, the metaphorical nature of signification. The ultimate "principle," however, is beyond signification, if by that is understood something existing *outside* phenomenal reality and its explanation in the hermeneutic circle. Anything in fact can be a "fan," a signifier for the moon, if we take the "moon" to signify everything. The instant of understanding is simultaneously the *dissolution* of the principle and of the signifying process, in the nondualism of the Real, the "true face," "suchness" (*jissō*), whose simultaneous singularity and openness is shown precisely by the infinite possibilities—but also the ultimate impossibility—of metaphorization. There are infinite other ways than a fan to point to the moon; depending on the circumstance and the person, some will be more effective than others in inducing understanding; but none will ever *be* the moon, the moon itself being a metaphor for the principle. And all this is most probably what Shunzei understood by the "deep mind" of poetry.

WITTGENSTEIN'S SILENCE, HEIDEGGER'S UNDERSTANDING

Does the "thought" of nonduality amount to what Derrida calls "the metaphysical reduction of the sign," that is, the process of erasing difference by reducing the signifier to the signified, the sensible to the intelligible, or simply expelling one from the other?[15] This is the same as to ask if the thought of the Middle Way is a metaphysics similar to that of classic Western philosophy. I feel that this question, while vexing for someone who would bring these two philosophical traditions in dialogue with each other, is ultimately an artificial one in being unnecessary. For the thought of nonduality is precisely the irreducibility of the empty to the phenomenal and vice versa, that is, the holding of the tension of their opposition in the indeterminacy of the middle, which is, perhaps, what long remained unthought in Western metaphysics and is brought to the fore by Derrida's own "concept" of dif- férance. In other words, it is because they are different that they can be the same, and the same because different, and the Middle Way thus announces that thought (the "is" and "is not") is possible only on the "ground" of what eludes it. When language, or metaphorization, has done its task of "explana- tion," and understanding is reached, there is only "silence."

Wittgenstein advised a similar silence ("What we cannot speak about we must pass over in silence") after clarifying the logic of what can be said and thought in propositions or tautologies, if only to affirm that "even when *all possible* scientific questions have been answered, the problems of life remain completely untouched," and that there are "things that can- not be put into words," being "mystical."[16] Wittgenstein was concerned with delimitating the sphere of the logical, while Madhyamika is focused on the possibility of liberation from "the problems of life," that is, suffer- ing, but both teach the limits of language. It is significant, in this regard, that Heidegger also saw the inadequacy of scientific logic and of classical metaphysics to account for the meaning of being and embarked on the existential analytic (in *Being and Time*) in order to work out the ques- tion of being when it is properly understood, not as the abstract object of an epistemological inquiry by a transcendental subjectivity, but in and through the fact of existence as being-in-the-world (*Dasein*). And it is with the existential analytic, the analysis of the temporality and historicality of being, one senses, that Western philosophy took a turn that brought it into the path of Eastern thought.

For our purposes in reading Shunzei's and Shinkei's Buddhist-inspired view of poetry as the symbolic manifestation of the Real, of the poem as a contemplation of the Real, Heidegger's account of the phenomenon of un- derstanding is, I believe, illuminating in that a poem, as an "explanation" of something (and not, rather, of nothing) presupposes understanding. It presupposes an intention (*i*) or orientation toward something, which in *Makashikan* is the principle (*ri*); otherwise it would be just words that cannot be "read." For Heidegger understanding is, like care and concern, the mode of being of Dasein. Dasein finds itself always already "thrown" in a totality of involvements with inanimate entities and with other Daseins that together constitute its world; as such Dasein always already has a grasp, albeit often preconscious, of their significance for it by the very fact of being-in-the-world. The same fact of "thrownness" into the "there" of its world, moreover, discloses to Dasein the significance of its own existence, not as mere presence, but as "potentiality-for-Being towards itself, for the sake of itself."[17] This disclosure is Dasein's understanding of its own temporality as what is "*not yet* actual and what is *not at any time* necessary," but nevertheless has the potential to be. In other words, being-unto-death, the existential angst, in revealing Dasein's temporality, is precisely the condition that would, in the Buddhist master narrative, open up the path or Way, awaken the thought of enlightenment (*hosshin* 発心), the potentiality for Being. As Dasein is a kind of being that *is* in terms of its possibilities, its understanding has the character of *projection*, a sketching out beforehand of its own potentiality for Being within the world as a network of significances for it. When Dasein works out the possibilities projected in understanding, it is engaging in interpretation (*Auslegung*), a process that renders *explicit* what has been implicitly understood *as* something. In terms of the *Makashikan* passage quoted above, the fan is interpreted *as* the "moon," the shaking tree *as* "the wind," and these in turn *as* the manifestations of the principle. These "signs" become intelligible, that is, meaningful, due to the projective character of Dasein's understanding, such that it always already has a preconception of what is to be understood, even when it first becomes explicitly aware of it only in the process of laying-out (*Auslegung*) or explication that is the interpretation. What this means is that understanding always precedes interpretation in the hermeneutic circle; nothing can be "read" intelligibly without a preunderstanding of its potential significance for Dasein. Particularly when Dasein is in a privative state of mind (and seeking the meaning of Being is such a state of lack), the more prepared it is to interpret what is disclosed to it through the agency of the sign.[18] I find this theory of the projective character of understanding illuminating in setting the condition of possibility for our ability to interpret poetry that is, on the face of it, just mere words.

The difference between the Heideggerian quest and the Buddhist one is perhaps that in the latter, the interpretation has already been explicitly laid out in the vast Mahayana scriptures and treatises as a guide to follow, although it is invariably also said that one must undertake the journey and experience it oneself. The *Makashikan* is itself such an *Auslegung* in the form of a pedagogy of explicating (in the sense of "unfolding") the processes of the mind to empower it to "see" Being. It is noteworthy that Heidegger's existential analytic in *Being and Time* broke off before its completion. On the other hand, his thinking is said to have taken a crucial turn (*die Kehre*) that took it beyond philosophy as rational inquiry and into the language of poetry. It is this turn, it seems to me, that brought him even closer to the concern of this book, which is ultimately to explicate how poetry and philosophy can come to travel the same path.

TEN

Beyond Meaning

Beauty Is the Aura of Contemplation

One of Shunzei's major concerns, as manifest in his judgments at poetry contests, was the importance of the materiality of the poem in evoking a "surreal" or supramundane realm. That is to say, he emphasized the symbolic nature of poetic language, its power to evoke or provoke a state of mind similar to the contemplation of ultimate reality in Zen meditation, or *shikan*. Tanaka Yutaka has shown that the most appropriate comprehensive term for Shunzei's critical ideal, one indeed that influenced the whole course of medieval poetry, is *kehai* けはひ・景 or *keiki* 景気, "aura, emanation."[1] One of Tanaka's most important theses in his book *Chūsei bungakuron kenkyū* is that the poetic ideals of the *Shinkokinshū* poets, like *yūgen* 幽玄, *yojō*, and *en* 艶, should not, as previously, be understood wholly as formal "aesthetic" principles, but within the context of the whole reexamination of the nature of poetic process and poetic expression initiated by Shunzei in the *Korai fūteishō*. Put another way, the major question here for a Western readership, which I attempt to answer in this chapter by retracing the path from the *Shinkokinshū* to Shinkei, is what constituted the "aesthetic" for a period in which the idea of "art for art's sake" was far-fetched, to put it mildly, and the margins of the secular and the sacred, and of poetry, philosophy, and religion, were, as we have seen, quite fluid indeed.

Shunzei's notion of aura is defined alongside *yūgen* in such statements as this:

> [A poem] should be such that in the mere reading out or chanting of it there is something that somehow sounds compelling and ineffably deep [*en ni mo yūgen ni mo* 艶にも幽玄にも]. If it is a good poem, there will seem to be, apart from its words and configuration, an aura [*keiki*] that accompanies it. For instance, it is like haze hanging over the spring flowers, like the belling of a deer heard before the autumn moon, the fragrance of the spring breeze about the plum tree by the hedge, or rain dripping over the crimson foliage on the mountain crest—something that floats and hovers about the poem.[2]

Readers of *Japanese Court Poetry* will recall here a very similar passage from Chōmei's *Mumyōshō* on the character of *yūgen*, "ineffable depth," and recognize also that *yojō*, or overtones, *omokage* 面影 (shadow, reflection), and *en* (compelling grace) all belong to the same semantic field as "aura" or emanation.[3] In this poetry, words that clearly manifest their meaning would not be as "compelling" (*en* in its primary meaning) as those that allow the imagination to contemplate, through the ambiguity of the poem's meaning, or indeed the absence there of any overt meaning, its extension into another realm. This is not, strictly speaking, a "descriptive" mode; nor is it "objective" in the sense that a photograph would be, since what is at stake is essentially the quality of the poet's mind, the inner eye set before a natural scene. In this sense, the symbolic "aura" given off by the poem's image is the shadow or reflection (*omokage*) cast by its author's contemplative gaze. In the poem itself, the object-image is never seen as an autonomous singularity, but always in combination with another, which alters and yet defines it, while being itself modified and made visible by it, in a relation of mutuality that Ezra Pound, defining the Image under the influence of his reading of oriental poetry, called "an intellectual and emotional complex in an instant of time."[4] Haze over spring flowers, dripping rain on the autumn hills, moonlight evoked by the belling of a deer—the essence of poetic feeling is based on an eminently contextual view of reality, and "aura" is the unseen fragrance emanating from the mutual contact. In phenomenological terms, the realm of poetry is one in which objects become manifest within a relation of engi, or dependent origination.

haru fukaki	In the soft currents
nobe no kasumi no	beneath the clouded haze of
shitakaze ni	deep spring fields,
fukarete agaru	Blown, it floats upward—
yūhibari kana	the evening skylark.

About this poem by Jien from round 17 of the mid-spring section of the "Poetry Contest in 600 Rounds," the spokesman for the opposing side objected that *kasumi no shitakaze* (literally, underbreeze of the haze) sounds odd, and the implication that the skylark would not rise but for the breeze is irrational. The spokesman for Jien's side replied that the poem is evoking the *aura* of the spring wind's lightness, which makes us feel that the bird is being buoyed up by its soft currents. Shunzei as judge upheld this latter defense, saying that while it is true that on the level of common sense, *fukarete agaru* (literally, blown, rises) is indeed questionable, yet it is precisely this line as such that suggests the whole aura of the hazy meadow stirring softly in the spring breeze.[5] In other words, a degree of poetic license is necessary to reveal the *hon'i*, or essential quality, of a scene, the "aura" that is a combined effect of visual and tactile elements acting upon each other. Here the delicate litheness of the spring breeze is manifest in the buoyancy of the bird's flight, and the exact quality of the bird's flight in turn manifests the spring breeze, a small yet complex detail captured by the clarity of the poet's inner eye and expanding to modify the character of the whole scene.

THE ONTOLOGICAL DIMENSION OF YŪGEN, INEFFABLE DEPTH

Yūgen, "ineffable depth," is a term used by Shunzei in a sense not easily distinguishable from his usage of *keiki* or *yojō*, an indication that they are variations of the same concept of symbolic ambiguity based on a Buddhist understanding of phenomena. "Were it not for poetry, no man would know their color and fragrance, and what then could we take to be the heart of things?" What "floats and hovers" over the poem may be said to be "the color and fragrance" of phenomena viewed in their essence as mutable appearance rather than the substantial entities hypostatized by the rational or utilitarian mind, the better to employ them in its own enterprise. Shunzei characterizes the poem below by Retired Emperor Go-Toba from the "Poetry Contest in 1,500 Rounds" as, among other things, *yūgen*.

kaze fukeba	When the wind stirs,
hana no shirakumo	subtly, pale clouds of flowers
yaya kiete	melt out of sight,
yonayona haruru	as nightly more lustrous shines
miyoshino no tsuki	the moon on the hills of Yoshino.

In the poem of the Left, *yonayona haruru/miyoshino no tsuki* (nightly more lustrous shines/the moon on the hills of Yoshino) has a more compelling beauty [*en*] than even a fully illuminated autumn sky. It truly feels as if one were gazing at the sheer reflection itself. In the poem of the Right, it is true, the words "Were I to say that today is truly regrettable" and so on clearly manifest their meaning [*tashikani kotowari kikoete*]. However, in the way of poetry, the unparalleled mode of ineffable depth [*yūgen*] in "nightly more lustrous" is the more desirable.[6]

What renders *yonayona haruru* more compelling and ineffably deeper than a wholly illuminated autumn sky is surely the way the moon's transparency is made to emerge/merge in a contrastive and disclosing relation to the diminishing cloudiness as the cherry flowers imperceptibly thin out over time (the force of *yaya kiete*). The essence of the scene, a subtly emergent clarity, is depicted as a dynamic process intimately fusing all the elements of the poem in an ineffably marvelous motility of surface coalescing into one single effect, the sense of being bathed in a sheer transparency of moonlight. In this sense, the poem is an experience of disclosure and not the expression of a clear meaning.

kimi narade	If not you, to whom
tare ni ka misemu	then should I show them?
ume no hana	Plum blossoms:
ka o mo iro o mo	a color and fragrance glowing
shiru hito zo shiru	for the one who truly knows.[7]

This *Kokinshū* poem refers to the aesthetic discernment of its recipient in terms of his "knowing" the color and fragrance (*iro o mo ka o mo/shiru*) of the plum blossoms. Genji alludes to this poem in praise of Prince Hotaru's exquisite taste when it comes to judging the subtle distinctions in varieties of incense. The critical usage of "color and fragrance" as a quality discernible only to the refined eye (*shiru hito zo shiru*) was current in the Heian period, as was the use of *kokoro ari* (literally, having a heart) to mean "sensibility," a heart alive to the *aware* or moving power of things. As we have seen from the *Korai fūteishō*, the "color and fragrance" of phenomena is by no means a wholly aesthetic formal quality for Shunzei, but their very heart or essence (*moto no kokoro*) as manifestation rather than substance. The true ontological nature of existence understood through the principles of temporality, emptiness, and dependent origination is that which is figuratively expressed as an ineffable fragrance, aura, or trace. When Shinkei quotes Yoshida Kenkō in *Tsurezuregusa* (Essays in Idleness, 1330–32), "Are we to gaze at the moon and flowers with the eye alone? To lie awake anxiously through the rainy night, and then stand before the petal-strewn drenched shadow of the trees, yearning after what has passed, this indeed . . . ," and so on, in the context of a statement in *Sasamegoto* defining *omokage* and *yūgen*, he was without doubt also acknowledging Kenkō's grounding of the medieval aesthetic on a Buddhist-inspired understanding of the object as trace or aura, an ineffable presence marking an absence and vice versa.

kokoro naki	Even to a self
mi ni mo aware wa	empty at heart is disclosed
shirarekeri	a moving power:
shigi tatsu sawa no	From the marsh a snipe leaps
aki no yūgure	into the shadowy autumn dusk.

Saigyō's (1118–90) famous poem provides a truly apt instance of the medieval view of poetry as a revelation, a disclosure of the Real from one discerning mind to another through the mediation of a figure. It is the reason why Shinkei in *Sasamegoto* calls poetry nothing less than the *darani* (literally, true word; Skt. *dhāraṇī*) of Japan, and why from such a lofty perspective, Teika and Ietaka might be judged mere "makers of poems" (*utazukuri* 歌作り), that is, craftsmen or artists, which is a notch lower than Jichin and Saigyō, who are the real "poet-seers" (*utayomi* 歌詠み).[8] The experience of a liberating disclosure figured by this poem is probably what the *Makashikan* means by the earlier cited statement, "From a single sign, you will obtain release from all and for all." Here what is "disclosed" to the inner eye by a bird leaping up and into the encroaching dark is, I believe, none other than the essential character of existence as an "apparition," a momentary appearance from within the ineffable depth of circumstance that determines it and is in turn determined by it. And framing the vision by the personal statement of the upper section is to register it as a moment of *aware* in Shinkei's sense of a *com*-passionate dialogical exchange, so that what the bird discloses is also the nature of the speaker as himself only a fleeting apparition, that is to say, precisely a *kokoro naki mi* 心なき身, literally, "a body without a heart" in the Buddhist sense of *anātman*, an absence of self-nature, an emptiness at the core, a sheer surface, shadow or reflection (*omokage*) without substance, and so on.

According to Kubota Jun, the main line of interpretation for *kokoro naki mi* takes it indeed to mean the self of a Buddhist recluse who has severed himself from the passions of the mundane world. A representative Muromachi-period commentary would be Tō no Tsuneyori's in the *Shinkokinwakashū kikigaki* 新古今和歌集聞書: "'Self empty at heart' means that having escaped the mundane world and cast off the six hindrances, one is devoid of a nature and of mind [*mushō mushin* 無性無心], and feels neither joy nor sorrow."[9] In this interpretation, the poem is rife with irony or the ambiguity of the paradoxical. For one might well ask, how can a subject without a heart sense *aware* in its common meaning of the moving power of things? The implied answer would be that it is precisely the egolessness of *mushin*, its blankness so to speak, that enables the bird to become spontaneously manifest upon it (*shirarekeri* is in the non-agentive passive voice). This means that *aware* as a dynamic motion of exchange between subject and object requires first of all a self-abnegation. What is evoked in the poem is the phenomenological experience of dependent origination, or *engi*, the coming into being momentarily of subject and object in a mutual exchange similar to that of spring wind and skylark, or cherry blossoms and moonlight, in the poems quoted earlier. And it is the sense that even such a fleeting manifestation, the sudden apparition of a bird in the darkening sky, is generated by a totality of mutually interrelated factors whose limits are wholly open, immeasurably deep and remote, that is called *yūgen*.

Yūgen, which like love is a totally unworldly consciousness, is a sense of the mystery of things that lies just under the surface of our obdurately self-aggrandizing, wholly trivial mundane existence in the early years of the twenty-first century. It is the uncanny feeling that what we are, and how things are, have their source in a dynamic totality infinitely more vast and beyond reckoning, which is nevertheless continually changing according to our actions within it. The taste and appearance of a glass of wine is the product of a certain soil and climate, a method of storage and handling, the passage of years, and certain unknown factors besides, all of which have worked together to produce just this "color and fragrance." "Smash a cherry tree and you will find no flowers within; it is in the skies of spring that the flowers bloom."[10] In this sense, things have their "real" existence outside themselves; they are the trace emanation of the concrete network of circumstances that have produced them. A corollary of this is that displacement, the motion of alterity, is of the essence (*hon'i* or Shunzei's *moto no kokoro*) of phenomena and of the symbolic poetry that would manifest them as such.

An interesting thing about Saigyō's poem is the fact that Shunzei, though giving it the most superlative praise, nevertheless judged the poem pitted against it (also by Saigyō) to be the winning one. Later generations apparently found this sentence inexplicable and fabricated stories about the poem. *Ima monogatari* 今物語 (Tales of Today) recounts how Saigyō, then traveling in the far north, journeyed back to the capital expressly to find out if his snipe poem would be included in the *Senzaishū* imperial anthology to be compiled by Shunzei. Told that it would not, he said, "Well, then, there was no reason to come at all," and went directly back north. *Seiashō* 井蛙抄 (Well-Frog Collection), after recounting this same anecdote, goes on to report how a priest on pilgrimage to the Sumiyoshi, where the god of poetry is enshrined, saw a vision while practicing his devotions in the night. In the dream-vision, he saw a crowd of people, civilians and priests, nobles and commoners, gathered in front of the shrine as if waiting for someone. And sure enough, in a while, a man dressed in the deep black robes of a priest appeared. He was escorted inside the shrine, from where soon afterward his voice was heard chanting in loud, clear tones the very poem by Saigyō that had been rejected for the anthology.[11]

Such tales, though apocryphal, indicate the high estimation in which the poem was held in the popular imagination. It was apparently the belief that Saigyō felt a deep personal attachment to this particular poem, and that it was religious to the core, on a par with ritual scripture in illuminating the Buddha's teachings, since it was deemed sacred enough to be chanted in a temple. The poem that Shunzei preferred to the snipe poem in round 18 of the *Mimosusokawa utaawase* 御裳濯川歌合 is the following:

ōkata no	What could it be
tsuyu ni wa nani no	in the common dew all around
narinuramu	that thus came to be?
tamoto ni oku wa	As to that which settles upon
namida narikeri	my sleeves—they are tears.

The mind of "from the marsh a snipe leaps" is ineffably profound [*yūgen*], and its body of figuration [*sugata*] is unsurpassable. The language of "what is it in the common dew all around" is seemingly trivial, but its mind is exceptionally deep; it must be said to be the winning poem.[12]

In fact this poem is similar to the other in its dyadic renga-like structure; bifurcated by the caesura at the end of line 3, it divides into two statements, which illuminate each other in the sense that a question sets off a response whose significance is visible only within that context. As Shunzei says, the diction is seemingly inconsequential, not at all "poetic," yet the question that is being asked is in fact a "deep" one: what is it *within* this transparent globule of water that gives us a clue to its origins? The answer is of course, wholly nothing; there is no inner substance in the dew that has made it what it is. Lacking a self-nature, it is a mere surface behind which there is no*thing*. How do things come to be, precisely what, or where, is their source? What is the set of atmospheric conditions—wind currents, barometric pressure, temperature, and so on, that manifest themselves as these dewdrops on the ground? And what are the factors that determine each of these atmospheric conditions in turn? It is indeed a question about climate and weather, the one remaining field still to be controlled by science, and about environment and ecology, but only as these are related to the philosophical issue of the ultimately immeasurable "formlessness" that grounds "form," the dewdrops that are external manifestations of something else. In a radical, renga-like shift made possible only in the gap of discontinuity between the upper and lower verses, and in the contrastive marker *wa*, the poem then pivots around and implicitly restates the question within the human context: what is it that becomes these tears? What is all this sorrow and suffering all around, the fire and the fury, signifying perhaps nothing, but clearly manifesting themselves in these tears, nothing but empty tears, yet welling up from deep down—where? In sum, the poem embodies a process of reflection tinged by an ironic self-alienation. The persona is clearly not simply weeping his heart out; nor has it occurred to him to say, "I weep, therefore I am." He is gazing at his tears from the outside and finding himself there, a creature of circumstance, a kind of trace, as tears and dew are mere ephemeral traces of a process without a core that remains constant throughout it. If this poem were a pair of renga verses, and the same goes for the previous one, they would be in the Distant Link mode due to the depth of the gulf that the mind must hurdle to arrive at the poet's intention, which is also the depth of its symbolic resonance as a disclosure of the ineffable nature of reality.

The question remains: why did Shunzei prefer this poem to the one on the snipe? Of the masterfulness of the latter, his superlative praise leaves us no room for doubt, but is that not perhaps the problem? Is not the "what is it in the dew" poem more moving in its very inchoateness, its lack of "artistic" articulateness? Is not this utterly simple(-seeming) utterance the very figuration of the helpless vulnerability of the human subject who must always find himself outside, always being so to speak *reduced* to tears? It is worth noting in this connection that Kamo no Chōmei's (1155–1216) long description of *yūgen* in the *Mumyōshō* employs exactly two analogies from the human plane (as distinct from natural phenomena) to illustrate the concept. One is the woman of unsatisfied and deeply suppressed passion who does not speak, yet gives off an aura by which we can faintly discern her condition. The other is the infant whose babbling does not make sense, yet nevertheless works on our emotion:

> Again, when an innocent child utters unconnected words whose import escapes our comprehension, such words, trivial as they are, nevertheless hold much appeal, as if there were something in them that merits our understanding. How can such things be easily learned or clearly expressed? One can only realize them for oneself.[13]

There is, at first glance, something childish and naive about a question like "what is it that becomes the dew"—science, after all, can answer it in a perfectly rational way. And then to say, quite simply, "mine are tears" seems nonsensical and unrelated to the question. But when one has intuited the poem's full implication, one realizes that there is no final answer, just as when we are confronted with children whose endless questions finally lead to the ultimate one about the final cause or origin. The child's babbling in the prelinguistic stage, before she learns to express herself within its conceptual system, can seem profound to an adult precisely because the sounds are coming from a source prior to a culturally determined and therefore finite kind of understanding, and because the adult will know, from the fullness of her own knowledge and experience, that the basic questions posed by human existence are wholly beyond the spheres of logic and science. From this perspective, speech that seems to understand all too well, that is perfectly fluent and articulate, like the snipe poem in comparison to this one, will not seem as sincere, as wholly open to the "ineffable" as this one, which borrows the awkward simplicity and vulnerable heart of a child to express an apparently "unconscious" or "preconscious" depth. The idea that children are closer to life's source is, of course, a common Romantic myth— Wordsworth's "The child is the father of the man" is the well-known expression of it. In Japanese classical criticism, the woman in a state of longing beyond the power of words to express, and the child who does not have the power to express what he feels, are exemplars of the "ineffably profound," because they mirror the human condition at its ground, before and beyond language and culture. In the mundane world, however, the mythical closeness of women and children to the source can also mean their distance from the political power lodged in the manipulation of language and culture, and can thus present very real problems. In other words, when figurative examples or myths are taken literally, the distinctions between men and women, and adults and children, can acquire a solidity that obscures the principles of nondiscrimination and emptiness that ground the existence of all humans alike, as well as of phenomena and event, and constitute the sum of Buddhism's contribution to human knowledge.

Ultimately, perhaps, in this gesture of preferment for the "common dew" poem, Shunzei was underlining a difference between coolly articulating a mystery on the one hand, and evoking in the very tissue of the articulation the suffering sense of deprivation that it entails, that is, a sense of the simultaneous poverty and excess of language before a truth that it would manifest. There is an essential tension and contradiction, after all, between language and a truth that is always described as "beyond words" (*gongo dōdan* 言語道断), and ultimately beyond meaning in the sense of an assertion constituted of a subject *and* a predication. Here it is significant that *Shinkokinshū*-style poems favor the open closure of a nominal phrase—namely, *aki no yūgure* (the autumn evening . . .), without a predication, or that a renga verse ending in a nominal is followed by the so-called final particle *kana*, whose function is precisely to evade the assertiveness of a predicate, or to make it open to ambiguous interpretation. *Kana* has no referential content, only a tonal value; it is a linguistic sign that apparently combines the interrogative value of *ka* and the vaguely exclamatory force of *na*. Thus in poetry it is a sign representing the gentle eruption of a wondering, yet deeply moved response; the cipher of an "emotive" moment without precise content or meaning. The technique of layering or doubling that bifurcates the five–line structure into two syntactically discontinuous parts also creates a gap, from which a wordless yet felt significance erupts, the kind that we have seen in all the renga and waka examples quoted. The point would seem to be to prevent the poem's closure into any easy meaning, to let significance leak out between the lines and be sensed as an aura or emanation. And this suspension of meaning, the openness of its indefinite deferment (the delay in *différance*), makes itself felt precisely because of the self-referential materiality of the words' presence. That is, the words are there to trace the shape of an absence, an absence, in turn, intended to open up a wordless disclosure in the reader's or auditor's mind.

THE POEM AS BODY, VOICE, AND FRAGRANCE

Shunzei's concern with the configuration (*sugata*) of the poem as chanted and heard, its aurality, reveals the traces of poetry's ritual function as a kind of oracular incantation, a revelatory performative activity. The passage defining *kehai*, or aura, cited on page 98 above, actually begins in this way:

> In poetry as a rule, one does not necessarily express an arresting conception or even conclusively assert a meaning [*koto no kotowari o iikiramu* 事の理 を言ひきらむ]. Poetry was originally known as "poem-chanting" [*eika* 詠 歌], and therefore it should be such that in the mere reading out or chanting of it there is something that somehow sounds compelling and ineffably profound. If it is a good poem, there will seem to be, apart from its words and configuration, an aura that accompanies it. For instance, it is like haze hanging over the spring flowers . . . [14]

He repeats this emphasis on aural figuration elsewhere and in the *Korai fūteishō* goes so far as to say that a poem is something "whose good or bad is audible in the encounter with the voice" (*koe ni tsukite yoku mo ashiku mo kikoyuru mono nari*).[15] This means that the poem is first and foremost a concrete sensual experience before it is an intellectual one. When chanted, the very fabric and tissue of the poem's body of figuration (*sugata*), its "textuality" in the Derridean sense, or "semiotic" character in the Kristevan sense, presents itself directly in the sensuous medium of the voice. The poem's configuration—a specific choice of words arranged in a deliberate way, which can only be registered abstractly on the page (unless the reader has a musical sense, or the poem is executed as an artistic piece of calligraphy), becomes materialized as the timbre, pitch, density, strains, and extensions of the voice.[16] And it is in the very opposition or tension between the poem as pure materialized body and as disembodied significance that the aura that is *yūgen* is released, if it is a good poem. Chanting a poem, it would seem, is like burning a cake of incense in order to release its fragrance.

ELEVEN

Ushin

Poetic Process as Meditation

A symbolic poetry such as is formulated by Shunzei in the *Korai fūteishō*, which uses words wholly as the indices of a nonlinguistic, "metaphysical," if you will—essence, is the very figuration of the poet's mind. The process of producing it becomes the crucial issue, particularly in the *ushin* 有心— literally, "having a heart-mind"—style, which I render as "Style of Meditation" for the same reason that I have often preferred to translate *kokoro* as "mind" in dealing with the critical vocabulary from the *Shinkokinshū* period on.[1] In Teika's explanation of this style in the *Maigetsushō* 毎月抄 (Monthly Notes, 1219), it becomes clear that it is here where the idea that poetic composition involves the discipline of mental meditation is on its home ground, and equally clear that for Teika, pure poetry is the figuration of a state of contemplation similar to Tendai *shikan* as Shunzei sees it, or to Shinkei's equation of the distant link with Zen meditation.

> Now among the ten styles, none surpasses the Style of Meditation [*ushintei* 有心躰] in embodying the essential nature of poetry [*uta no hon'i* 歌の本 意]. It is a configuration that is extremely difficult to conceive; you cannot make it come naturally by mulling this way and that. Indeed, it is precisely

by thoroughly clarifying your mind and immersing it in that realm [*yokuy-oku kokoro o sumashite sono ikkyō ni irifushite* よくよく心を澄ましてその一境に入りふして] that you may, on rare occasions, compose in such a style. And therefore what is called a good poem is in each and every instance nothing other than that which reflects the depth of the poet's mind. However, if in an excessive desire to push the mind yet deeper, you twist and turn things too much, then you will instead come up with that utterly distorted, convoluted species of poem called *irihoga*, whose configuration is unstable and incoherent, and that is more dreadful than one that does not evince the mind at all. This margin is perilously crucial; you must exercise the greatest caution here.[2]

What is at issue here is the same "deep mind" that Shunzei had such difficulty verbalizing in the *Korai fūteishō* until he found its most appropriate expression in the meditational practice of "stillness and insight." Teika was, like his father Shunzei, a devoted reader of the *Makashikan*; his close affinity to this text is evidenced by the fact that at seventy-two, when he retired from the world, the priestly name he chose for himself was Myōjō, "Clear Tranquility," from the opening line of the Preface. Thus it is reasonable to assume that in this passage Teika, like Shunzei, identified the realm of poetry in essence, which is also that of the "deep mind," with the realm of *shikan*. As for internal evidence, there is the very language of the *Maigetsushō* text: composing in this style requires that the poet "wholly clarify" and "immerse" his mind in "that realm." That realm is the meditational experience of the emptiness of the sign, a freeing of the mind from the apparent solidity of meaning in mundane discourse as well as conventional poetic usage. By dissolving the seemingly fixed relation between signifier and signified, the "sign and non-sign" in the *Makashikan*, words are set free, and the mind as well is liberated into the realm of "clear tranquility" that gives birth to language as it were for the first time. Here the poet's subjectivity, which is constituted by his finite and particular circumstance, is emptied as well, as he confronts the meaning of meaning, which is also the inalienable meaning of things on their elemental ground.

The passage also reveals that *ushin* is poetry operating at the very margins of language: "this margin is perilously crucial" (*kono sakai ga yuyushiki daiji nite haberu*); the liberation of language can give birth to the most authentic, originary expression, or set free within its vertiginous network of mirroring and mirrored denotations and connotations, the mind can also fail and produce "that utterly distorted, convoluted poem called *irihoga*, whose configuration is unstable and incoherent." Here we should recall Chōmei's report that the new style espoused by Teika's group was in fact pejoratively labeled *Daruma uta*, "Dharma poems,"[3] that is, akin to the incomprehensible, seeming "non-sense" of the Zen *mondō*, or dialogues, where neither the question nor the answer signifies, precisely because it is aimed at breaking away from the common sense of everyday discourse. We should also note that Teika's greatest admirer, the Muromachi poet Shōtetsu (1381–1459) himself, would confess: "At times when I lie sleepless and Teika's poems come to my mind, I get the feeling that I am going mad [*monogurui ni naru kokochi shihaberu nari* 物狂ひになる心地し侍る也]. When it comes to composing in an involuted style, none can rival the poems of Teika."[4]

Like Teika, Shōtetsu was drawn to this thin, perilous edge where words begin to blur and turn wholly permeable, yet he would persist in his pursuit of what was perceived to be a deviant and obscure style. "How inferior my poetry must seem to others, since I always try to avoid composing as they do"—thus Shinkei quotes Shōtetsu, and adds, "Such wisdom should chasten one" (*SSG* 26: 150).

While similarly basing his practice on meditation, Teika's poetry is obviously more radical in diction and conception than Shunzei's. He was, for one, more emphatic about pursuing his own poetic vision to the utmost, even if it strained conventional poetic usages. For "the fact is that the Middle Way of poetry [*uta no chūdō* 歌の中道] can only be realized spontaneously by oneself. It is not something you can follow by having another point it out to you."[5] It is significant that Shinkei would later quote one of his poems in *Sasamegoto* as an example of "enlightenment without a teacher." The following passage in the *Maigetsushō* describing his view of the "excellent" or ideal poem (*shūitsu no tei* 秀逸の躰, while clearly influenced by Shunzei's "aura" concept, is equally trained on a view of poetic process as a meditation transcending both the fixed formulations of language and of thought itself.

First of all, the configuration of what deserves to be called an excellent poem breaks through the myriad determinations and is not fixated on things [*banki o mo nukete mono ni todokōranu* 万機をもぬけて物に滞らぬ], so that it is not manifestly in any one of the ten styles yet seems somehow to enfold all of them, and while evoking overtones [*yojō ukabite*] makes one sense the presence of a man of authentic mind and correct bearing. What people ordinarily understand by an excellent poem is one that is innocent of striking features [*mumon* 無文] and reads smoothly, uncomplicated in conception and calmly flowing in diction. This is a superficial view. If such a poem were to be considered a masterpiece, then no doubt we would be composing masterpieces with every poem. True excellence is to be found rather from within a process of composition that reaches out to the very margins where the nature of thought itself becomes clarified through and through [*eigin koto kiwamari ansei sumiwatareru* 詠吟事極まり案性澄みわたれる], so that the poem simply issues forth, spontaneously and offhandedly, as it were, without the mark of a conceptualization deliberately designed to deal with the specific topic. The mind of such a poem is, to begin with, deep, sublimely tensile in its inner rhythm, and masterful in the way it seems to expand beyond the words themselves [*takumi ni kotoba no hoka made amareru yō nite* 巧みに詞の外まで余れるやうにて]. Its configuration is lofty, its words, which would ordinarily sound improbable together, nevertheless follow one another smoothly; it evokes a compelling, subtle ambiance, a shadowy reflection by no means common [*omoshiroku kasukanaru keishu tachisoite omokage tada narazu* おもしろく、かすかなる景趣たち添ひて面影ただならず], and such is this ambiance that the mind is wholly drawn into it. Such a poem, however, is not one you should set out deliberately to compose. It will come of itself when you have perfected your practice.[6]

The primary thought threading through this long passage is the one with which it opens, and that is the idea that poetic process is a breaking through boundaries: of the ten style classifications, first of all, but also of the predetermined semantic values of words and their equally conventional syntactic combinations (the force of *banki o mo nukete mono ni todokōranu*). What is at issue is clearly the strenuous labor involved in a truly creative act, when the poet must at all costs struggle to break out of the prison house of the language system, the accumulated discriminations of established rule and precedent, such as were of great concern to the conservative Nijō school, which dominated the poetic milieu during Shinkei's time. However, while it is certainly a necessity that poets liberate their own voices, be able to hear their own thoughts, it would, I believe, be a mistake to interpret this passage as a radical attempt to put tradition down, or as a call for individual self-expression. Teika's oft-quoted slogan "old words, new heart" [*kotoba wa furuki . . . kokoro wa atarashiki*][7] cautions us against such a reading, as does the typical *Shinkokinshū* practice of *honkadori* 本歌取, allusive variation on old poems. Indeed, it can be said that an authentic engagement with tradition, in Mikhail Bakhtin's sense of a dialogical communion with voices in the past, first came to the forefront of Japanese poetic history in the age of Teika and Shunzei. When Shunzei went so far as to compare the unbroken continuity of poetry's "deep mind" in the waka anthologies to the transmission of the Dharma from the Buddha to his disciples and the Zen patriarchs through successive ages, he was expressing his sense of a vital link with past poets through his own practice of dialogical communication with them in his own poetry.

The breakthrough that is Teika's subject is rather that which Shinkei refers to when he defines *ushin*, the Style of Meditation, as poetry that is "wholly [the product of] a practice in the ground of the mind [*hitoe ni shinji shugyō no uta* ひとへに心地修行の歌]" (*SSG* 50: 189). It is poetry

> in which the mind has dissolved [*kokoro torake* 心盪け], and is profoundly at one with the numinosity of things [*aware fukaku*]; poetry that issues from the very depths of the poet's being and may truly be said to be his own waka, his own authentic renga [*waga uta waga renga*]. (*SSG* 50: 188)

This is a liberation not of the mundane subjectivity as such, a psychosocial entity bounded by the finitude of particular sociohistorical circumstance and linguistic convention. On the contrary, it is the *dissolution* of such a limited personality into an unbounded "universal" realm in which every man finds his true, authentic self (what Teika calls *kokoro naoku* 心直く, "the authentic mind") if he would but break out of the mundane and set free the buddha that is within him.

READING TWO USHIN POEMS BY
TEIKA AND SHŌTETSU

It is unfortunate that we have no extant examples of poems classified as *ushin* by Teika, since the authenticity of the manuscript called *Teika jittei* 定家十躰 (Teika's Ten Styles) has been called into question.[8] Our abiding concern, however, is to map out Shinkei's reading of his predecessors, and, happily, he himself cites two poems below in the course of his discussion of the *ushin* mode in *Sasamegoto*. The first is by Teika himself; the second, by Shōtetsu (*SSG* 50: 188):[9]

harusame yo	Ah, the spring rain:
konoha midareshi	In a whirl of withered leaves,
murashigure	the winter shower
sore mo magiruru	even after it had vanished,
kata wa arikeri	could yet baffle the senses![10]
Lord Teika	Teika

mi zo aranu	Void is the self.
aki no hikage no	As the autumn sunlight with
hi ni soete	each passing day
yowareba tsuyoki	dwindles starker in life
asagao no hana	the morning glory flower.[11]
Priest Shōtetsu	Shōtetsu

Both poems (in the original) are a precise and economic figuration of a state of mind; in each, the words are wholly adequate to the thought. In the sense Shinkei means by *kokoro torake*, the mind is fused or dissolved into its "object," so that you could not alter a word in it without thereby disturbing the exact contour of the thought. In particular, Shinkei had superlative praise for the first line in both cases, which is "truly beyond the imagination of the kind of author who must borrow another's voice" (*SSG* 50: 189). And it is true, indubitably, here that it is precisely the first line as such that makes the crucial and "marvelous" (*gemmyō*) difference, for it enables the remaining four lines to fall into place, the way, indeed, that a good tsukeku illumines the maeku (and vice versa) in renga; this is no doubt what Shinkei had in mind in isolating the crucial impact of the initial line in determining the meaning of the rest.

In Teika's poem, the first line simply says "spring rain" plus the vocative-emphatic particle *yo*, which invokes the spring rain while simultaneously establishing it as the focus of concern. The line is not quite, but does function as an apostrophe does in English poetry, according to Jonathan Culler's analysis of it as the personified figure of the lyric voice itself.[12] The rest of Teika's poem, in a precise yet wholly radical procedure, discloses what the spring rain is by sheer displacement, by showing closely what it is not. That is, the phenomenon is evoked as an absence precisely traced by another presence, the winter shower, which is not the main subject but its supplement, though it occupies fully four lines of the poem and moreover exists only in the persona's memory. It is as if both winter shower and spring rain existed only in the gap of the difference separating them, one being the outside of the inside, a minimally contrasting pair. Still, the poem's subject remains ineluctably the minutely fine and soundless dripping of spring rain everywhere as the persona sits and eventually loses his consciousness of time and place, becoming one with the spring rain in a state of meditative trance in which both rain and self lose their mutual distinction and merge into one, undifferentiated and beyond thought. In one stroke, Teika here has inscribed the *honi*, or "essential nature," of both spring rain and winter shower (*murashigure*, where the prefix *mura-*, here used in the sense of "a clump" of cloud precipitating a shower, is crucial) through a precise drawing of the difference between them, while relying on the principle of the ineffable emergence of phenomena from emptiness. The instantaneous appearance and disappearance of a passing winter shower, "baffling the senses," is like the sudden ruffling of a wave of thought on the calm, even surface of the sea of emptiness, setting up vibrations in the subject's mind, disturbing the tranquility of his spring rain *samādhi,*an advanced stage of meditation wherein the mind has settled into an immovable concentration on a single entity. None of all this is on the verbal surface; it is all in what Shinkei calls "what is left unsaid" (*iwanu tokoro*), the "aura and overtones" that the aspiring poet should attend to in order to reach the ultimate in poetry.

Like Teika's *harusame yo*, the exact value of *mi zo aranu* (literally, the body/self is not!) in Shōtetsu's piece is quite ambivalent as such: does it refer to the poet's self, the autumnal light, or the morning glory? Or all three? As a mere linguistic string, it indicates a negation of the existence of self, but taken with the emphatic deictic *zo* and against the rest of the poem, it evokes an experience of suddenly being *taken out of oneself,* as if the self swooned or had been sucked out, or, and I think this is closest to the point, one were walking along and suddenly at the next step there was only empty air underfoot. It is not the sensation of falling but the immediately prior moment, the sudden loss of firm ground. In other words, the force of the first line embodies the mind's reaction to the sheer contradiction figured in the dynamic image of autumn sunlight growing weaker with the days as the morning glory, conventional symbol of frail evanescence, becomes more vital. This paradox, which comes to a head in the opposing pulls of line 4, *yowareba tsuyoki* (literally, as it weakens it gets stronger), is the node of the poem's configuration or gestalt, a most subtle, subliminal point, as if the vitality seeping out of the sun were being absorbed in exact proportion by the frail flower in a miraculous exchange that discloses the permeability of margins (of the physical body, of the self as substance), and inscribes time itself with its proper fullness and significance. It is also in this rift that opens up between sunlight and flower, this gap of a taut difference that yet vitally connects both, that the self is swallowed up. Thus the first line signifies an experience that is a kind of death, the extinction of the small, the narrow, the so-called substantial mundane self with firm boundaries, the self that is, from an enlightened standpoint, only a conventional fiction.

TWELVE

Poetry and the Instantaneous Illumination of Zen

Shunzei, it will be recalled, states in the *Korai fūteishō* that since poetry manifests the significance of phenomena through its "deep mind," and because poetic experience is best understood within the Mahayana philosophical context of the three truths, it can be the circumstance (*en* 縁) that leads one to the Buddhist path. In *Sasamegoto*, Shinkei recounts the story of how Shunzei, beset by grave doubts in old age about his neglect of strict religious practice in favor of poetry, was visited by the god of Sumiyoshi who graciously relieved him of such crippling anxieties, saying: "Do not belittle so the Way of poetry. By means of it, you will accomplish without fail rebirth in the Pure Land. Poetry is a discipline in the direct route to enlightenment in this body [*kadō sokushin jikiro no shugyō nari* 歌道即身直路の修行也]" (*SSG* 45: 182–83).

Let me quote this section more fully, because it is one in which Shinkei unequivocally identifies poetic practice with Zen meditation, and the poem with the dharani, or True Word.

> In the sessions held here among country folk, a verse that cannot be understood by everyone alike, even if it is composed by a master, is regarded as to that degree inferior.

In all the arts, there is a vast difference in attitude between learning and mental application [*keiko to kufū to* 稽古と工夫]. You may spread out before your eyes all the teachings of the sages, anthologies of the ages, but without experiencing for yourself in your practice the chill and the heat of it [*reidan jichi no tokoro nakuba* 冷暖自知のところ], you will not arrive at the ultimate. Priest Saigyō himself was reportedly always saying that "the Way of poetry is wholly the practice of Zen meditation [*Kadō wa hitoe ni zenjō shugyō no michi* 歌道はひとへに禅定修行の道]." Verily, to attain the Way there is no other teaching apart from the direct route of instantaneous enlightenment [*tongo jikiro* 頓悟直路].

According to Tsunenobu, "Waka is the wellspring of reclusion [*inton no minamoto* 隠遁の源], the direct route nurturing the awakening of wisdom [*bodai o susumuru jikiro nari* 菩提を勧むる直路也]. The principle of Suchness and of the Real [*shinnyo jissō no ri* 真如実相の理] is contained within its thirty-one syllables." The import of these words earned Teika's sincere praise. . . . [1]

In this way, the five-part structure of the poem [*hen-jo-dai-kyoku-ryū*] corresponds to the five great constitutive elements, the five Buddhas of the mandala, the five wisdoms; to wit, the all-encompassing manifestation of the cosmic universe. Again, the six types of poetry are the six realms of illusion, the six types of action, the six constitutive elements in fusion; in a word, the Buddha-Body in essence. . . .

In essence, the Way of poetry is the True Word of our country [*kadō wa waga kuni no darani nari* 歌道は我が国の陀羅尼]. When you employ it as an instrument of vain sophistry, it means that your reading of the sutras and commentaries, as well as your practice of Zen meditation, are all equally blind delusions. (*SSG* 45: 182–83)

This whole book has in one sense developed as an analytical presentation of the thinking about poetry represented by the abstract statements above. On the various levels of poetic structure, poetic process, "aesthetic" ideals, and, not least, through analysis of concrete waka and renga examples, I have everywhere attempted to demonstrate the practical application of the principles thus enunciated by the *Shinkokinshū* poets in isolated places and brought together as a comprehensive poetics by Shinkei. No doubt on one level, words like "Zen meditation," "True Word," "instantaneous enlightenment," and so on are merely a language, a vocabulary for speaking about poetry—an intellectual system whose distinctions and categories happened to be a convenient epistemic framework for explaining the distinct activity of poetry. Poetry is surely the same everywhere, regardless of the different critical languages used to analyze it, which would depend upon the ontol-

ogy and epistemology paramount at each time and place. Here we are dealing with the question of the relation between "form" and "content," language and meaning, or the truth value of analogy and metaphor. If it were
possible to separate the two terms of these dichotomies, then one would
be justified in seeing differences only in the formal languages of criticism,
and that which is signified by poetry would be the same everywhere. If,
however, one believes that there is a seminal relation between the two, and
I believe that there is one, in the pragmatic sense that language determines
attitudes and conditions our very way of thinking, then these Buddhist
terms and categories, when used in describing Japanese symbolic poetry, are
not a mere garment but manifest the "substance" within as well, and one
would have to concede Shinkei's so-called "identification" of Buddhist and
poetic practice.

The issue is complicated (yet in one sense facilitated) by the fact that
the ultimate Buddhist standpoint of nondualism recognizes no intrinsic
distinction between polarities, including that of theory and practice, or
what Chih'i in the *Makashikan* calls "explanation [or preaching] and silence" (*setsumoku*). Ultimately, therefore, it is *not* a question of establishing the truth of an assertion, but of analyzing how the assertion could be
true. In sum, it is all a question of reading, and what I am doing is writing
a tsukeku to Shinkei's riddle maeku in order to comprehend it, or in the
process of trying to do so. Again, ultimate truth or reality has no face; only
the temporal gesture of understanding does. As I have attempted to show
in the foregoing discussion, the Mahayana doctrines of mutability, emptiness, and dependent origination constitute the epistemological basis of the
symbolic poetry developed in the *Shinkokinshū* period, while the concept of
the nondualistic "deep mind" as ground or originary source (*shinji* or *moto
no kokoro*) of all phenomena is the basis of its poetic practice.

Expressed more narrowly, the most decisive influence of Buddhist philosophy upon medieval poetry, and I refer here to the avant garde poets of
the *Shinkokinshū* anthology and their descendants in the Muromachi period, is in its attitude to language, meaning, and expression. Language in
this poetry is not being used to represent and transmit meaning; rather, it
is a heuristic device for experiencing existence or true reality as it is understood in Mahayana Buddhism. Meaning in Buddhist epistemology is always
relative and contingent, and the essential nature of phenomena is the same;
both are at ground empty. But viewed from the other side, it is precisely

this ground of emptiness that makes both meaning and phenomena possible, that enables them to enter into relation with each other. Expressed radically, there is no such thing as a singular, self-sufficient entity; there are only relations, permeable margins, shifting boundaries, transformations, and mergers. That is the essential nature of the dharmas, and the ultimate aim of human knowledge, which is wisdom or enlightenment, is to actively experience this nature in oneself as well, to discover, that is, one's original mind, to awaken to this first principle (*ri*) or truth, which is both marvelous and terrible at the same time. Marvelous because it makes for a broad, generous, and liberated mind; because it leads to a breakdown of borders, a way out of contrived, narrow views and positions, and can be the basis for the survival of human civilization, as well as for the conservation of nature in the twenty-first century. Yet such a truth is also terrible. It negates the comfortable sureties of our mundane existence, which is based on sameness and repetition, self-centeredness, personal attachments, belongingness, distinctions of age, rank, gender, and so on, in sum, on a sense of order and permanence.

On one level, the common one, *mono no aware* is accurately, I believe, translated as "the pathos of things," their sorrow and their tears, because life is in truth not as we would rather wish it to be. This sense of disappointment can lead to sentimentality and nostalgia, both of which possess their own grace in the otherwise vulgar rush and armored transactions of daily life. Or it can lead to a sense of irony and paradox, a brand of stoicism that endures in the face of all odds and the certitude of death. As ironic stoicism and graceful nostalgia, *mono no aware* has permeated the Japanese character until modern times, although it is not clear, given the psychological dislocations of the Pacific War and Japan's consequent single-minded transformation into a first-class economic power, that this particular character has survived the twentieth century. *Mono no aware* has its circumstantial origins in the historical experience of failure and defeat, which is why although individual American minds might understand it, it is or has been foreign to the construction of the American character as transmitted in history books and popular culture. Detached from the wholly mundane, however, and viewed from an enlightened or transpersonal perspective, *mono no aware* is the sense of wonder, mystery, and love that I have earlier discussed as *yūgen*, and it is this sense that poetry ideally evokes, in the medieval view of it.

POETRY AS THE TRUE WORD (DARANI)

A sense of wonder and mystery is not something that can be said or expressed as a meaning. It can only be "sensed"—and here I have in mind Shinkei's term *kansei* 感情, "a feeling as sensed," which means both "sensibility" as the capacity of a subject to feel, and "sensuousness" as the quality that phenomena have of moving, eliciting or drawing a response. The ubiquitous term *en* 艶 occurs everywhere in Shinkei's writings to describe things as various as phenomena, feelings, events, the poet's mind, and poetry itself. It is thus tempting to read it as a universal term for "beauty," except that this beauty is not, as in classical Western aesthetics, primarily bound up with the perception of external form, but rather with the vitality that animates it. Etymologically, *en* signifies "sensual allure," the color, fragrance, shape, sheen, texture, and motility of a vital surface—in sum, the dynamic qualities that are manifestations of life as *eros* and have the power to draw us toward the other. *En* was used by Shunzei to mean the compelling beauty of the evocative, the indirect and ambiguous, that which cannot be pinned down and deprived of the sensuous mobility of life itself. As is well known, one of Teika's characteristic styles was *yōen* 妖艶, where the first ideograph designates a female ghost, a kind of witch, a creature from a supernatural realm, so that the whole means "bewitching" or "seductive allure," a surreal, decadent, strangely fascinating kind of beauty.

Together with the concepts of "aura" (*kehai*), "reflection" (*omokage*), and "overtones" (*yojō*), discussed earlier, the term *en* indicates two things about medieval symbolist poetry: one, that the poem was seen as a sensuous experience with a power to draw a response; and two, that this sensuousness returns, not specifically to the object so depicted, but to the ultimate principle that is its founding ground. In other words, the sensuous is displaced from the plane of the wholly material (this is in fact an abstraction of our bifurcating, calculating minds) to that of the nonclinging mind, as when Shinkei defined *en*, not as a quality of the verbal surface as such, but as the aura or compelling grace of an illumined heart/mind (*kokoro*). That is to say that in Shinkei, *en* is the fascinating, charismatic quality of the hidden realm of principle as it subtly manifests itself in phenomena when seen through the mind's eye. What symbolic poetry does is to invest the sensual with the sheen of numinosity, or to figure a thought, the one thought, with the feel and tactile sensation of the material. In all the arts of the word, this sensory figuration of the mind in its pure unadulterated form is possible solely in poetry. It is not, for instance, an accident that medieval Nō developed as a symbolic theater equally trained on the potency of the mind to configure the poetic through a concentrated attention to the *jo-ha-kyū* of the various aspects and levels of performance as a singular event.

And it is in this sense of the poem or renga verse as a direct and immediate, that is, living, perception of the principle that Shinkei was moved to call it the True Word (*darani*). Also called *mantra*, in Buddhist practice these were incantations meant to concentrate the mind and so make it more supple and acute. They were also, however, regarded as symbolic, and even mimetic *embodiments* of enlightenment, of the Real, from an "esoteric" standpoint that has already discarded the mundane duality between mind and matter, or mind and language, in such a way as to identify the world with the purified Buddha-realm.[2]

Poetry as the True Word, the word that truly *speaks*, is not a predetermined meaning within the linguistic system, but a voice come to life, a truth become manifest, as it were, for the first time. This word may not allow itself to fall into the worn grooves of conventional meanings but must make the language itself opaque and strange in order to force readers or auditors to figure out its significance for themselves and thus experience its truth directly. In other words, the same requirement that a poet must aspire to know "the chill and the heat" of it on his own applies to readers as well. This "chill and heat" is not a meaning, but the experience of the Real, or of things on their home ground. In renga tsukeai specifically, this experience is like a lightning flash that momentarily reveals the maeku before it falls back again into the common light of day, so to speak, or disappears into the formlessness of the One. The experience of momentary illumination is the same, whether the genre is renga tsukeai, the Distant Link waka favored by Teika and his group, or, later, the haiku created by Bashō. If the poem is good, it will reenact for readers centuries later the same mind-opening flash, or tense fullness of significance, that it generated when first created. Such poetry does not age; being brief, "simple," and distilled, it contains no extraneous elements or dated mannerisms that tie it wholly to a specific historical period (which does not, of course, preclude the necessity of knowing how to read it). In this sense, it may be said that words in waka or renga of the highest type enact an event, perform a ritual of illumination within the compass of thirty-one syllables or in the space of the gap from one verse to the next in renga. In Shinkei's advice to Sōgi when the latter submitted his latest work for his criticism, we may observe what the process of composing such verses entails:

> In general you should avoid the excessively elaborate [*aya tsukisugi* 文付き過ぎ], the redundant [*kudoki*], and the fleetingly eye-catching [*omoshiroki tokoro*]—therein inevitably lies much that is worldly [*bonzoku* 凡俗] and self-affected [*watashi-meki* 私めき]. The quality of coldness and slenderness [*samuku yasetaru* 寒く痩せたる] is of the highest, although it is, to be sure, not attainable by everyone. But if your discipline is shallow, your mind unsettled, and you persist in elaborating vainly upon the mere surface of the verse, it might indeed seem interesting for a moment, but will quickly disenchant in the next as the words lose their vital tensility [*kotoba take o ushinai*]. It is of the utmost importance, when composing, to calm your mind absolutely and while attending to the words and configuration of your verse, to distance yourself from its meaning [*waga ku no kotowari o hanarete*] and send it off to another place [*yoso ni noki*], as if you were contemplating the distant sea or gazing at an autumn dewdrop. (*Tokoro*, letter 3, p. 289)

The terms "distant sea" and "autumn dewdrop" are particularly enlightening in this passage, because they imply a mental contemplation of something so vast or so infinitesimal that the whole apparatus of logic and thought ("meaning," or *kotowari* above), which are based on distinctions, must fail before it. Along with the previously cited expressions from *Sasamegoto*, "dissolve the mind" (*kokoro o torake*) and "let the mind settle minutely in the realm of grace" (*kokoro o hosoku en ni nodomete*), this passage defines a way of seeing beyond the fixed and particularized forms of phenomena, a going beyond the fixed meanings of words, and out into the blurred and indeterminate territory into which everything merges and fades. In other words, contemplation, also called mental application (*kufū*), is a process of expanding the mind so that it may encompass and transcend the limited meaning of the maeku's words as such, and then reconstitute them in another guise, which is the tsukeku. It is the process of deconstructing or "breaking" the maeku, in wholly opening the mind to it, and then reconstructing it in another form, something that is possible only, and paradoxically, because ideally, the poet's mind is grounded on a field beyond distinctions and the language system that fixes them as such.

THIRTEEN

Linking by Words and by Mind

Understanding, Interpretation, and Iterability

YORIAI: LINKING BY CONVENTIONAL WORD ASSOCIATIONS

The feeling of tension and liberation generated by a good link is no doubt the mark that the poet has grappled with the integral meaning, "intention," or feeling of the maeku through the contemplative process. That process of stepping out of one's subjectivity or "self-affectation" (*watashi-meki*), as Shinkei calls it, in order to grasp the mind of another was a difficult one. This may be gleaned from Shinkei's frequent criticism of the common tendency to link up solely through isolated words in the maeku, without attempting to really understand and relate to what it is actually saying. He was referring in particular to the practice of linking through conventional word associations (*engo* 縁語) or verbal correspondences (*yoriai* 寄合). These were pairs of words or phrases that had a natural propensity for drawing together due to semantic similarity or opposition, so that the occurrence of the one in the maeku automatically summons the other in the tsukeku; examples

are the pairs "snow = melt," "wet sleeves = tears," "young shoots = pick,"
"black = white," "dream = reality."[1] In most cases, however, the "magnetic"
affinity between the words of a *yoriai* pair is due to their co-occurrence in
countless waka, *monogatari*, and other works of the classical literary canon.
Any reader of waka will be familiar with the pairings "crimson leaves =
deer," "wild geese = old village," "orange blossoms = cuckoo / the past," "the
world = cast off the self," and so on. As a collective poetry, renga in particular would not have been possible without the whole system of shared
associations established by centuries of monolithic waka compositions on
the same themes or *topoi*, the same combinations of natural phenomena
to inscribe the seasons. Such fixed and familiar pairings had been compiled in *yoriai*, or word-association dictionaries, for the benefit of renga
beginners from as early as the 1300s, and represented a communal store of
materials from which one could draw during the extemporaneous sessions
themselves. "In the middle period, what was called linking was no more
than verbal correspondences that had been determined beforehand for the
majority of cases, without regard for the mind [*kokoro*] and the rhetorical
inflexion [*tenioha*] of the maeku," Shinkei observes (*Oi* 418). In this regard,
it is important to note that Shinkei was not objecting to *yoriai* per se, but
rather to their use in an automatic, mechanical fashion, without attention
to the integral conception or feeling of the verse in which such words were
embedded. Contrary to what was apparently the popular opinion, he did
not hold that two verses linked solely through associative word pairs, or
yoriai, had in fact achieved a connection.

> In the commentaries of our predecessors in the middle period, we find verses
> being classified as a *yoriai* link or a *kokorozuke* link, and it seems that it was
> deemed perfectly acceptable for the *yoriai* link to wholly disregard the *kokoro*
> [of the maeku]. It is difficult to agree with this view. There cannot be a *linked*
> verse that does not connect to the meaning or feeling [*kokoro*] of the maeku,
> can there? In waka, the distinction between the Close and Distant links is
> made on the basis of the presence of a conceptual or feeling connection in
> *both* cases. A linking continuity that does not run through both upper and
> lower verses is *an impossibility*. (*Oi* 418; emphasis added)

That is, a "link" that completely ignores the meaning, conception, or feeling
of the maeku in favor of a mechanical recitation of word associations is a
contradiction in terms.

uguisu no	Mixed in among
kaigo ni majiru	the hatching eggs of the warbler,
hototogisu	a cuckoo's.
unohanagaki ni	A green plum lies fallen on
nokoru aoume	the hedge of deutzia flowers.
Shūa	Shūa

Here Shinkei objects that the only connection lies in the conventional verbal correspondences (in the classical poetic lexicon) between "warbler = plum" and "cuckoo = deutzia flowers." This is, incidentally, also a typical case of *yotsude-zuke* 四手付, a "four-cornered" verbal link composed of two correlated pairs. There is no attempt to "read" the maeku's meaning, the idea of a mother abandoning her young to be brought up by someone else, or of taking advantage of another's labor of nest-building. What Shūa does is the typical renga move of transforming the images in the maeku into other terms, while retaining its configuration, but the move is not accompanied by an interpretive illumination of the maeku's meaning. Thus the two verses are deployed like two parallel lines that do not intersect, or a conversation without a common ground. Certainly, there is wit and cleverness—what Shinkei meant by "eye-catching" in the letter to Sōgi, in Shūa's mimicry of the maeku as an abstract design, the "concept" of a foreign intruder in a collectivity (the cuckoo among the warblers, the green plum among the deutzia flowers), but it is not hard to imagine what would happen to a sequence in which the linking techniques were mainly of this wholly verbal or abstract kind; the whole would quickly become a monotonous game.

KOKOROZUKE: LINKING BY FEELING OR CONCEPTION

A central issue in Shinkei's concept of linking as *kokorozuke* 心付, and one decisive for his view of it as dialogical relation, is a concern for the organic unity of the verse as an integral utterance by a subject who has something to say. The task of the renga poet is to confront and interpret that utterance, signifier of a particular mind, in a dialogical motion of understanding, and not to evade it through clever words. Renga in his view, if it is to aspire to be serious art, cannot be a merely entertaining game of words; rather it must be a dialogue between the heart/minds (*kokoro*) of speaking subjects. I use these terms here in the Bakhtinian sense. The leading theorist of dialogism in language, M. M. Bakhtin draws a distinction between the typical object of linguistics, which is to describe and analyze language as an abstract system of signs or a code, and the activity of the human sciences, which is dialogic in nature, that is, involving the subject in the necessarily context-bound, contingent process of expression and responsive understanding in relation to another. The following passage will give an idea of the orientation of Bakhtin's thought; if one reads "verse" for "work," his subject might as well be linked poetry.

> The work is a link in the chain of speech communion. Like the rejoinder in a dialogue, it is related to other work-utterances: both those to which it responds and those that respond to it. At the same time, like the rejoinder in a dialogue, it is separated from them by the absolute boundaries created by a change of speaking subjects.[2]

In an earlier essay, "Discourse in the Novel," Bakhtin tended to set up an opposition between poetry and the novel by treating them as monologic versus dialogic genres.[3] This binary opposition cannot hold, however, when one considers the use of poetry in classical Japanese literature. Not only does it fly in the face of the existence of Japanese poetic sequences of collective composition, renga and haikai, where dialogue is constitutive of the genre itself. There is also the dialogical operation of waka in poetic exchanges and poem citations (*hikiuta* 引歌) in Heian narrative prose itself, and the same mediation of older poems in the intertextual process of *honkadori* (allusive variation on an older poem).

A change of speaking subjects, and within the same work, is precisely what is instituted by the gap/link between any two verses in renga. Therefore, like Bakhtin, Shinkei assigns a crucial meaning to the unique, "unrepeatable" integrity of the whole verse utterance, that is, its *subjective* aspect in living discourse, which anticipates a response, as distinct from its "value" within a reified semiotic system.

Dialogue requires a listening to the other and an understanding response. To disregard the maeku poet's meaning or intention is to ignore him as the subject of his own utterance, to turn a deaf ear to his voice, and merely treat his words like entries in a dictionary, or in the impersonal language system of conventional associations. What is illumined then is the system and the book, perhaps the poet's cleverness or wit, but certainly not the voice that speaks the words of the maeku as the other in a dialogic exchange transpiring at a concrete point in time. In short, here, as in his larger philosophy of beauty and existential knowledge, Shinkei was valorizing the temporality of the word as experienced—that is, "read," by the poet in relation to the mind of its author.

> Verses that are concerned primarily with *yoriai* use too many implements and do not cohere into an integral meaning [*gusoku ōki ni torite ikku no kotowari naranu nari*]. Such artificially designed verses are a mere collection of old objects. Reading them is like seeing the Kamo Festival procession pass a thousand times; there is nothing there to startle the eye. (*Ichigon* 1)[4]

Isolated from the specific temporality of the moment, fixed associations are a redundancy, without point or power. Moreover, an excessive concern with the words of the maeku as such

> is like fixing your eye on the target in archery practice and neglecting your own posture, so that you cut a bad figure. As one is taught there to merely be aware of the target's presence and for the rest pay close attention to your own figure [in relation to it], so in renga you need know only that the maeku is there. Forget about verbal correspondences and let your mind instead roam around [*kokoro o megurasu*]. (*Ichigon* 1)

We have already seen how Shinkei advised Sōgi not be become fixated by the verse's words and meaning as such (and we have to assume that he means the dictionary meaning) but to distance himself from these through a process of detached contemplation. Distancing is a way of "encompassing" the maeku by seeing it in a larger perspective, and it is also a way of liberating the imagination, which is essentially what *kokoro o megurasu* 心を巡らす, "letting the mind roam around," signifies. Now, when forced to release his hold on conventional word associations, when deprived of the security of the dictionary, so to speak, in the process of linking up to the maeku, the renga practitioner might initially feel lost and abstracted. But there are certain techniques, according to Shinkei's instructions to Kenzai in *Ichigon*, that are useful. One is to attend to the maeku's *tenioha*, the particles and inflexional suffixes that constitute the joints of the maeku's syntax, and then use one's imagination to find the substantive words (*tai no kotoba* or nouns, verbs, and adjectives) that correspond to that syntactic framework. The same may be said of important adverbials like *mata* (again), *ge ni* (indeed; just so), and interrogative pronouns like *nani* (what; why), *ikani* (how), and so on. Since such syntactic and inflexional signifiers are in effect the bearers of the maeku poet's precise intonation, by responding to those in particular, the verse will naturally link up to the other in terms of both form and conception without deliberately isolating substantive words in it for *yoriai* pairings. "For this reason, the skilled poet's renga is said to 'approach' [*yoru* 寄る], while that of the unskilled 'attaches' [*tsukeru* 付ける] itself to the maeku" (*Ichigon* 2). This is indeed a noteworthy and revealing distinction. An "approach" is in effect a mode of illuminating the maeku by setting it in a context or framework, thus rendering its meaning visible while leaving its formal "identity" intact. The process of "attaching," on the other hand, obscures the meaning or intention of the maeku, since one adds on to its substantive words others, which may be correlated to them by coded associations but are frequently irrelevant to the sense of the verse utterance as a whole. "Attaching" then ends up "effacing" the maeku by pasting irrelevant words onto it.

This does not mean, of course, that one ignores the substantive words of the maeku. In *Ichigon*, Shinkei lists three ways by which one links up to, "engages" (*toriyoru*), the maeku; namely, through its (1) particles and inflexional suffixes (*tenioha*); (2) its sense, significance, or feeling (*kokoro*); and (3) its substantive words (*tai no kotoba* 体の詞). Only if it is impossible to proceed through any or all of these three ways does one have recourse to *yoriai* correspondences as the primary mode of connection. In practice, obviously, the conventional system of associations is everywhere necessitated by renga's rules of thematic sequencing; Shinkei's concern is that the association be set within an original, meaningful statement in relation to the maeku and not just hammered on. It is perhaps like the difference between dovetailing joints or nailing them together.

> In this way [using fixed *yoriai* pairings], as one continues to repeat generally the same things while ignoring the difficult issues of the meaning [*kokoro*] and syntactic intonation [*tenioha*] of the maeku, the whole session ends up becoming so monotonous, one would think everyone's honor rested on making it so. Needless to say, such conventional associations are essential at the beginning stage of one's training. But when one has reached the highest stage and composes wholly according to the inspiration generated by the maeku's meaning and syntactic intonation, such coded associations reveal their inadequacy. Even the talented will find it fruitless to keep reflecting on the same associations over and over again. It is in a session where the different thinking of each member takes the verse to an unexpected realm that the backbreaking labor of the author is manifest [*manza ono'ono aranu sakai to anjichigaetaru sakusha funkotsu naru ya* 満座各あらぬ堺と案じちがへたる 作者粉骨なる哉]. (*Oi* 419)[5]

The great difference between waka and renga, according to Shinkei, is sim-ply that in the one, "there is one mind in the upper and lower verses," while in the other, "there are two authors" (*Ichigon* 2–3). In other words, the ge-neric separation between upper and lower verses in renga signifies the inter-vention of another "author" (*sakusha*) or subject, a different voice, and the labor of that subject in relating to the mind of the other is precisely what makes renga essentially distinct from waka. The language might be simi-lar, the high poetic realm aspired to the same, but the actual, continuous intervention of another voice as a formal feature of renga structure is what makes the crucial difference. Without the joint of a difference that inscribes the presence of two authors exchanging one mind, renga might as well be waka. Or it might as well be a game of "words merely rolling off the tip of the tongue." On the contrary, it is this labor and work of meeting across a palpable divide that is precisely what makes renga absorbing reading even today. It is precisely its collective and performative nature that makes it unique, but this "collective" must not be taken to mean sheer similarity and uniformity, but rather the interpersonal communication of authors who are mutually distinct and think differently (*anjichigaetaru sakusha*), and are thus able to open up new realms of thought (*aranu sakai*).

Shinkei's repeated advice to practitioners to leave the mechanical and redundant and exercise the imagination is no doubt an indication that the reality of popular renga sessions in his time was quite different. Some modern scholars have indeed faulted him for an "elitism" that prescribed the poetic ideals of the old aristocracy—that is, the whole symbolic and philosophical aesthetics represented by *ushin* and *yojō*, for a genre that alleg-edly belonged to commoners. An early evaluation of his literary historical achievement concluded that he formulated a "metaphysical poetry" that set literary history back at least a century in inhibiting the irrepressible spirit of the commoners that would later burst out in the comic renga genre called *haikai*.[6] Possibly, such early evaluations were based on a reading of his criti-cal works and commentaries that was influenced by a schematic view of literary history as a Marxist class struggle; no doubt, Shinkei himself would have applauded the move as indicating the contextuality (here, the postwar intellectual milieu, whether advocating democratic or socialist principles) of interpretation and understanding. There is also the complex question of Shinkei's exact role in the formation of the so-called *ushin renga*, the "elegant and refined" renga that would become the orthodox mode in Sōgi's time. Here, all that can be said is that his role was major and crucial, but when the larger picture is considered, it will be seen that his emphasis on *kokoro-zuke* (linking by mind rather than words alone) had even greater consequences for comic renga and the Shōfū style of the Bashō school. Perhaps, too, Shinkei's occasionally denunciatory prose and tone of authority do not sit well with modern liberal and permissive attitudes.[7] Moral force and conviction are indelibly inscribed in Shinkei's criticism, in part motivated by the war-torn history of his age, in part by his Buddhist calling, but they are not qualities that we associate with a modern aesthetic sense founded on a construction of its autonomy from other spheres of life and scientific disciplines. The modern bifurcation of ethics and aesthetics tends toward fixed attitudes and prejudices, or a laissez-faire indifference, that are wholly inadequate to the challenging global sociopolitical conditions in which we now live. Shinkei's so-called "elitist" attitude could not have been short of radical, since he demanded of commoners that they develop a sense of quality and high-mindedness, as well as a sense of themselves as thinking subjects with their own minds, rather than passive objects of the linguistic system, poetic or otherwise, which is a mere redundancy unless it is used with self-reflection as well as imagination. The man who declared that "it is better to criticize the Dharma and fall to hell than merely to make offerings to numberless Buddhas" (*SSG* 47: 184) can certainly not be accused of elitism, unless commoners and peasants are not intrinsically capable of critical thinking, and that would indeed be a patronizingly elitist attitude. Again, his teaching that rules inscribe distinctions, for the sake of convenience, upon a ground that is intrinsically empty of distinctions, discourages a narrow-minded adherence to them. Nor can it be said to be the pronouncement of an elitist. As for reverencing tradition, what he taught was to comprehend the minds of old poets, not to imitate their words. In sum, Shinkei's poetic philosophy, his advocacy of a poetic mode of being or Way, which is based on the primacy of mind, can only be interpreted as elitist if one believes that a common, mundane way of thinking is sufficient for a truly human existence.

LINKING AS RESPONSIVE ANIMATION OF THE PRIOR TEXT

As a performative activity, the excitement of renga as a unique poetry, whether in the "refined" or comic mode (the two are the same in being based on an essentially ironic sense of existence) is the palpable sense one has in reading it that one is watching the very process by which minds work. To an extent greater than for any poem composed by an individual author, though similar to the Distant Link poems in waka, renga demands of the reader that active, responsive kind of understanding, that dialogic, participatory consciousness, that Shinkei required of the poet himself. If one does not palpably sense the tension of a linked opposition between the two verses, or experience that surge of fullness that comes when one has understood the link, then one has missed what *linked* poetry is about. Shinkei's metaphor for verses that might read impressively in isolation, but do not actually connect, is quite revealing. He compares them to "impeccably dressed, lifeless corpses set out in a row." On the other hand, a verse might seem inconsequential as such, yet "in engaging the previous verse, even the most trivial words come to life with an appeal they have never had before" (*SSG* 5: 124). For "in the Way of renga, it is in the previous verse where your own vital spirit [*tamashii*] lies" (*Tokoro*, letter 3, p. 286). In all these, vitality and life stand for the palpable tension linking the two verses, charging them like an electric current.

This charge is not really a matter of divining the maeku poet's intention, however. There are, strictly speaking, no "singular" intentions in renga. Each verse is primarily a *turn* (in both senses of the word) in an ongoing process of conversation, and no one holds the stage long enough to hold forth in a monologue clarifying his particular "intention." Or, to put it in another way, the poet's intention resides as an internal cause (*in* 因) in the shape of his speech, and the next poet brings in his own speech as the external condition (*en* 縁) illuminating the former, charging it with significance. Where in this "significance" can the former's singular intention be isolated? Is it not so that that intention was itself already influenced by the mae-maeku (the verse before the one immediately preceding) to begin with? In this sense, the discourse of renga belongs to no one in particular and simultaneously to everyone, so that when Shinkei speaks of the "vital spirit" (*tamashii*) of the verse as lying in its maeku, he is underscoring the nature of renga as transpersonal, intersubjective discourse. Meaning here is the process of charging the maeku with significance, illuminating its "mind" with one's own, and meaninglessness is to leave the maeku a "lifeless corpse," unspeaking, alienated, and thus breaking the vital chain of temporal discourse that speaks itself in everyone, and that everyone causes to speak by the very motion of understanding inscribed by each verse.

In this way, in the modern controversy over authorial intention as the ground for "objectivity" in any literary critical enterprise, renga practice would cast doubt on the status of the poet's intention as an entity wholly contained by and articulated in his verse, in the sense of determining it.[8] Since the verse is conditioned by its maeku, and that in turn by its maeku, and so on, the attempt to grasp the other's intention will involve the critic in an infinite regress. This is not to say, however, that renga espouses an unprincipled or nihilistic relativism. As we have just seen, *kokoro-zuke*, linking by mind, requires attention to the other's utterance as a whole, a certain fidelity to the other's words as constituting a meaning, which is not, however bound by his intention, if by that is understood something singular and simple, and thus quantifiable, or an entity external to the words themselves. Since renga is a performance of discourse as a speech chain and not a lyric poem by a single author, the idea of an individual intention is, strictly speaking, incoherent. The point, rather, is the link itself, the motion of understanding the other's words by applying one's own mind to them, which means construing them, reading and interpreting them *con-textually*. And it is precisely because of temporality and dependent origination that understanding—and with it, meaning—cannot be other than contextual. The gap enabling the introduction of another mind also entails a "breaching," or, if you will, a "deconstruction," of the maeku, in the sense of an opening of it up to the light of understanding, which is also, for Shinkei, the creative access to new worlds (*aranu sakai*).

Indeed, when one takes it as axiomatic that there is no such thing as a purely individual intention in the chain of discourse, a verse that illumines the maeku, casts it in a new light by fidelity to its integral meaning, may be said to have an "objectivity" distinct from the alleged objectivity of recovering another's "intention" intact. This is not to banish intention, but rather to say that the construal of intention is precisely the task of reading and interpretation. The process can be compared to translation. Any good translation will illumine the original text, yet no two translations, even in the same target language, are exactly alike in their reading of the original text. A reader conversant with both languages can tell whether a "link," so to speak, or a creative transposition, has occurred, but it is not possible to predict the configuration a translation will take, just as in renga, the same verse will elicit different responses from different poets. This reveals the incommensurability of literary translation and so-called "machine translation." It explains why certain texts, no matter how old, achieve a continuing afterlife through the responsive understanding of their readers.

That such an understanding requires the labor of training is shown, however, by the fact that even Sōgi, who was to become the master renga poet of his time, was susceptible to the redundancy of formulaic, unspeaking *yoriai* early in his career. This may be gleaned from another passage in the letter quoted earlier:

> Regarding your most recent verses, I must say that I find every one of them interesting. However there are among them a number whose handling is a little uncertain [*obotsukanaki*], and I shall comment on a few of those here.

aki mo nao	Even autumn is yet
asaki wa yuki no	shallow: the snowy sky slowly
yūbe kana	taken by evening.

To this you added,

mizu kōru e ni	Over the frozen water of the bay,
samuki karigane	the cold cries of the wild geese.

> This verse is overstated and artificially contrived [*kekkō no mono* 結構の物]; it does not approach the manifest intention and feeling of the hokku. It is desirable when composing the *waki* 脇 [second verse] and subsequent verses to leave a few things unsaid. To exhaust the images of Water and Winter in this way would make it difficult for the poet of the third verse. It seems to be the common practice when composing verses on, say, Autumn, to link up to the maeku by using words like "wild geese," "deer," "dew," and so on, even though the meaning does not actually connect. On the contrary, the verse that truly links up to the maeku from the depths of the poet's mind may ignore such conventional associations [*engo*], and yet seem fully to connect. (*Tokoro*, letter 3, pp. 279–80)

Sōgi's verse seems rather good and evocative as such. Yet Shinkei says in no uncertain terms that it does not connect to the manifest intention and meaning of the maeku, called hokku here, because it happens to be the opening verse of a sequence. What it does is to elaborate on the Winter theme announced by the "snow" through the images of the frozen inlet and the cold cries of the wild geese, but at no point does it intersect or "interface" with the feeling and intention of the maeku as an *integral* expression. The meaning of Sōgi's verse as such is clear, but it is curiously wooden and inert, lacking the vital power to move. Precisely because it uses too many "implements"[9]—here "water," "frozen," "bay," "cold," and "wild geese," it presents a solid front against the maeku, and the two verses end up completely estranged from each other; there is no charge going through. By *sakai ni irisugi* 境に入り過ぎ, which I have rendered as "overstated," Shinkei clearly means becoming so fixated by the overt meaning of the maeku's words as such, being so caught up by their conventional associational boundaries (which in renga is equivalent to their "dictionary" meaning), that one ends up merely elaborating or embroidering on them with more words, and thus coming up with an unconnected statement, instead of opening one's mind to the maeku's *kokoro*—its meaning, intention, or significance, and letting it come through. *Sakai ni irisugi* literally means "going beyond the boundary," that is to say, overshooting the mark; according to Shinkei, it is a tendency common to the quick-witted and is as bad as falling short of the mark. If we pursue Shinkei's archery metaphor, becoming fixated on the target is the same as missing it. An "approach" that opens up the mind of the maeku is not the same as an "attachment" to its surface, its words. One needs to step back and listen with the mind's ear in order to see and hear the object as a whole and thereby create something new. Once more, Bakhtin on the act of understanding:

> Recognizing and encountering the new and unfamiliar. Both of these aspects (recognition of the repeated and discovery of the new) should merge inseparably in the living act of understanding. . . . The exclusive orientation toward recognizing, searching only for the familiar (that which has already been), does not allow the new to reveal itself (i.e., the fundamental, unrepeatable totality).[10]

"That which has already been" is "like seeing the Kamo Festival procession pass a thousand times," a repetition. The sign is eminently iterable; due to the existence of the linguistic code, it functions, remains legible—and thus productive—even when estranged from its context.[11] The tsukeku is always an iteration of the maeku, but not wholly so, since it would then repeat the mae-maeku, and it is precisely this returning to the (provisional) origin, so to speak, the karmic circle, that is strictly proscribed by the *uchikoshi* rule in renga. In other words, when Shinkei underscores "the different thinking of each member" (*ono'ono anjichigaetaru sakusha*) as that which produces new worlds, or urges Sōgi to resist "fixation" (*sakai ni irisugi*) in linking up to the maeku, he is implying that in order to avoid the karmic circle, one must recognize the old and familiar, yes, but also discover in the maeku author's *kokoro*, what it intends to say, something else, and so "allow the new to reveal itself," if only for a moment, before the new in turn withers and gives way to another "event," another context.

FOURTEEN

The Chill and the Meager (*Hieyase*)
Poetics and the Philosophy of the Privative

I should point out that the hokku to which Sōgi composed the tsukeku quoted on page 132 is by Shinkei himself.[1] It not only gives us concrete evidence of how the two poets' mutual participation at sessions in Musashi during the Ōnin War were extremely useful learning experiences for Sōgi, but also indicates the close and immediate relation between performance and critical evaluation in the renga milieu. Emphasizing the vital role of critical evaluation in the dialogical poetics of renga, Shinkei held that it is harder to appreciate another poet's brilliance than to compose a verse oneself. Shinkei's hokku is an invitation to appreciate the way in which a snowy evening in winter may be felt to be even more deeply moving than the autumn dusk (viz., "even autumn is yet shallow"), which is the classical image of *aware* in the poetic tradition. In order to respond to the feeling of the snowy sky slowly dimming at evening—a single, integral image that has all the austerity and *sabi* 寂 quality of an ink-wash painting, Sōgi might for instance have centered his verse on the remoteness of the cries of the wild geese behind the vague impenetrability of falling snow and darkening shadows. That single image, the faintness of the sound, would have pointed up the stillness of the hokku and brought it to the fore. To illustrate what Sōgi's tsukeku might have been, let me quote another pair of verses whose feeling resembles that of those that failed here:

furitsumoru	Foothills under
yuki no yamamoto	a deepening pall of snow
kururu hi ni	as twilight falls.
kane hitokoe no	Far away in the cedar grove,
ochi no sugimura	the muffled boom of a bell.[2]
Shinkei	Shinkei

Here we may justly appreciate Shinkei's tsukeku as an example of his celebrated aesthetic of the "chill and meager" (*hieyase* 冷え痩せ), or of the "cold and slender" (*samuku yasetaru* 寒く痩せたる). These terms refer on the level of poetic rhetoric to a tautly precise economy of diction, the use of only a "few words" (*kotoba sukunaku* 言葉少なく) to evoke a single effect. Although the tsukeku have fourteen syllables in both cases, in Shinkei's verse we can say that there are only two "words," *kane hitokoe* 鐘一声 (single boom of a bell) and *ochi no sugimura* をちの杉むら (distant cedar grove), in contrast to the five in Sōgi's verse. The difference demonstrates that many or "few" is not literally a question of the number of lexical items used, but rather a matter of their strict choice and arrangement *in relation to* the feeling, intention, or significance, that is, the *kokoro*, of the maeku. In contrast to this taut, economic "coldness" and "meagerness," a verse that includes words irrelevant to the maeku's *kokoro* is "flabby and warm" (*futori atatakanaru* ふとり暖かなる); its superfluous words are like excess flesh radiating their own heat, apart from any exercise of the bones and sinews of the mind. Or a verse might tease the wit and fancy, but without the sense of existential irony, itself an economy, that gives wit its true expressive power, its products will always seem like "an artificially contrived object" (*kekkō no mono*), "a vain elaboration on the surface of the verse" (*uwa'uwa to ku no ue o nomi momi*).

A negative valuation of the painted, decorated surface in favor of a bare yet vital simplicity, a reticent expressiveness, a quiet austerity: these are qualities that have long been recognized as characteristic of the quintessentially Japanese arts that had their origins in the Muromachi period. I refer to the arts of teahouse architecture and the cult of *wabicha*, the rock garden, ikebana, Nō, and black-ink painting and calligraphy, whose austere qualities are the same as those foregrounded in Shinkei's aesthetics. It is not clear, however, that such an aesthetics of the cold and austere was to the popular, or even aristocratic, taste. As Haga Kōshirō reminds us, *yūgen* as commonly understood in Higashiyama culture connoted not only courtly grace and refinement but a flowery, showy splendor.[3]

SABI AND HIEYASE AS THE AESTHETICS OF RECLUSION

Shinkei's valorization of *sabi* and *hieyase*, an aesthetics of the chill, lonely, and "reduced" in the sense of "distilled," was not, in fact, the dominant taste of his time. This art is wholly unworldly; it belongs to a philosophy of renunciation, the mind-set of the *intonsha* 隠遁者, or "recluses"—priests, wandering renga poets, aristocrats reduced to genteel poverty, or warriors out of favor with their lords—who produced much of what we now consider the characteristically "medieval" literature and art. Whether they actually lived in seclusion or were employed in some intellectual or artistic capacity by the shōgun or one of the various territorial lords, the "recluses" professed a symbolic rejection of worldly illusion and adherence to the existential truths of emptiness and temporality.

Reclusion is a time-honored tradition in Japanese culture. Historically, as we see already in the earliest chronicles, it is a consequence of political defeat. There is no need to mention the famous exiles—dispossessed princes, former ministers, the defeated Heike, a few emperors—throughout Japanese history. In literature, Ariwara Yukihira, and then Narihira in the *Tales of Ise*, who doubtless provided the models for Genji's exile in Suma and Akashi, are early examples, along with Sugawara Michizane, falsely accused of treason and banished to Kyūshū, whose story would still be providing material for Kabuki plays in the Edo period. The *wabihito* 侘び人, a poor, dispossessed man lamenting his fall from society, is a recurrent figure in both medieval waka and renga. It is significant in this regard that in the cult of *wabicha* 侘び茶, founded by Murata Jukō in the late fifteenth century on the inspiration of Shinkei's aesthetics of the chill and meager, material poverty and plainness acquire a positive character as signs of an authentic existence grounded in the Buddhist understanding of the essential truth about life and death.

Shinkei's attitude that the moving character (*aware*) of art is based on an understanding of privation is evident in an anecdote he recounted to his student Kenzai 兼載 (1452–1510) about Ton'a, one of the leading *shakuhachi* (bamboo flute) musicians in the country in the years before the outbreak of the Ōnin War.

> Shinkei recounted the following. Among Sōa's disciples, the one called Ton'a was a master whose art surpassed even his teacher's. Among Ton'a's disciples in turn was the man called Priest Jōzen. When someone asked Ton'a to appraise this priest's music, he answered, "He surpasses me both in the quality of his sound and in dexterity, but he is nevertheless inferior to me." Asked what this could mean, he replied, "Living as I do apart from the world, I know nothing of flowers and colors but feel in all things the pain and sorrow of mutability. I play with this contemplation [*kannen* 観念] in my heart, and consequently everyone is drawn to my music. Now that priest, being rich, noble, and perfect, has none of this sensibility and therefore his music lacks all appeal." This means that in both waka and renga, it is essential in every verse to have this contemplative spirit [*kannen no kokoro*].[4]

Readers of Kawabata Yasunari's novel *Yukiguni* (*Snow Country*, 1947) will perhaps remember the powerfully chilling, purifying effect of the poor mountain geisha Komako's samisen playing on Shimamura, and note the affinity of Kawabata's art to the medieval aesthetics of privation, or emptiness, enunciated by Shinkei.

An apparently negative aesthetics whose beauty is wholly distant and inward cannot be to the mundane taste, which tends toward the immediately perceptible, novel, or unusual. Shinkei attributed the so-called decline of renga in the middle period, after its initial flowering in the age of Gusai and Nijō Yoshimoto, to a worldliness and technicality that inevitably overtook it along with its overwhelming popularity.

> Thereafter the art of renga became common and acquired the look of elaborately crafted objects [*mimijika ni saiku-gamashikute*]. As a predecessor said, the likes of it had never been seen before, not even in waka. Indeed, even those verses considered memorable and transmitted down to our time all give the same impression of being fabrications [*mina tsukurimono nado no gotoku naru*]. Sounding worldly and familiar to the ear [*bonzoku ni mimi ni chikaku*], it is no wonder that they appeal to those enthusiasts who have yet to attain to the Way. (*Iwahashi batsubun* 326)

In such comments, Shinkei reveals his priestly calling; surely only a priest would frown at the popular exercise of renga as a game of clever words, a verbal craft with no higher aim than the pleasure of the moment. For the same reason, and no doubt also from moral conviction, he could not evade his vocation as a teacher or his nature as an intellectual.

Even Nijō Yoshimoto, whom modern scholars invariably cite for under-scoring renga's character as a temporal event, and its aim as "the pleasure of the session" (*tōza no ikkyō* 当座の逸興), nevertheless took seriously the question of whether renga could be a cause of enlightenment (*bodai no in-nen* 菩提の因縁). His reply, justifying poetry as religious practice, is worth quoting at length:

> In general, among the numerous buddhas of past and present ages, there are none who did not chant poetry. There is no question about the deity-buddhas and the saints of antiquity, since it is by means of poetry that they guided the sentient creatures.[5] And is not renga in particular what people of sensibility now practice with fervor? Hence in recent times, Bukkoku-zenji 佛国禅師, Musō-kokushi 夢想国師, and others engaged in it night and day.[6] Doubtless there is a reason why; it certainly seems that there is merit in it.
>
> Reflecting earnestly on this matter, [one sees that] in renga, the thought of a moment does not continue into the following moment. In it the realms of glory and ruin, of happiness and grief lie side by side, the one slipping into the other in a manner no different from the condition of the floating world. Today comes while we think of yesterday; autumn comes in thoughts of spring; leaves color as the flowers fade—is this not to contemplate the truth of the "whirling petals and falling leaves"? In the Way of waka, poets of the past were so obsessed by it that there are cases where one went so far as to wish to exchange his life for it or died from bitterness after suffering some adverse criticism. There are no such examples in renga. Since it is no more than the playing out of the pleasure of the session [*tōza no ikkyō o moyōsu*], there is neither obsession nor fixation, and since none has any thought be-yond the task at hand, there is no opportunity for bad thoughts to flourish. But expressing my opinion so frankly, I shall surely be criticized for splitting hairs and forcing too labored a construction on the matter.[7]

Since the concept of impermanence or temporality is a fundamental one in Shinkei, as in all classical literature, he would surely agree with Yoshi-moto's construction of the constantly shifting thought in renga as a per-formative demonstration, or contemplation, of it. Moreover, renga's nature as an "event" produced extemporaneously by several poets within set time limits discourages fixation in favor of allowing the excitement of temporal-ity, the unpredictability of engi, to flower. The fact remains, however, that Yoshimoto's understanding of *yūgen* in his renga treatises does not reach beyond a graceful refinement, which he opposed to *zoku* 俗 as the vulgar in mind, language, and poetic conception,[8] while Shinkei's privative aesthetics searches beyond outward refinement to address the issue of the symbolic distillation of existential truth.

SKILL, TECHNIQUE, PIGMENTS, AND THE FICTIONS OF MUNDANE REALITY

As we know, from the 1990s on, when all areas of life have become places of entertainment and commerce, the dissipation of mind and feeling over the unreal, there *is* something essentially evasive and ultimately dangerous about passively surrendering the mind to the facile or allowing it to get absorbed in the instrumental. Popular renga as Shinkei characterizes it was concerned primarily with verbal dexterity, wit and technique, and not sensibility or *aware*, and thus gives the impression of being artificial fabrications (*tsukurimono* 作り物) or skilled handicrafts (*saiku* 細工).

The difference between what we now call "arts and crafts," the so-called useful or, alternatively, decorative arts, and poetry lies in the issue of expression. Poetry in Shinkei's understanding is a symbolic expression of the ultimate truths about human existence; it is, to put it briefly, an expression of feeling as *aware*. Implements and accessories of daily life are primarily utilitarian in purpose; their forms are expressive only of their function. This is true also of the decorative arts, whether their design is abstract or literary; their function is still to adorn and ornament a space and a surface. No matter how intricately wrought an object—a brocade robe, painted china, lacquered food boxes, a fan—its decoration will always be a layer added on to the thing itself and not, as in the best poetry, the organic and necessary form of its self-expression. As in all high art, form is not merely a *means* of expression; it is itself the figuration and material body of the aesthetic-religious experience. What the consciousness responds to is the sensuous materialization of another consciousness and its response to the existential experience all human beings share; this is particularly true of literature, the art of language, the most human of symbolic forms.

Still, it cannot be denied that skill and technique as such are always popular and impressive. Renga was, after all, an extemporaneous verbal performance, and no doubt it was always a temptation to play up to the audience by displays of witty repartee, double entendre, esoteric allusions, rapid-fire composition, and so on in a bid for attention and personal power. Certainly, awesome displays of the synthetic products of technology—missile launches, sophisticated gadgetry, the latest deadly weaponry, cars, computers, and celebrities—always seem inevitably in our own time to dazzle the eye and numb the mind to the verities of existence. Poetry based on hard thinking and self-reflection has little chance against such blinding forces; only an education that transforms the mundane mind can release it from its abject worship of the machine, and from becoming machinelike itself. Shinkei observes:

> The art of renga in our time is like a great sword, a thing wrought in silver, or a woven quiver surmounted with a cock's feathers. Practitioners everywhere can hear only the immediately impressive, recognize only the marvelous in one another's work. It is wholly an art of decorating in pigments flecked with gold and silver, and utterly lacks the integral, sinewy line of the black-ink painting of the Chinese [*irodori hakudami nomi nite, sara ni hitofushi no sumi-e karamono wa miezu to nari* 色どり箔彩のみにて、さらにひとふしの墨絵唐物は見えずと也]. Thus their work is renga only in the intention, having wholly abandoned and lost its configuration, diction, and quality—so a predecessor said. (*Tokoro*, letter 3, p. 288)

The distinction between painting with pigments and with only black ink and water is Shinkei's most revealing metaphor about pure poetry, and Japanese poetry, given its brevity, could not afford to be less than pure. The line between a successful poem or verse and a non-poem is very clear in premodern Japan. As in *sumi-e* painting, the link from the artist's mind to his hand and brushstroke is wholly direct and immediate; a stroke once made cannot be erased, and so honest and austere is the medium of ink, water, brush, and paper that it faithfully registers, like a musical instrument, not only the slightest tremor and unsureness, but also the most delicate or most powerful state of mind. The calligraphy and abbreviated *sumi-e* paintings of the Zen masters and Zen-inspired artists is a case in point. *Sumi-e*, moreover, because of its abstract formality and monochromatic appearance, is to that degree more susceptible to the kind of symbolic figuration that is Shinkei's view of poetry, one that is based on *musō* 無相, the emptiness of form, an aesthetics in which things are not grasped as in mundane reality but in their essence.[9] The art of painting with colors is in contrast quite open to the illusion of representation and naturalism. The viewer tends to identify what is depicted on paper to external reality and, indeed, colored painting was used in Japan for just this purpose, as visual representations of "real" scenes from everyday life or from fictional narratives, as in the

Genji picture scroll and other such *monogatari* illustrations in the *Yamato-e* Japanese (in opposition to Kara-e, or Chinese) style. For a symbolic art of expression, colors would be extraneous accessories, a mere distraction from the essential, and this is Shinkei's point. Colors can obscure the truth, just as phenomena narrowly viewed do; they can "fabricate" and play upon the surface of things, just as words can and do, and impress the eye and seduce the ear in doing so.

The dichotomy between pure and popular literature that would excite debate among modern novelists like Akutagawa and Tanizaki in the early decades of the twentieth century is what is reflected in Shinkei's drawing of a crucial distinction between colored painting and the black-ink wash, between pure poetry and the renga "fabrications" of the popular milieu. The apparent prejudice against fiction (*tsukuri monogatari* 作り物語, invented tales) and the corresponding valorization of poetry and poetic prose as "pure" literature in traditional Japanese thinking had at least one of its roots in the Buddhist rejection of mundane reality (*zoku* 俗 or *bonzoku* 凡俗), that which is linguistically and sociologically contingent, and hence constructed, as the only and ultimate reality. A novel that depicts this world as such as real, without the sense of paradox and irony that would liberate it from such a fixed determination, can in fact mislead naive readers and suck them into the very illusory fantasy that is the root of human suffering. Shinkei's objection to the use of renga to contrive illusion is perhaps correlated to a fictionalizing tendency that would later come to the fore in the haikai of the Edo period. What Earl Miner has called the "thinginess" of haikai, the density of quotidian objects and images in it,[10] as rendered with a wit that is not necessarily a criticism of life but rather an affectation of urbane sophistication in the ways of "the floating world," gives it the feel of the familiar surface of social life that one associates with the novel or fiction. It is no accident, in this connection, that one of the most brilliant Genroku haikai poets, Saikaku, would later find his niche in fiction writing. Nor is it surprising that his contemporary Bashō found it necessary, when he found his own voice, after rejecting the formulaic renga of Matsunaga Teitoku, and after experimenting with the absolute freedom of Danrin-school "dadaism," to trace his new style back to the founding ideals of "Saigyō's waka, Sōgi's renga, Sesshu's paintings, and Rikkyū's tea,"[11] that is, to the medieval poetics of *sabi* and Zen emptiness that is Shinkei's theme: "But if your discipline is shallow, your mind unsettled, and you persist in elaborating vainly upon the surface of the verse, it might indeed seem interesting for a moment but will quickly disenchant in the next, as the words lose their vital tensility [*omoshi-rokuhaberu tomo mizameshi, kotoba take o ushinaihaberu ya*]" (*Tokoro*, letter 3, p. 289).

THE VITAL TENSILITY OF THE SUBLIME

Take, usually appearing in the classical critical vocabulary in the compound *take takashi* 長高し (lofty, sublime) signifies the height or length of an object, its reach and extension in space. I have rendered it "vital tensility" above, because that is most appropriate in the context of Shinkei's aesthetics as a whole. On the plane of poetic diction, *take* is further defined by another recurring phrase in Shinkei, *hitofushi ni iinagashitaru* 一節に言ひ流したる. This has the sense of "a single sinewy, undulating line," the same modifier he employed for describing *sumi-e* above, which may also be read as "a line undulating from a single node," the graph for *fushi* appearing at times as 筋, which is properly read *suji*, "sinew, line," or as 節, "joint, knob, node," that is, the point in a tree trunk or branch, say bamboo, from where main stems grow. Whether *fushi* is sinew or joint, the phrase *hitofushi ni iinagashitaru* connotes a tense vitality or power that manifests itself in *take* as a tensile extension, the supple quality of growing plants or a ballet dancer's body. As a characteristic of renga diction, tensility points to the integral unity of an utterance whose words are chosen with economic precision to dovetail into each other aurally and syntactically in relation to the *kokoro* of the maeku. Another verse submitted by Sōgi for Shinkei's evaluation illustrates the principle more clearly.

To the following third verse from around the same time,

irie o samumi	Clumps of grasses withering
karuru murakusa	in the cold along the inlet.

you added,

mizu keburu	By the river's foggy waters
kawabe no ashibi	at morning, the miscanthus fires
kesa kiete	have died out.

This too manifests a somewhat contrived conception and does not approach the feeling of the maeku. It would have worked better had you evoked the pale cast of the aging moon on the water, the desolation [*sabishisa*] of moonlight glinting behind the terribly wasted grasses in the old inlet. . . . I myself suffer from this infirmity of crowding two or three things into a verse that should properly have only one integral image. It is desirable to observe this principle as closely as possible and design the verse so that everything coalesces into a single monochromatic unity [*tada mono isshiki nite shitatetaku ya* ただ物一色にてしたてたく哉]. (*Tokoro*, letter 3, pp. 281–82)

Aurally and conceptually, the image design of Sōgi's tsukeku is interesting and coherent as such. It attempts, moreover, to link up to the maeku through the lexical correspondences "inlet = river," "clumps of grasses = miscanthus," and the thought that the "cold" is caused by the extinguishing of the miscanthus fires, although he could just as well have reasoned the other way round, that the fires could not stay lit due to the cold winds. But such *yoriai* pairings and deliberate logic, a result of attending too closely to the maeku's words as such, have the contrary effect of fragmenting it instead of drawing the two verses together into a "single node," that joint of a turn that connects and separates at the same time. As Shinkei suggests, a verse centering upon the late-night moon upon the water would have been sufficient. It would have been the single image, set in a spare and tightly drawn diction, that might have resonated with the maeku, set the two verses flowing together into a "single undulating" current beneath the surface. Below is a comparable tsukeku by Shinkei.

fuyugare no	In winter-withered
nobe ni sabishiki	fields the color of loneliness
iro miete	apparent.
yūhi no shita no	The glinting line of river
mizu no hitosuji	beneath the dying sun.[12]

Mizu no hitosuji (literally, single line of water) is the one image here that tenses up the maeku with a surge of significance. The "joint" of the connection turns around the relation of similarity and difference between withered fields and the white incandescence of flowing water at sunset. There is nothing fixed or predetermined about this relation; it is metaphorical in nature and first comes into existence through the poet's mind. It is not a function of discursive thinking, not an explanation, but a product of a meditation on the interrelation of all phenomena. As symbolic poetry, it goes beyond a simple drawing of analogies, namely, winter-withered fields = the color of loneliness = the glinting line of river at sunset. It further invites an introspection upon that which itself grounds the making of the metaphor. Here, that is the thought that *sabi*, cosmic stillness and silence, or the subjective experience of an impersonal existential loneliness (*sabishi*) beyond consolation, is itself based on *śūnyatā*, the principle that self and phenomena are wholly contingent and temporal, that they are mere forms (*iro* 色, literally, color, appearance), empty, yes, yet full at the same time, for there is nothing apart from form. The water that is, poetically speaking, both formless and colorless, takes on or becomes the reflection of the slanting sun, and it is this that is "the color of loneliness" in the context of the link, this becoming something else that is simultaneously the sign of an emptiness at the core and may in fact be felt as "lonely" if one does not wish to be as transparent water. In the maeku as such, loneliness is the withered form of the grasses as a manifestation of seasonal process. The keenness of Shinkei's tsukeku is in the way he grasps *miete*, "become apparent" both literally and contemplatively; the image of the glinting river is a perfect visual "analogue" of the maeku's "lonely color," giving it a momentous intensity of feeling, while simultaneously opening a slowly widening window of contemplation upon the Real. What we see, in sum, is "what is left unsaid," Shunzei's "aura," or Shinkei's own "vital tensility," the words' extension into the "surreal" realm of nonmundane perception.

Incidentally, this link gains an interesting dimension when read, as I believe Shinkei intended it to be, as an allusive variation on Jakuren's famous poem *SKKS* 361:

> sabishisa wa   Loneliness—
> sono iro to shi mo   a feeling not lodged within
>   nakarikeri   this form, that color:
> maki tatsu yama no   pines rising on the mountain
> aki no yūgure   in the gathering autumn dusk.

Both of Shinkei's premier students, Sōgi and Kenzai, left commentaries on this poem, an indication that it was very much a part of their milieu's poetic consciousness. "Since the needles of the pine do not take on color, they function here as a verbal allusion"—thus Sōgi. And Kenzai: "Pines are evergreen trees. 'Not lodged within that color' means that colors as such do not have the quality of loneliness."[13] Jakuren's point is the ultimate indeterminacy of the origins of feeling and perception, and that *sabishisa* is this very ambiguity. One can almost sense Shinkei's playful smile when he composed the reply to the maeku's "the color of loneliness / apparent" as in turn a confirming, yet differing, response to Jakuren: non-form inheres in form, absence of color in color, and anything at all, when seen contemplatively, is *sabi*. We should note also his characteristic transposition of the *Shinkokinshū* autumnal sensibility to the wintry modality of the spare, the chill, and distilled.

"Spare in diction, chill and meager" (*kotoba sukunaku hieyasetaru*) and "undulating from a single node" (*hitofushi ni iinagashitaru*) together constitute Shinkei's ideal of good renga diction. The one refers to a precise and utterly disciplined choice of words, in such a way that not a single one is superfluous or misplaced *in relation to* the maeku, and the whole gives an effect of purity and a taut coldness. "'As lapis lazuli heaped in a crystal bowl' means to aim for an effect of purity and cold" (*SSG* 12: 137). The other refers to the way in which words are pulled into a syntactic and phonological relation that gives them a vital tensility and suppleness, "'like a five-foot stalk of blue-flag iris newly watered.' The effect is one of spaciousness and a cool wetness" (*SSG* 12: 137). The two, purity and tensility, are inseparable qualities belonging to the style of loftiness or sublimity (*take takaki tei* 長け高き躰) which occupies the central place in his aesthetics. This "loftiness," which is less an imposing height than a distancing from the inside, an inner dimension of spaciousness, cannot be considered apart from the spiritual strenuousness that a poet brings to the process of composition.

> What is called a masterly verse [*shūitsu* 秀逸] depends on none other than this quality of the soul. It is such a verse as must issue from a man whose spirit is minutely permeated by beauty and made tranquil by it [*kokoro o hosoku en ni nodomete* 心を細く艶にのどめて] and whose mind is deeply imbued with a sense of life's moving power [*yo no aware o mo fukaku omoi'iretaru* 世のあはれをも深く思ひいれたる]. In this way, a word or two might well spell all the difference in the total configuration of a poem. But this difference, which is variously perceived as a quality of refinement, gentleness, or tensility [*shina. yū. take*], as a certain meagerness and coldness [*yase. samuku*], or a compelling remoteness [*rōrōshiku*]—such a verse about which floats the wordless fragrance of the mind [*iwanu kokoro no nioi* 言はぬ心の匂ひ] can only issue from the lips of the contemplative man.... It is because the keen poet dissolves his mind [*kokoro o torake* 心を盪け], because the verse issues from the depths of his being, that its composition takes time, and a session might well continue until dusk. The verse of the untalented, on the other hand, merely rolls off the tip of his tongue, and thus requires no time at all. And since it is possible to spend long years of training without acquiring the [mind's] ear, there are many such people who become merely dexterous and nothing more. (*SSG* 14: 140–41)

KŪ, OR THE EMPTINESS OF FORM

Poetic process entails a "dissolution of the mind," that is, a letting-go of the ego that is simultaneously a closing of the habitual distance between the mind and its primal ground or *shinji* (mind-ground). It is also a seeing-beyond the fixed and particularized forms of objects, or meanings, and out into the indeterminate and blurred territory of *kū*, the emptiness of form. This process, which we saw expressed in the letter to Sōgi as "contemplating the distant sea or gazing at an autumn dewdrop," is apparently both a distancing and a concentration; it means to contemplate something so infinite, or infinitesimally small and indivisible, that the whole apparatus of discursive reasoning, which is based precisely on dichotomies, is rendered impotent before it. The two terms of this metaphor for poetic process are therefore not mutually exclusive, but are at base the same, in that they both liberate the mind into the open dimension of *śūnyatā*. As a manifestation of the powers of the poetic mind, it doubtless has affinities with the *shikan* meditation practice of moving from the provisional (or conditioned) phenomena to the realm of emptiness, and then returning to phenomena with an illumined sense of their indeterminacy as both conditioned and empty, or neither, hence at one with the middle truth:

> Next is to explain the forms of contemplation. There are three: entering emptiness through the provisional [*juke nikkū* 従仮入空] is called contemplation of the two truths; entering the provisional through emptiness [*jugū nikke* 従空入仮] is called contemplation of equivalence; entering the Middle Way using the two truths as expedient means, and thus illuminating the two truths, so that each state of mind becomes tranquil and flows of itself into the sea of wisdom, is called contemplation of the supreme truth of the Middle Way.[14]

It is noteworthy that in Guanding's Preface, the bodhisattva's adornment of perfect mastery is described in terms of an ability to freely "enter samādhi through one sense-faculty and arise from samādhi to expound the dharma with another sense-faculty, or . . . simultaneously both enter and arise from samādhi with the same sense faculty, or . . . neither enter nor leave it with any particular sense faculty," and so on.[15] The mental flexibility required to break through the maeku's words and construe it in a way that remains faithful to its syntax would seem to entail the passage from provisionality to emptiness and back that is expounded in the *Makashikan*.

The thinking that is specific to poetry as a Way, the poetic mode of being that was Shinkei's vision of an authentic existence, is wholly distinct from the mundane (*zoku, bonzoku*) way, which is always, as a matter of habit, colored by self-consciousness (*watashi-meki*), biased and conditioned. It is not the use of reason to determine the physical nature of phenomena in order to harness them to man's use. Here, knowledge is not power in the sense of objectification, and consequent possession and exploitation. It is merely the liberation of the mind from any preconceived ideas about anything at all; the sweeping it clear of the clutter of trivia; the dissolution, through close analysis, of fixed positions. Language, and the thinking that transpires through it, is an institution of discriminations and predeterminations. "White" is different from "black"; "you" are different from "me"; "reason" is not "passion"; "evil," not "good"; "friend," not "enemy"; and so on. But as Buddhism teaches, these differences are just names; it is blindness and positively harmful to oneself and others to take them for real. For the fact of the matter is, as Western thought has also recognized since Saussure's analysis of language as a system of differences whose units have no positive value, and since Einstein's theory of relativity, "white" is so because there is "black," and "green" and "red"; "I" am "I" because of "you," there are "friends" because there are "enemies," and all these distinctions, this network of *différance*, and external phenomena as well, have a dependent origination (*engi*), mutually causing each other to come into existence and exit into nonexistence. Springing from categories of the mind, none of them could possibly exist without the others; they all stand and fall together. Therefore, in order to see things as they are, in the pristine, primal light of the pre-(or post-)linguistic stage, one must abjure thought, "clarify" or "settle" the mind, retract it, so to speak, from its habitual attachment to things so that it may return to itself (its home ground) and things may also return to themselves. In this state, there is no more "you" or "I," object or subject, there is only the being or suchness (*jizai* 自在 or *shinnyo* 真如; Skt. *tathatā*) of all things, the one thought that is the ground of all thought (*ichinen sennen* 一念千念), the wind hidden in the great void, "the perfect fusion of the three truths" (*santai ennyū* 三諦円融) of the empty, contingent, and middle, the melting away of all distinction. As expressed by the scriptural epigram, *shohō jissō* 諸法実相, all the dharmas *as such*—singly, severally, and in dynamic totality are coextensive with each other in the sense of mirroring, or being traces of, each other, ad infinitum. Thus they may be said to spring from a single node, which is like the eye of a storm or the still point of a vortex, and are all wholly real in the ultimate sense, beyond the question of life and death.

Clearly, this is not a standpoint of philosophical skepticism so much as the end of philosophy and the beginning of poetry and religion, or of life lived in accordance with the Way. This end point of arrival, which can only be reached by a leap of faith and of courage, is beyond contemporary skepticism. (Consider, for instance, the resonance of the following: "'Not to be overpowered though one stood alone before the August Seat in the Great Hall of State of the Imperial Palace.' This means the poem must be resolute and strong" *SSG* 12: 137). This end point does not rest in seeing everything as "empty" because conditioned, nor in seeing *différance*, the enabling gaps between things, as the only reality. That is still to remain within the plane of language—and for contemporary theorists of the linguistic turn, "there is only language," the endless play of signifiers, the proliferating gaps between signifier and signified, Chih-i's sign and non-sign. That is still to hold back from the abyss of being, Heidegger's *Abgrund*, with the mental categories still intact. As Shinkei states,

> If you did not set your mind upon enlightenment [*satori* 悟り], how could you free yourself from the delusions [literally, arising-and-ceasing] in the Way of poetry? And yet even the highest enlightenment of the emptiness school [*kūmon daigo* 空門大悟] is considered inferior in that it is still based on a relativizing discrimination [*ushodoku* 有所得]. In the Tendai school of form *is* emptiness, the ten worlds—including the six worldly and the four saintly realms, are all ultimately one, undifferentiated and beyond form [*Tendai sōsokukū-mon ni wa, jukkai rokubonshishō issō musō to ieri* 天台相即空門には、十界六凡四聖一相無相といへり]. (*SSG* 49: 187)[16]

HIKKYŌ-KŪ, OR THE EMPTINESS OF EMPTINESS

In effect, Shunzei's "deep mind" and Teika's *ushin* realm of meditation are radicalized by Shinkei within the post-*ushin* realm of absolute emptiness (*hikkyō-kū* 畢竟空), the utter effacement of margins and the wholly open dimension of *śūnyatā*, which is none other than the realm of *mushin*, "no-mind" and suchness. Such a standpoint is not easy to grasp; how does one "grasp" the empty except through the discriminations, binary oppositions, and analogies of language? This is the same as to ask, how do you transmit a significance except through the categories enabled by that same language? But the question has become irrelevant for the seeker at least, since from the standpoint of absolute emptiness, there is nothing to grasp; emptiness is itself empty; it is a principle (*ri* 理), not a being or substance. The network of differences that enable meaning in language is indeed crucial in reaching the final destination, but having arrived there, tasted of its fruit, so to speak, one does not tarry but returns to the mundane world in order to show the Way to others: "In every art, it is important to bear in mind that in the beginning, you progress from the shallow into the deep, but having arrived there, you again emerge into the shallow" (*SSG* 49: 187).

There is no way to comprehend this statement except in a wholly pragmatic and, on another level, in a political sense, as an expression of commitment to humanity. Grasping the absolutely empty is after all an oxymoron; upon that ultimate locus, one has let go of the distinction between deep and shallow that was crucial to attaining illumination but is meaningless for the illumined: "Through the cause, you arrive at the effect [i.e., the fruit of wisdom]; thereafter through the effect you return to the cause" (*SSG* 49: 187). Or as it is everywhere stated in the *Makashikan*, "pursue the high to transform the low" (*jōgū kege* 上求化下). High and low are contingent categories established relative to a concrete course of action; there is nothing immanent in them. For if you did not believe that differences are relative and contingent, there would be no point in educating the ignorant, redressing inequalities, or reforming criminals; in short, the whole idea of a Way would become irrelevant. The Way of the beings who figure as Buddhism's "saints," the buddhas and bodhisattvas, is not to remain in the rarefied regions of enlightenment but to make that in turn into a cause or "means" (*hōben*) to guide others out of "the burning house" of mundane suffering. There is wisdom, and then there is compassion (*jihi*). Mahayana Buddhism joins them inextricably, as if wisdom as such is barren fruit if it does not scatter and implant the seeds of others' salvation. This may be called Buddhism's political dimension, its compassionate involvement in the world through a pedagogy of the mind.

> As the formless Dharma Body manifests itself in the form of the Reward Body in response to circumstance, so poetry based on form is one manifestation of poetry grounded in emptiness [*usō no kadō wa musō hosshin no kadō no ōyō nari* 有相の歌道は無相法身の歌道の応用也]. One should not therefore make light of its temporary efficacy as a means [*hōben no gon'yō orosoka ni omoubekarazu* 方便の権用おろそかに思ふべからず]. (*SSG* 49: 187)

The Buddha's "reward body" is Buddhism's concession to the human expectation of reward or gratification for effort; it is not as such the ultimate truth, which has no form, but it is made available to beginners as a promise of the delights of enlightenment. In terms of literary history, Shinkei means to acknowledge the necessity and efficacy of poetry of the ordinary sort—facile, near and familiar, its meaning immediately comprehensible. This is poetry that can be learned and explained through rules of composition, as in the waka of the dominant Nijō school of his time, in contrast to the more imaginative and radical productions of the Kyōgoku-Reizei school with which Shōtetsu and Shinkei were affiliated; it is renga verses using the Close Link, based on coded and conventional verbal associations. These are also after all wholly positive responses to circumstance, and responsiveness, in poetry as in any human endeavor, is already the beginning of action. Everything can be turned into account in the economy of mental liberation. "You progress from the shallow into the deep"—the trite and trivial can open the way to the profound—"but having arrived there, you again emerge into the shallow." For "the mind of the true poet [*makoto no kajin* まこと の歌人] must not be fixated on either form or formlessness, the Close Link or the Distant Link; it must be like the undifferentiated mind-ground of a buddha [*hotoke no shinji no gotoku narubeshi* 佛の心地のごとくなるべし)" (*SSG* 49: 188).

The crucial principle in poetry as a mode of being is responsiveness, an absolute openness that is possible, however, only on the ground of nondistinction. This ground may not, ultimately, be compromised. One may as a teacher use the familiar and concrete as examples, establish the validity of an assertion through logic, magnify the small, and reduce the inflated. However, without at some point, at the advanced level (and Shinkei warns against the conflation of levels), exposing the basis of these arguments and analogies on a wholly relative and therefore conditioned set of criteria, in other words, without teaching the ultimate emptiness or conditionedness of all criteria, one is promoting a dangerous, eventually harmful, way of thinking. Thus Shinkei, after affirming the validity and use of conditioned forms as a *means* or an opening into the unconditioned and formless, adds this qualification: "However, to teach and convert others by preaching a doctrine based only on conditioned discriminations [*ushodoku* 有所得] is an offense even more heinous than if you had plucked out the eyes of all the creatures of the three thousand realms" (*SSG* 49: 188).

Itself a tautly drawn metaphor, this statement confirms that the ultimate aim of poetry as a Way is the transmission, not of particular meanings or charming sentiments, but of a way of *seeing*, a mode of being. It is to liberate the mind's eye, clarify the mind's ear, and thus empower the individual to discover for himself the validity of an assertion, the truth of a situation, precisely by *seeing through* them, or projecting them against a horizon more vast. Wisdom or true knowledge is in this way a cold eye, a chill, penetrating ray powerful enough to lay every assertion waste, in order to reveal that only love and compassion can thrive in the ruins. As a religion, Buddhism is thus like any other in affirming the inviolate claims of humanity and other creatures, both sentient and nonsentient, against any intellectual, philosophical, or political system at all that claims absolute validity beyond contingent circumstance.

THE CREATIVE PROCESS IN SUM

Creative process is in this way rooted in a clairvoyance, a way of seeing that penetrates through the ordinary appearance of things, their seeming solidity, and into the hidden and higher realm of principle (*ri*), where they have their true being, as indicated in the Tendai principle of absolute impartiality, "the perfect fusion of the three truths" (*santai ennyū*), or as Shinkei refers to it in the previously cited passage from the *Iwahashi* Epilogue: "The man who is ignorant of the Way is blind to the shifting of the four seasons, unaware of the deeply fascinating Principle [*en fukaki kotowari* 艶深 き理] coursing through the forms and colors of the ten thousand realms. He spends his whole life before a blank wall with a jar pulled over his head" (*Iwahashi batsubun*, p. 327).

In other words, going beyond the mundane and predetermined meaning (*kotowari*) of words and phenomena into the more expansive realm of a higher principle (*en fukaki kotowari*, or *ri*) that relativizes and deconstructs them is precisely the mental process necessary to achieve a profound connection with the maeku. Contemplation is the mediating process by which the poet transcends the limited meaning of the maeku and comes up with a verse that does not connect to it overtly through its words and configuration. It is because the advanced poet is composing from such a "cosmic" base that his verse manifests a suppleness and inner spaciousness that cannot be accounted for merely by its linguistic properties. And it is also through the words' sheer transparency, the absence of any superficial intention or fixed message in them, that we sense the authentic operation of his mind in the instance of tsukeai, which is in the most inspired moments like the powerful implosion of a revelation. It is surely in this sense that Shinkei did not hesitate to call all poetry of the first rank *shingon*, the True Word, a *dharani* incantation that empowers the mind by liberating it from the bondage of the mundane.

En is, as we have seen earlier, Shinkei's term for an inner grace, what in the history of Western critical thought has been understood as the unity of the beautiful and the true.[17] It is also, as in the passage above, the fascinating or compelling quality of the hidden realm of principle as it subtly manifests itself in phenomena. Again, it is synonymous with *aware*. As we saw in the *Sasamegoto* passage on poetic process, it is the realm upon which the poet settles his mind (*en ni nodomete*), in which his mind is "deeply imbued with a sense of life's moving power" (*yo no aware o fukaku omoi'iretaru*). That same passage tells us that *en* is "the compellingly remote, wordless fragrance of the mind" (*rōrōshiku iwanu kokoro no nioi*), drawing us from the fixed, narrow, and everyday into a universal immanent realm where nothing remains still, and each is a mirror of everything else in a constantly shifting, yet subtly poised network of interrelationships. "Tensility, meagerness, and coldness" (*take. yase. samuku*) refer to the unintoxicated strenuousness of that mind as it manifests itself in the diction and figuration of the verse, while "refinement and gentleness" (*shina. yū*), though evoking the graceful, courtly sensibility of the *Genji* world—that object of nostalgia for Shinkei, Shōtetsu, and, of course, Teika and Shunzei before them—refers even more relevantly to the gentle, compassionate heart of the buddhas and bodhisattvas, for whom human existence is not a matter of indifference but potentially replete with the fullness of being. In sum, "refinement and gentleness" are synonymous with *aware*, a responsiveness to the moving power of being that lodges in everyone and everything. In this way, Shinkei's ideal of *en*, inner grace, spiritual charisma or radiance, is a paradoxical, dialectical concept. As a measure of mental development, it is the quality or emanation of an ideal person who possesses both the chill, penetrating gaze of a sage and the responsive heart of a human being in the world. *Michi*, "the Way," the poetic mode of being, the fusion of beauty and truth that is *en*, is also ultimately grounded in the twin Buddhist ideals of wisdom and compassion.

FIFTEEN

The Mode of Ambiguity
Is the Dharma Body

"The mode of ambiguity that is constituted solely of nuance" (*omokage bakari o nomi yomu fumyōtei* 面影をのみ詠む不明體), also described as a verse "whose diction and figuration have an ineffable remoteness" (*sugata. kotobazukai no yōon no ku* 姿・言葉使ひの幽遠の句) is said by Shinkei to be the style of the ultimate realm of enlightenment in poetry, and is further identified with the Dharmakaya, the Buddha-Body in essence. It may be viewed as the home of *en*, and of symbolic poetry, in that its aim is to make apparent the very realm of principle and of being from which the inexpressible fragrance of the mind emanates. Here is the passage from *Sasamegoto* illustrating this ultimate mode with two poems as well as two illuminating citations from the sutras.

> People in these rustic parts do not care that their verses are all flabby and awkwardly stumbling [*futomi-tsumazukitaru*]; being most impressed with skillfully painted surfaces [*irodori takumi naru*], they brush aside those verses whose diction and figuration have an ineffable remoteness [*yōon*].
>
> A venerable old sage has said that the same holds true for all the arts, but in the Way of poetry in particular, one sets the highest value on sensibility,

nuance, and overtones [*kansei. omokage. yojō*]. In truth, the ineffably profound and moving resides precisely in what is left unsaid, in what is empty of overt meaning [*ikani mo iinokoshi kotowari naki tokoro ni yūgen. aware wa arubeshi to nari*]. In waka as well, the so-called "mode of ambiguity" [*fumyōtei*] that is constituted solely of nuance [*omokage*] is the awesome mode of the ultimate realm. . . .

aki no hi no
usuki koromo ni
　kaze tachite
yuku hito matanu
sue no shirakumo
　　　Teika

On the thin cloak
of autumn sunlight, rippling
　a wind rises, without a
pause, the figure moves on
a cloud in the blank horizon.
　　　Teika

aki no hi wa
ito yori yowaku
　sasagani no
kumo no hatate ni
ogi no uwakaze
　　　Shōtetsu

Frailer than the thread
the spider hangs   suspended
　the autumn twilight
along a distant web of cloud,
a passing wind upon the reeds.
　　　Shōtetsu

These superior poems [*shūka*] are truly in the mode of the Dharma Body [*hosshin no tei* 法身の躰], manifestations of spontaneous enlightenment without instruction [*mushi jigo* 無師自悟]. Their meaning is difficult to grasp in the language of words. . . .

He who would see me in the world of form,
Seek me in the realm of sound,
Is a man who walks the wrong path
And will not see the Tathāgata.
[*Kongōhannya-kyō*]

Awakening to my original non-arising and non-ceasing,
I passed beyond the way of language,
Was set free from all chains of delusion,
And leaving cause and condition far behind,
Understood that my own void is equivalent to the great void.
[*Dainichi-kyō*]

(*SSG* 43: 178–79)

The outward simplicity of these two poems belies their ambivalence and minute subtlety, which resist any single reading and present an impossible task for the translator. An explication of what is at work here on the level of poetic rhetoric will show their complexity. In Teika's piece, *usuki* 薄き (thin) is a pivot word modifying both *aki no hi* 秋の日 autumn sunlight) and *ko-romo* (robe, garment, covering; rendered above as "cloak"). *Koromo* 衣, while also resonating with *yuku hito* 行く人 (passing figure, traveler) in the lower section, through the mediation of the stock metonymic expression *tabigoromo* 旅衣 (travel robe), refers in the upper section (the first three lines) as such to the frail reflection of the evening sun as, paradoxically, a thin cloak veiling things. The third line, *kaze tachite* 風立ちて, sets this still, tranquil scene in motion; its first meaning is "a wind rises." However, in relation to "the thin cloak of autumn sunlight," and as an effect of the unusual trans-linear semantic string *koromo ni / kaze tachite*, "*on* the cloak / a wind rises" (the exact value of the locative particle *ni* is ambiguous), the verb *tatsu* 立つ also comes to be infected by its second sense of "cut, rip apart, interrupt" (*tatsu* 断つ・裁つ). That is to say, a wind rises, and the object upon which the sunlight is faintly reflected, later to be further implicitly identified with the "white cloud," is torn to pieces and scattered.

Viewed from Shinkei's concept of tsukeai, the upper and lower verses are in a *hen-jo-dai / kyoku-ryū* relationship in which each verse echoes and trans-forms the other. With the fourth line and part of the fifth, *yukuhito matanu* 行く人待たぬ / *sue* 末, literally, "the end [the future, the destination] / that does not wait for [pause, halt for] the traveler"—in the sense that it creeps up from behind him, taking him unawares—the drift of the poem's "mean-ing" emerges on the surface, but the ineffable uncanniness of that experi-ence, which may be imaged as the sudden opening up of a rift, a yawning abyss, can be sensed concretely only through the dynamic operation of the poem's total configuration, its gestalt. It is only through the working of the paradox embedded in the zeugma *tachite / yuku* as a departure or setting out (発つ, yet another semantic value of *tatsu*) that is also a breaking down, an "arising" that is also a scattering, that the subtle resonance between the images of the lone, vulnerable traveler hurrying toward his destination in the risen wind and the cloud scattering before him becomes actualized as a single node, a tactile mental sensation of aporia or mental stoppage. Again, the elliptical ambiguity of the lower section is such that "traveler," "end/ destination," and "white cloud" may each function as the subject or object of the verb *matanu*, "not waiting, without a pause." The traveler hurries on, not waiting for the end; the white cloud scatters, not waiting for the traveler. *Sue no shirakumo* 末の白雲, "the white cloud in the horizon," furthermore, also identifies the end/destination as both "unknown" (*shira-*, "white," "colorless," but also the negative base of the verb *shiru* 知る, "to know") and equivalent to the cloud itself, so supple is that simple particle *no* when used in poetry both in its genitive and subject-marker functions. Indeed, the "wind" itself may also be read as the subject of the verb *matanu*—the wind arises and moves on, not pausing for the traveler. Finally, the cloud, metonymical adjunct of the scene, is transformed into the metaphorical image of the traveler; this cloud trailing off in the horizon is his end and destination. The thin cloak of autumnal light, the traveler's cloak, the white cloud, the traveler himself—everything is transformed into permeable surface in this poetic choreography of the tearing of the veil of illusion.

Thus read or "laid out" (from *auslegen* in the Heideggerian sense), the configuration of the poem shows itself to be riddled with gaps or spaces opening up among the phrases, between and even within the words, blurring their semantic boundaries, causing the structural line divisions to radically shift and slide against each other.[1] The net effect of this outwardly tranquil and smoothly flowing, yet inwardly vertiginous, rhetorical surface is to dissolve the distinctions among sunlight, traveler, and cloud through the force of a mysterious wind, to baffle our sense of space and time, erase the difference between beginning and end by contracting—that is, reducing *almost* to nothing—the mediate duration that establishes them. In contemporary terms, the poem's gestalt is the dynamic figuration of a deconstructive event, an aporitic experience that concretely demonstrates Shinkei's definition of creative process as a dissolution of mental categories and implicitly illustrates what he means by saying that the mode of ambiguity is "constituted solely of nuance" (*omokage*, also, reflection, shadow, trace) or that it is a figuration of the Dharma Body in all its indefinable essence. With a skill most crafty and an intensely concentrated mind, Teika makes bodily apparent the abstract concept of the absence of self-nature in all the dharmas (*shohō mujishō* 諸法無自性). Through a minutely intricate turning and layering of the words' meanings and linked associations, he brings forth the experience of the mutual interpenetrability of all phenomena, which is also their unraveling distension or expansion into the infinite space of emptiness.

Shōtetsu's poem is clearly an allusive variation on Teika's, so closely does it match it as a crafty figuration of a minutely elusive feeling. The imagistic elements of autumnal light, cloud, and wind are the same, but there is a difference in the crucial supplement: the "cloak" in the one is a spider's web here, but they have the same function. Rhetorically, *sasagani no kumo* (spider's web 細蟹の蜘蛛 / cloud 雲) in line 3 is a "pause word" (*yasume kotoba* 休め詞) that results in a similar double vision fracturing the poem's meaning. Juxtaposing the subliminal image of the glinting spider's web with the distant wisp of cloud, the poem features a startling shift from the infinitesimal to the infinite, from the momentary stillness of sunlight lining the cloud to the sudden movement in the reeds that effectively dissolves both web and cloud as the faint evening light is extinguished. The frail, yet piercing, glint of the spider's thread before its scattering in the winds of darkness constitutes the node of the poem and marks its precise difference from Teika's. Where the one is like a deep, almost imperceptible tremor deep in the bowels of the earth that gradually spreads to the surface, Shōtetsu's gestalt is an ingathering of dispersed forces into the tension of a still, chill point.

Singly and together, the two poems recall one of Shinkei's metaphors for poetic figuration: "In their immensity, even the empty space constrains them; in their minuteness, the space in a poppy seed is yet too big for them. Like Jōzō 浄蔵 and Jōgen 浄眼, poetic inscapes room marvelous transformations [*shimpen* 神変]" (SSG 12: 134). As evidenced by the pointed quotations from the *Diamond Wisdom Sutra* (*Kongōhannya-kyō* 金剛般若経) and the *Great Sun Sutra* (*Dainichi-kyō* 大日経) terminating the section in which they appear, these "ultimate" poems are operating right at the far margins of language, deliberately stretching meaning, logic, and syntax to their utmost limits, using the subtle ambiguity of poetic language in order to reveal the silent, inexpressible principle at the heart of the ten thousand dharmas. Opaque on the surface, hollow within, they have no express statement to make, no meaning to impart. They are merely and wholly the charged forms of a penetration into the emptiness of the sign; they are a symbolic miming, a performance, a virtual *dharani* or embodied truth.

It is also on this lofty plane of principle, in these poems that manifest solely the turns and shifts of the poetic mind, that Shinkei's concept of linking as *hen-jo-dai/kyoku-ryū*, the structure of a signifying, revelatory transformation, finds its highest expression. As he insists again and again, it is to these subtle shifts between upper and lower verses in waka, these minute turns of the poet's mind, and not the words as such, that the renga practitioner should attend in order to reach the highest realm in poetry.

When renga practitioners read the imperial anthologies of successive ages and various other poem collections, they are only looking to find words for attaching verses together. They neither discern the mind [*kokoro*] in the poems nor comprehend their refinement, inner suppleness, deeply moving quality [*shina. take. aware fukaki tokoro-domo*], and the manner in which the upper and lower parts link and connect to each other [*jōge no kusari, tsug-isama* 上下の鎖り、継ぎさま]. Linking wholly on the basis of words eventually results in a sequence of verses that merely stand in a row, without their hearts/minds drawing together [*narabeokitaru bakari nite, kokoro wa yorazu ya*]. If you compose verses with a discerning eye for the way in which the two parts are connected in waka, with a feel for the places where the mind shifts [*kokoro no tenjihaberu tokoro-domo* 心の転じ侍る所ども], then you will find that the myriad phenomena are in themselves immanently linked together [*banshō onozukara tsukeaitaru* 万象自ずから付け合ひたる]. The study of one who has entered the ultimate boundary cannot be confined to the level of book learning. He must train his mind upon the myriad phenomena and the numerous fields of endeavor and turn them into a force for enlightenment in his own poetry [*bambutsu shodō no ue ni kokoro o tsukete, waga kadō no satori no chikara to subeshi* 万物諸道の上に心を付けて、我が歌道の悟りの力とすべし]. (*Iwahashi batsubun*, p. 323)

Here, by *kokoro*, Shinkei is clearly not talking about the meaning of the poem's words, what can be paraphrased or explained in prose. Rather, his subject is the motion of the poet's mind, what in Western terminology would be called "the creative imagination," as it manifests itself in the invisible and subtle connection between upper and lower verses, or in our perception of a cosmic shift that instantaneously gives birth to, in the sense of revealing, the true suchness (*shinnyo*) of reality. This sums up the universal dimension of Shinkei's poetic vision. True creativity is always a bringing forth of the ground of existence, as it were, for the first time. Imagination is rooted in the intuition, which is also given in Zen meditation, that the myriad dharmas are all phenomenological reflections or transformations of each other. All poetry of the first rank, that which breaches the margins of mundane thinking, reaches beyond what has been previously produced in the books of the tradition. Those books are not mere dictionaries but potential fields for understanding the poetic mind itself through the dialogic exchange of a responsive reading. But beyond them, the poet can find his own voice only by leaving the books and applying what he has learned to a broad experience of the world as such (*bambutsu shodō*). For "there is a vast difference between learning and mental application," enlightenment is a "knowing by oneself the chill and the heat" of things, it is a matter of direct and personal, *lived* experience. It cannot be transmitted, no one can point it out to you. Training, which involves reading the best of the tradition and studying with the right teacher, is being set upon the right path, but the great event of *satori*, the encounter with the mind's ground that lies at the end of the Way, is a solitary experience, a breaking-through that is also the opening up of a whole new nondualistic, unconfined realm.

> Apart from training your mind upon what is ineffably deep and of immovable dignity, there are no secrets in the Way. A keen intelligence is usually the envy of many a frustrated renga practitioner. But when you have entered the ultimate and become accomplished in a supple diction, the ten thousand worlds before your eyes will spontaneously turn into your own intelligence. (*Iwahashi batsubun*, pp. 321–22)

Of the absolute value that Shinkei attributed to poetry and the poetic mode of being, there is no question at all. In a critical biography shaped by his own poetry and commentary, I have tried to show that for him, poetry is man's most sensitive response to historical circumstance on the most universal and human plane, which is that of language. That the history of his age was one of factional turbulence and war was decisive in shaping his view of poetry as an existential practice of mental liberation. What might be called, for lack of a better term, the apotheosis of language in pure poetry is inseparable in Shinkei from his concept of poetic practice as a Way involving the whole person—sensibility, intellect, and ethics—and not merely an expertise with words. Consequently, it becomes no less than a civilizing influence, a field of training in wisdom and compassion for every man at a time when he feared that precisely these qualities were being lost in the destructive power struggles that led into the protracted civil wars that would rage on, in fact, for more than a century after his own death. Access to violence is always the desperate manifestation of an insecurity based on a delusion. It is more than interesting that Shinkei would write that, according to Hitomaro, the country's first major poet, "to be born in this land and be ignorant of the Way is to be like a bird who would fly in the sky without wings, a fish who would live in the water without fins" (*Iwahashi batsubun*, p. 327). It indicates that the mental liberation promoted by poetic activity is a kind of empowerment, an enabling of the human being to function freely and without psychological obstruction in his environment. So absolute was Shinkei's confidence in poetry's mind-opening power that, priest though he was, he nevertheless placed it on the same level as Buddhist teaching itself. As he tells the young Zen priest Kenzai:

> You must not think that this Way is inferior to the Buddha's Dharma [*kono michi o buppō nado yori otoru ni omoitamaubekarazu*]. In India, they preach

the *dharani* in Sanskrit; in our country, when the divine beings wish to soften their light [of wisdom and inner power] in order to transform others, they express themselves in poetry [*shimmei wakō kedo o naseba waka o nobu* 神明和光為化度和歌をのぶ]. This means that it is the True Word of this land [*kore sunawachi kono kuni no darani nari* これ則此国の陀羅尼なり]. It is not even in the slightest degree different from awakening to the fact of life and death, the divine responsiveness of the gods and buddhas, and the principle that the Buddha preached in a lifetime. (*Iwahashi batsubun*, p. 327)

The reason that in Japan, the practice of poetry, whether as waka, renga, or haikai, has historically been more widespread than we know from other traditions is that it was tied in with the concept of the Way and the Zen Buddhist thinking exemplified by Shinkei's poetics. This has the ultimate effect of rendering ambiguous the line between sacred and secular; as a Way or progression, it promises that even the man of ordinary intelligence may someday be able to liberate the buddha, the responsive, creative imagination within him, from the outward dross of the wholly mundane. No doubt freedom is a good desired by everyone. However, in the concept of the Way that informs the Japanese existential practice of the arts that had their inception in the medieval age, freedom is not a natural and inalienable right; it is not something one possesses to begin with, but a *virtù* and power that one attains to. A person is born in bondage to the circumstances of his birth, his social place, his history, culture, and language. Release from them is possible only through an utmost positive effort of mental detachment, which is the same that is required to reach the consummate realm of freedom, that is, self-being, suchness (*jizai*) in the arts. Suchness is not primarily the right to be or do anything, but merely *to be* in such a way as to harmonize with one's surroundings: to be without past or future, in such a way that one can see into the past and future; to be nothing in particular so that one can be anything; to be poor so that one may be enriched, and so on. Here emptiness is an immeasurable inner spaciousness, which is the ground of potentiality, the stillness that generates all sound and motion, clarifies problems by dissolving their seeming solidity.

In Shinkei's cosmic vision, tsukeai, or linking, is the dynamic operation of the immanent power, itself formless or beyond form, that suddenly assumes form and becomes perceptible through the *innen* or circumstances embodied in the maeku. As he declares near the grand end of *Sasamegoto*:

What is called the true Buddha or the true poem has no predetermined configuration. It is merely a feeling or an inner power that manifests itself

according to the time and in response to circumstance [*makoto no hotoke,*
makoto no uta tote, sadamareru sugata arubekarazu まことの佛、まことの
歌とて、定まれる姿あるべからず. *Tada toki ni yori, koto ni ōjite, kansei*
toku o arawasubeshi to nari ただ時により、事に應じて、感情徳を現す
べしとなり]. (*SSG* 60: 202)

This study of renga and medieval symbolic poetry commenced with an
observation about the manifest absence of a total semantic coherence in
the 100-verse renga structure as a working hypothesis. In a brief analysis
of *yukiyō*, the progression of the sequence as a whole, I concluded that the
principle of integral semantic unity is irrelevant there, for in sequencing, the
individual meaning of the verses functions merely to mould a continuum,
to define a formal shape in the evolving movement of the whole through
thematic and aesthetic continuity and change. In the subsequent long account of *tsukeai* as embodied in Shinkei's concept of *hen-jo-dai/kyoku-ryū*,
it became clear that here, also, meaning functions merely to make apparent
the invisible connection between things, and ultimately, the universal principle that grounds them. In short, the search for any particular or total synthetic meaning in the renga sequence is doomed to failure, for renga is precisely this unique and paradoxical genre whose very structure is founded on
the sheer relativity of meaning and of the language that contains it. Renga
is, as it were, language at war with itself, deliberately using its conditioned
and contingent meanings as the medium of a higher discourse that is transpiring outside and beyond it, but—and here is the ultimate paradox—possible only through it. The whole thrust of the medieval aesthetic of *yūgen*,
yojō, *aware*, and so on (these terms differ only in emphases and points of
view) is to reveal the dimension of openness that makes meaning itself possible. The valorization of the deep mind, the decisive concern for poetry
as a process of mental liberation, and the construction of poetic value itself upon the poem's affect as a finger pointing at the moon, so to speak,
are all indications of the essential existential orientation of medieval critical
thought. How is this concealed moon, this wind hidden in the great void,
to manifest itself except through the shifts and turns of language, except
through the interstices that language leaves open even as it strives to make
itself solid, and upon which rests the very possibility of a poetry of the True
Word beyond words? The only alternative is silence equal to the silence of
the universe, since we are not all like Kasyapa, who when the Buddha held
up the flower in his hand had only to smile his mysterious beatific smile to
signal his intuitive understanding of the principle in that wordless dialogic

exchange expressed by the Zen epigram, *ishin denshin* 以心伝心, "by mind transmit the mind." And yet, in Shinkei's "deep" view of renga, is not an authentic tsukeai that issues from the very ground of the mind, that chill, meager, and formless realm beyond fixed determination, in each and every instance precisely to uphold the flower and await the trembling forth of Kasyapa's smile?

A flower turns in the wind, an infant grows, a decaying tree crashes deep in the forest.

> The realm of mindfulness is not at all as remote as you might think. It is merely to awaken, with the grace and deep compassion of the poetic mode of being, to the knowledge that the mundane world is caught in a dream, an unreal fantasy; to realize that the poetry of laments and of love, of journeying, impermanence, and so on, all resolve themselves into this event, all end in this awakening; and that their aim is simply to draw forth even that single tear, that one thought of temporality. Thus mindfulness is nothing else than to wholly compose the mind to detach it from men's craving for the illusory, to awaken to the single great event of existence and abide within that knowing. (*Tokoro*, letter 2, p. 272)

> So long as you cultivate tranquility and grace through the Way of poetry, and deepening your consciousness of temporality have shed even a single tear, then you will have understood the moving power of all things, and would know that to employ them in a trivial, slapdash fashion in poetry is utterly to miss the point. . . . When you have arrived at the ultimate, the most essential is to compose in a calm, unhurried manner from a deep introspection that reflects the profoundly moving nature of each and every phenomenon, and thus to truly hold high the Way. (*Oi* 421)

A smile, a tear, a moving power; temporality, the paradox of motion, the gap that elicits a smile or a tear, a breakthrough. Being and time, process, the edges of things, the margins holding the center in place, the supplement that enables the essential. Labor and management, East and West, subject and object. Form and formlessness, the one in the many, the many in the one. Grasses in the wind. Renga.

Reference Matter

Notes

Introduction

1. Martin Heidegger, "Dialogue on Language," in id., *On the Way to Language*, trans. Peter D. Hertz (New York: Harper & Row, 1971), pp. 1–54.

2. Jacques Derrida quoted in Marilyn Ivy, "Consumption of Knowledge," in *Postmodernism and Japan*, ed. Masao Miyoshi and H. D. Harootunian (Durham, N.C.: Duke University Press, 1989), pp. 40–42.

3. David Loy, "The Clôture of Deconstruction: A Mahayana Critique of Derrida," *International Philosophical Quarterly* 27, 1 (March 1987): 59–88; 59–60.

4. The notable exception is William R. LaFleur's *The Karma of Words: Buddhism and the Literary Arts in Medieval Japan* (Berkeley: University of California Press, 1983), which has a chapter on the poet Shunzei's use of Tendai Buddhism.

Chapter One

1. For a translation of the standard rules of Muromachi-period renga—which is also a demonstration of its thematic and lexical categories, see Steven D. Carter, *The Road to Komatsubara: A Classical Reading of the Renga Hyakuin* (Cambridge, Mass.: Harvard University Press, 1987), pp. 41–72.

2. In this book, I capitalize words with a specific technical meaning in renga or waka poetics, viz., "Spring" as a thematic category, "Mode of Ineffable Depth" as a stylistic category, and terms with a specific connotation in Buddhist philosophy, viz., the "Real" for *jissō* 実相. The reader is referred to the Glossary for the most important terminology and concepts featured in the book.

3. I use the equivalence sign = to indicate a conventional association between two terms and the slash sign / for an alternative association to the same term. For other examples of such marked pairs, see "Things That Must Be Separated by More Than One Verse," in Carter, *Road to Komatsubara*, pp. 52–58.

4. Piero della Francesca quoted by Roland Barthes in id., *Empire of Signs*, trans. Richard Howard (New York: Hill & Wang, 1982), p. 11.

5. *Minase* text in *Rengashū*, ed. Ijichi Tetsuo (Tokyo: Iwanami Shoten, 1960). *NKBT* 39: 345–66.

6. In 1488, when the three poets composed the sequence as a prayer offering

to memorialize the retired emperor Go-Toba at the site of his detached palace at Minase (Osaka), Sōgi 宗祇 (1421–1502) was 68; Shōhaku 肖柏 (1443–1527), 46; and Sōchō 宗長 (1448–1532), 41.

Chapter Two

1. *Nihon kagaku taikei* 日本歌学大系 (hereafter *NKT*), ed. Sasaki Nobutsuna (Tokyo: Kazama Shobō, 1956–63), 4: 350. The *Sangoki* is one of several counterfeit treatises attributed to Fujiwara Teika (1162–1241) that nevertheless wielded a great influence on medieval poetics. The first of its two sections is believed to have been written by Teika's great-grandson Fujiwara Tamezane (1266–1333) before 1313.

2. The *Sasamegoto* text used in this book is the one edited by Kidō Saizō in *Rengaronshū Haironshū*, ed. Kidō Saizō and Imoto Nōichi, *NKBT* 66 (Tokyo: Iwanami Shoten, 1961), 119–204; it is cited here and subsequently as *SSG*, followed by the *Sasamegoto* section and page numbers. For a complete, annotated translation of the treatise, see Ramirez-Christensen, trans., *Murmured Conversations: A Treatise on Poetry and Buddhism by the Poet-Monk Shinkei* (Stanford: Stanford University Press, 2008). This book is in one sense an extended introduction to the other, as conceived within the context of medieval Buddhist poetics and contemporary poststructuralist theory.

3. Shinkei does not explain the disappearance of *ryū* in this equation, but his reason can only be that a renga verse pair is not in fact a single integral poem that needs a "Dissolve" to carry it through to the end. Or one could say that in renga, the "Dissolve" happens in the openness of the space between the two verses.

4. "Short verse" is the two-line 7–7–syllable verse, and "long verse" the three-line 5–7–5–syllable verse. Renga is an alternation of these two.

5. Gottlob Frege, "On Sinn and Bedeutung," in *The Frege Reader*, ed. Michael Beaney (London: Blackwell, 1997), pp. 151–71.

6. *Oi no susami*, *Rengaronshū* 2, ed. Kidō Saizō, *Chūsei no bungaku* ser. (Tokyo: Miya'i Shoten, 1982), p. 143. Buddhism forbids the taking of animal life, and hunting is therefore a sinful activity. *Oi no susami* (Solace of old age, 1479) is Sōgi's most sustained critical commentary on verses by his predecessors, including those by his mentor Shinkei.

7. I agree with the editor of *Sasamegoto*, Kidō Saizō (pp. 156–57n10), that *omokage no tōku/naru* (literally, the image growing distant) in the maeku as such may be understood to refer to someone from whom the persona has grown estranged, which is why I have rendered the term as "the image of a face."

8. Kidō is describing how Sōzei's style of linking, characterized by the stark autonomy of the single verse, and the clarity of the opposition between maeku and tsukeku, directly transmits the tradition of the Nambokuchō (1338–92) masters. Kidō Saizō, *Renga shironkō* (Tokyo, Meiji Shoin, 1973), 1: 28–29. Sōzei (1386?-1455) was, along with Shinkei, one of the so-called "seven sages of renga" (*renga shichiken*) who revived the art in the Muromachi period (1333–1573). For the literary history and major figures of mid-Muromachi renga, see Esperanza Ramirez-Christensen,

Heart's Flower: The Life and Poetry of Shinkei (Stanford: Stanford University Press, 1994; hereafter cited as *HF*), esp. chap. 3.

Chapter Three

1. Ferdinand de Saussure, *Course in General Linguistics*, trans. Wade Baskin (Glasgow: Collins/Fontana, 1974), pp. 120, 122.

2. See the anthology of readings edited by Mark C. Taylor, *Deconstruction in Context: Literature and Philosophy* (Chicago: University of Chicago Press, 1986), for an understanding of the various conceptual threads and philosophers who contributed to the dismantling of the metaphysical tradition in Europe.

3. "What then is truth? A movable host of metaphors, metonymies, and anthropomorphisms. . . . Truths are illusions which we have forgotten are illusions; they are metaphors that have become worn out and have been drained of sensuous force, coins which have lost their embossing and are now considered as metal and no longer as coins." Friedrich Nietzsche, "On Truth and Lies in a Nonmoral Sense," in *Philosophy and Truth: Selections from Nietzsche's Notebooks from the Early 1870's*, ed. and trans. Daniel Breazeale (Atlantic Highlands, N.J.: Humanities Press International, 1979), p. 84.

4. Jacques Derrida, "Différance," in id., *Margins of Philosophy*, trans. Alan Bass (Chicago: University of Chicago Press, 1982), p. 9.

5. Ibid., p. 13.

6. I refer to Roman Jacobson's influential theory of the poetic or literary function as specifically oriented toward the message for its own sake, its verbal form, as distinct from functions of language that emphasize each of the other constituent elements (viz., addresser, addressee, context, contact, and code) in any speech event. See his "Linguistics and Poetics" in id., *Language in Literature*, ed. Krystyna Pomorska and Stephen Rudy (Cambridge, Mass.: Harvard University Press, Belknap Press, 1987), pp. 62–94. Jacobson states that "this [poetic] function, by promoting the palpability of signs, deepens the fundamental dichotomy of signs and objects" (pp. 69–70). Hence structuralists and formalists exclude truth-value as in principle outside the bounds of poetics.

Chapter Four

1. Jonathan Culler, *On Deconstruction: Theory and Criticism After Structuralism* (Ithaca, N.Y.: Cornell University Press, 1982), p. 94.

2. Edmund Husserl, "Essential Distinctions," in *The Hermeneutics Reader*, ed.Kurt Mueller-Vollmer (New York: Continuum, 1985), p. 175.

3. Edmund Husserl, *Cartesian Meditations*, trans. Dorion Cairns (The Hague: Martinus Nijhoff, 1970), p. 10.

4. Here it must be noted again that the phenomenal "object" is not the one simply given to perception as a "real" physical thing out there. Rather this object, or *noema*, is what is constituted in the mind through the act of intentionality, or *noesis*. Intentionality, in turn, names the orientation of the mind toward something,

or the fact that consciousness is always consciousness of something; it is always "intended" toward an object. Phenomenology studies the structure and operation of conscious mental acts, e.g., cognizing, doubting, recalling, conceptualizing, etc., in an attempt to found a more solid ground for knowledge and understanding than the unthinking acceptance of beliefs about the world as given or as observed by the positivist empirical sciences. I find the phenomenological attempt to analyze cognition, understanding, and subjectivity useful for literary analysis. In particular, the concept of "horizon" (as also the fusion of horizons) is, I believe, crucial in the mutual overcoming of prejudices and fixed positions.

5. Dermot Moran, *Introduction to Phenomenology* (New York: Routledge, 2000), pp. 161–62.

6. Husserl, *Cartesian Meditations*, §19, p. 44. Also cited in Moran, *Introduction to Phenomenology*, p. 162.

7. The table is summarized from *Shogaku yōshashō* 初学用捨抄 (Do's and Don'ts for the Beginner), a Muromachi-period renga manual attributed to Sōgi, but most likely by a Shinkei disciple like Kenzai 兼載 (1452–1510). *Rengaronshū* 2, ed. Kidō Saizō, *Chūsei no bungaku* ser. (Tokyo: Miya'i Shoten, 1982), pp. 423–24.

8. Hans-Georg Gadamer, *Truth and Method*, trans. Joel Weinsheimer and Donald G. Marshall (New York: Crossroad, 1989), pp. 306–7, 374–75.

9. The difference between Seasons and Human Affairs is described by Sōgi in *Oi no susami*: "In composing verses on the four Seasons, one can rely on the atmospheric effects of the scenery, so that even if the verse itself is not so minutely conceived, it will nevertheless seem graceful as long as the configuration is sound. . . . Verses on Love, Laments, and Reminiscences, on the other hand, must be composed with precise attention to even the smallest syntactic particles in the maeku." *Rengaronshū* 2, ed. Kidō, p. 158. Sōgi's observation suggests that the complexity of subjective expression in the Human Affairs themes, as marked by the maeku's specific inflexion ("the smallest syntactic particles"), requires a more strenuous effort on the part of the tsukeku poet.

10. John D. Caputo, *Radical Hermeneutics: Repetition, Deconstruction, and the Hermeneutic Project* (Bloomington: Indiana University Press, 1987), p. 40. Caputo is here construing Husserl's concept of intentionality, the grasp of an object by consciousness, as an interpretive act. In Husserl's writing, however, the emphasis seems to be on the intentional act as a constitution, that is, as a continuous synthesizing of the various "views" of the object into ultimately the same identity, which can always be verified as the truth. In other words, Husserl's concept of intentionality is an attempt to fix the unstable Heraclitean flux into singular moments of cognition and re-cognition that constitute a transcendental phenomenological knowledge. See Husserl, *Cartesian Meditations*, pp. 46–49.

11. Jacques Derrida, *Positions*, trans. Alan Bass (Chicago: University of Chicago Press, 1981), p. 26. An illuminating analysis of how Derrida's concept of *différance*, while constituting a major insight in Western philosophy, yet falls short of the radicality of Mahayana thinking may be read in David Loy, "The Cloture of Deconstruction: A Mahayana Critique of Derrida," *International Philosophical Quarterly*

27, 1 (March 1987): 59–88; 59–60. As should be evident by now, I myself have found Derrida's thought of différance and method of deconstruction extremely suggestive, even productive, in analyzing medieval Japanese poetry and poetics, although I have also found useful and so employ the thoughts of hermeneutic and phenomenological philosophers whom Derrida has deconstructed on the way. This is because I believe that from a nondualistic perspective, no deconstruction is ever final; a maeku as prior text, whether ancient or modern, will always reveal facets that can be read otherwise than it has been.

Chapter Five

1. *KKS* 469: Love. Anonymous.

2. *KKS* 697: Love. Tsurayuki.

3. *KKS* 471: Love. Tsurayuki.

4. As a testimony to the ambiguity here, *ayame mo shiranu* may also be read as the disordered state (lacking a coherent design, and thus not to be "read") of the lover's mind.

5. *SKKS* 251: Summer. "Composed on the topic 'Cormorant River' during the hundred-poem contest sponsored by the Regent and Grand Chancellor."

6. It is also possible to read *yaso* as "arrow" + emphatic particle *zo*; it would then be a metonymical reference to "warriors" and reverberate with the fishermen's "cormorants" (used to capture the fish) as a death-dealing instrument; we would then have a case of polysemy with three referents.

7. *Yakumo mishō*, §6, *NKT* 3: 83.

8. *Mumyōshō* in *NKBT* 65: 62. A *hampi*, also the other name for *yasume kotoba*, or pause words, was a short robe with sleeves reaching only halfway down the arms. It was worn between inner and outer robes and thus gave its name to this waka figurative device, whose most important feature, as distinct from the preface, is its medial position.

9. Wang Wei, "Song of Wei Cheng" (also known as "Sending Off Yuan Er to His Post in Anxi"), in *Wang Wei*, ed. Tsuru Haruo, *Chūgoku shijin senshū*, 6: 81:

送元二使安西
渭城朝雨裛軽塵
客舎青青柳色新
勧君更盡一杯酒
西出陽關無故人

10. Du Fu, "Jueju," in *Du Fu 1*, ed. Kurokawa Yōichi, *Chūgoku shijin senshū*, 9: 125–26:

絶句二首［之二］
江碧鳥逾白
山青花欲然
今春看又過
何日是歸年

Chapter Six

1. The one hundred verses of a renga sequence are referred to according to the way they were recorded by the calligrapher on the renga manuscript (*kaishi* 懐紙) during the session. The *kaishi* consisted of four sheets of paper, each folded along the middle and sewn together, along the right-hand edges, with the other three at the session's end. Each sheet or "fold" (*ori* 折) thus had two sides, the front (*omote* 表) and back (*ura* 裏), and the verses recorded—from top to bottom and right to left, on the eight sides as follows: fold 1 [front 8, back 14]; fold 2 [14, 14]; fold 3 [14, 14]; fold 4 [14, 8]. Thus the first eight verses are expressed as "the front of the first fold," the next fourteen as "the back of the first fold," and so on. The fourth and last sheet also had the special name "remaining-trace fold" (*nagori no ori* 名残の折) in the sense of its being a trace of all that had gone before. The fact that a sheet is, oddly enough, expressed as a "fold" or break between what precedes and what follows it (the front and the back), indeed the whole system of *kaishi* terminology, is an indication that these physical divisions constituted a set pattern of breaks or pauses, against which the actual progression of the sequence could be intelligibly measured.

2. Nijō Yoshimoto, *Tsukuba mondō*, in *Rengaronshū, Haironshū*, ed. Kidō Saizō and Imoto Nōichi, *NKBT* 66 (Tokyo: Iwanami Shoten, 1961), pp. 86–87.

3. Ichijō Kanera, *Renga shogakushō* 初学抄 (Notes for Renga Beginners), in *RS*, 2: 298.

4. *Katahashi*, in *Rengaronshū* 3, ed. Kidō Saizō, *Chūsei no bungaku* ser. (Tokyo: Miya'i Shoten, 1985), p. 148.

5. Zeami Motokiyo, *On the Art of the Nō Drama: The Major Treatises of Zeami*, trans. J. Thomas Rimer and Yamazaki Masakazu (Princeton, N.J.: Princeton University Press, 1984), p. 83. Text in *Karonshū Nōgakuronshū*, ed. Hisamatsu Sen'ichi and Nishio Minoru, *NKBT* 65 (Tokyo: Iwanami Shoten, 1961), p. 417.

6. *NKBT* 65: 417; I give my own translations from here on in the interest of clarifying the links with renga *jo-ha-kyū* in Zeami's original texts. In headnote 49, the editor of the *NKBT* text, Nishio Minoru, observes that Zeami here apparently adopts in his explanation the Japanese practice of translating and writing commentaries on the Chinese classics and Buddhist scriptures.

7. For a description of the grammar of Nō dance, see Monica Bethe and Karen Brazell, *Dance in the Noh Theater* (Ithaca, N.Y.: East Asia Program, Cornell University, 1982). See also *Nō as Performance: An Analysis of the Kuse Scene of Yamamba* (Ithaca, N.Y.: East Asia Program, Cornell University, 1978) by the same authors, esp. pp. 6–8 on *jo-ha-kyū*.

8. Nishio Minoru observes that the explanation of *ha* as a breaking up of the Prelude is an original idea with Zeami (*NKBT* 65, p. 418n1). As we have seen, Shinkei's concept of the "turn" or shift in poetic structure is precisely what founds his analogy between *hen-jo-dai-kyoku-ryū* and *jo-ha-kyū*. The question of influence is always a tricky one. It would first be necessary to examine the textual relationship between Zeami and Nijō Yoshimoto, and then between Yoshimoto and Shinkei. Between Zeami and Shinkei, a direct textual influence is not very likely, since the Nō treatises were transmitted in secret only to Zeami's heirs and were not in fact

made public until modern times. There is, incidentally, also a close relation between the ideas of Zenchiku 禅竹 (1405–1468?) and Shinkei, and they were contemporaries. See Haga Kōshirō, *Higashiyama bunka* (Tokyo: Haniwa Shobo, 1962),
pp. 174–84. For a study and translation of Zenchiku's Nō treatise *Rokurin ichiro*
六輪一露, see Arthur H. Thornhill III, *Six Circles, One Dewdrop: The Religio-
Aesthetic World of Komparu Zenchiku* (Princeton, N.J.: Princeton University Press,
1993). Haga views Zenchiku and Shinkei as representing the highest development
of Higashiyama aesthetic philosophy. Yet it is not known whether there was any
personal contact between them, and of course the same restrictions of secret transmission in Nō would apply there as well. In his glowing account of Higashiyama
culture in *Hitorigoto*, Shinkei mentions both Zeami and Zenchiku, among many
other outstanding figures in the various arts (*Hitorigoto*, p. 474). My feeling is that
what ultimately unites the artist-thinkers of the Muromachi period is their reading
of their art within the framework of Mahayana intellectual philosophy, particularly
the concept of Emptiness, and that this worldview was something they shared with
their audience. In Shinkei's case, the correlation is particularly inevitable, given his
formal priestly training and his position as bishop of Jūjūshin'in Temple in Kyoto's
Higashiyama hills.

9. *NKBT* 65: 417–18.

10. See Zeami Motokiyo, *Sandō* 三道 (The Three Elements, 1423), also called
Nōsakusho 能作書 (The Book of Composing Plays), *NKBT* 65: 470–81. Zeami, *On
the Art of the Nō Drama*, trans. Rimer and Yamazaki, pp. 148–62.

11. Zeami Motokiyo, *Shūgyoku tokka* 拾玉得花 (Gathering Gems and Realizing
the Flower, 1428), *NKBT* 65: 462. Zeami, *On the Art of the Nō Drama*, trans. Rimer
and Yamazaki, p. 138. This work contains Zeami's ripest understanding of *jo-ha-kyū*
as a universal principle of nature, the life process itself.

Chapter Seven

1. *Chikuenshō* (ca. 1278), *NKT* 3: 414–15. This treatise contains the teachings of
Fujiwara Tameie (1198–1275) on such matters of diction and style as poetic flaws,
the six modes (*rikugi*), and allusive variation (*honkadori*), as recorded by his son
Tameaki (fl. ca. 1263–1295).

2. *Chōtanshō*, *RS* 1: 153–54.

3. Tanaka Yutaka, *Chūsei bungakuron kenkyū* (Tokyo: Hanawa Shobō, 1969), pp.
353–55. Tanaka's analysis of Shinkei's concept of linking in this volume is to my
mind the most incisive work by a contemporary Japanese scholar on the subject.

4. From the revised *Sasamegoto* text edited by Ijichi Tetsuo in *Rengaronshū
Nōgakuronshū Haironshū*, ed. Ijichi Tetsuo, Omote Akira, and Kuriyama Ri'ichi,
NKBZ 51 (Tokyo: Shōgakkan, 1973), p. 121. The use of the verb *tsūjiru* in the passage
is significant for my earlier hypothesis of the link as an instance of hermeneutical
understanding.

5. The *Renju gappekishū* is in *Rengaronshū* 1, ed. Kidō Saizō and Shigematsu
Hiromi, *Chūsei no bungaku* ser. (Tokyo: Miya'i Shoten, 1972). Entry 561, p. 140,
under *yo* lists the verbal correlates *sumu* (dwell), *sutsuru* (cast off), *mayou* (to be

deluded), *izuru* (leave), *take* (bamboo), *ashi* (reeds), *yume* (dream), and *tsuyu* (dew). The *Renju* was compiled as a manual for beginners by Ichijō Kanera sometime before 1476.

6. *SKKS* 997. Love. "From the poetry contest at the residence of Taira Sadafumi." Also in *Kokin rokujō* V: 33865.

7. *Genji monogatari*, *NKBZ* 12: 187–88. For the passage in English, see Murasaki Shikibu, *The Tale of Genji*, trans. Edward Seidensticker (New York: Knopf, 1977), 1: 48.

8. *Nakagawa no yado* (mid-river abode) is a reference to the location of the Kii governor's house, where Genji encounters the Locust-Shell Lady.

9. *Shūi gusō* 3314. Miscellaneous, "Dawn."

10. *Fūgashū* XVI.1784. Miscellaneous. Also *Shūi gusō* 391, where the poem appears as one from a "Hundred-Poem Sequence on Living in Solitude" composed in Bunji 3 (1187).

11. *Shinkokinshū* XVIII: 1780. Miscellaneous.

12. One of the poems composed for the *Santai waka* (Poems in the Three Modes) held in Kennin 2 (1202).3.21.

13. From the *Shōtetsu monogatari*, *NKBT* 65: 208–9.

14. *Guhishō*, *NKT* 4: 298. The same opinion appears in abbreviated form in the *Sangoki* (see Chapter 2, n. 1, above), *NKT* 4: 351.

Chapter Eight

1. The verse "In a flash of lightning" is the tsukeku in one of Shinkei's illustrations of the Distant Link, and is discussed from that perspective in the preceding chapter.

2. *SKKS* 591. Winter. Lord Minamoto Saneakira (910–970).

Chapter Nine

1. Shunzei, *Korai fūteishō*, ed. Ariyoshi Tamotsu, in *Karonshū*, *NKBZ* 50: 273.

2. I shall take up the significance of indicating phenomena by their "color and fragrance" later.

3. See Tanaka Yutaka, *Chūsei bungakuron kenkyū* (Tokyo: Hanawa Shobō, 1969), p. 14.

4. Shunzei is referring to the *Makashikan* 摩訶止観 (The Great Stillness and Insight), the famous treatise on the method and concept of Zen meditation in Tendai Buddhism. It is composed from the lectures of Tendai's founder, Chigi 智顗 (Ch. Zhiyi, 538–597), as recorded by his disciple Shōan Daishi 章安大師 or Kanjō 灌頂 (Ch. Guanding, 561–632), who also wrote the introduction from which Shunzei quotes the line cited. Tendai was the long-established religion of the Heian court, and its major canonical texts, of which the *Makashikan* was one, were basic reading for the court intelligentsia. Shunzei's son, Teika, also records in his diary, the *Meigetsuki* (明月記), reading the complete text over a period of months. The opening line cited by Shunzei from Shōan Daishi's preface means that it was Zhiyi

who first fully explicated and appreciated the marvelous powers of *shikan*, or meditation, in the history of Chinese Buddhism.

For the complete text translation of the introduction and first chapter, see Neil Donner and Daniel B. Stevenson, *The Great Calming and Contemplation: A Study and Annotated Translation of the First Chapter of Chih-i's Mo-ho-chi-kuan* (Honolulu: University of Hawaii Press, 1993). They render this first line from the Chinese as: "Calming and contemplation as luminosity and insight: [this teaching] had not yet been heard of in former generations" (p. 99; see also n. 1 there.) Sekiguchi Shindai notes eight variant renderings of this line in Japanese Buddhist translations; Shunzei's (*shikan no myōjōnaru koto, zendai mo imada kikazu*) is closest to that of Archbishop Kenshin of the Ryūzen'in in the eastern valley precincts of Mount Hiei. *Makashikan*, trans. Sekiguchi Shindai (Tokyo: Iwanami Shoten, 1966), 1: 365; hereafter cited as *Makashikan*.

5. Here follows an analogy between the historical transmission of the Dharma from the Buddha to the disciples and patriarchs through generations down to Zhiyi, and the handing down of the poetry of successive reigns through the anthologies from the *Man'yōshū*, *Kokinshū*, and so on.

6. *Makashikan*, 1: 124–26, 130.

7. Ibid., 24.

8. As quoted in the *Wakan rōeishū*, a Heian anthology of Chinese and Japanese verses that was popular reading even in the Muromachi period. Text from *NKBT* 73: 200.

9. *Makashikan*, 1: 23. The *Chūron* is the Chinese version of Nagarjuna's *Mūlamadhyamaka-kārikā*, as translated and edited by Kumarajiva based on the version by Pingala (ca. 300–350); it is the edition that represents the Chinese and Japanese understanding of Nagarjuna's philosophy. This is the famous verse 18 in chap. 24 of the *Chūron*.

10. "These things are not two" refers to a quotation cited some lines previously in the *Makashikan*: "The *Shiyaku* says: 'The Buddha and his disciples practice two things [*ji* or *koto*]: preaching and silence'" (*Makashikan*, 1: 30).

11. "It is like holding up a fan . . . in the great void" is the statement of two lines that is quoted in the *Wakan rōeishū* immediately before Bai Juyi's dedication. The authority of the *Makashikan* is clearly being used to clarify Bai's appeal to the efficacy of poetic language and imagery in promoting understanding of abstract Buddhist principles. See entries 587 and 588 in the *Wakan rōeishū*, *NKBT* 73: 200.

12. Guanding is here alluding to his earlier warning that one should not inflict harm on oneself by becoming obsessed with the texts, referring to Zhiyi's three works on the three types of meditation: direct or instantaneous, gradual, and irregular. *Makashikan*, 1: 29.

13. See preceding note for "the three kinds of texts."

14. *Makashikan*, 1: 31; *T* 46:1911.3b. For a study and annotated translation of the introduction and first chapter, see Donner and Stevenson, *Great Calming and Contemplation*; their translation of this passage is on pp. 126–27. In rendering *mon*

as "sign" instead of their "text," I am attempting to draw the *Makashikan* into the contemporary theoretical discourse of the sign.

15. I refer to Derrida's critique of the classic Western concept of centered structure, using the contemporary concept of the sign, in "Structure, Sign, and Play in the Discourse of the Human Sciences," in id., *Writing and Difference*, trans. Alan Bass (Chicago: University of Chicago Press, 1978), pp. 278–93, especially p. 281.

16. Ludwig Wittgenstein, *Tractatus Logico-Philosophicus*, trans. D. F. Pears and B. F. McGuiness (London: Routledge & Kegan Paul, 1961), p. 149: 6.52; p. 151: 6.522, and 7.

17. Martin Heidegger, *Being and Time*, trans. John Macquarrie and Edward Robinson (New York: Harper & Row, 1962), p. 183.

18. The brief account of understanding and interpretation is from ibid., pp. 182–95.

Chapter Ten

1. In Tanaka Yutaka, *Chūsei bungakuron kenkyū* (Tokyo: Hanawa Shobō, 1969), pp. 21, 27–29. *Kehai* is synonymous with *keiki*, the aura given off by a natural scene, and the term Shunzei uses in the quotation below. Konishi Jin'ichi also deserves recognition here as one of the first to note the importance of Tendai *shikan* in Shunzei and *Shinkokinshū* poetry in his early article "Shunzei no yūgenfū to shikan," *Bungaku* 20, 2 (1952): 12–20.

2. *Jichin-oshō jika'awase* 慈鎮和尚自歌合 (Priest Jichin's Solo Poem Contest), in *Utaawaseshū, NKBT* 74: 472.

3. The passage is translated in *JCP*, p. 269.

4. In Pound's essay on vorticism in the *Fortnightly*, (September 1, 1914, later endlessly disseminated in various critical sources on his role in the formation of modernist poetry.

5. [*Shinkō*] *Roppyakuban utaawase*, ed. Konishi Jin'ichi (Tokyo: Yūseidō, 1976), p. 42. The topic for this round is "Skylark." Left and Right refer to the names of the two competing teams of poets during a poetry contest.

6. Round 271 of the *Sengohyakuban utaawase*, in *Utaawaseshū*, pp. 486–87. The competing poem from the Right by Fujiwara Kanemune (d. 1242) is: "Hana yue ni / oshimu kyō zo / to iu naraba / kaerite haru ya / ware o uramimu" (Were I to say / that today is truly regrettable / because of the flowers, / will spring instead resent me / when it returns?) The *Kokinshū*-like wit in the conception is not unappealing, but it lacks the other's rich ambiguity, that is, the *yūgen* quality prized by Shunzei.

7. *KKS* 38. "Sent to someone with a spray of plum blossoms." Ki no Tomonori.

8. *SSG* 41: 176. For the critical context of the opposition *utayomi / utazukuri* within the discourse of *ushin*, see Amagasaki Akira, *Kachō no tsukai* (Tokyo: Keisō Shobō, 1983), pp. 149–58.

9. As quoted in *Shinkokinwakashū zenhyōshaku*, ed. Kubota Jun (Tokyo: Kōdansha, 1977), 2: 355. The "six hindrances" are the five senses and psychological consciousness, or mentation.

10. From Zeami's *Yūgaku shūdō fūken*, in *Karonshū Nôgakuronshū, NKBT* 65:

445; Zeami Motokiyo, "Disciplines for Joy," in *On the Art of the Nō Drama: The Major Treatises of Zeami*, trans. J. Thomas Rimer and Yamazaki Masakazu (Princeton, N.J.: Princeton University Press, 1984), p. 119. The poem, of uncertain authorship but apparently popular from the early Muromachi period as a Zenlike epigram, reads: *Sakuragi wa / kudakite mireba / hana mo nashi / hana koso haru no / sora ni sakikere.*

11. The relevant passages from *Ima monogatari* and *Seiashō* are quoted by Kubota Jun in *Shinkokin wakashū zenhyōshaku*, 2: 355.

12. From round 18 of *Mimosusokawa utaawase*; cited in Kubota 2: 357, and Tanaka, *Chūsei bungakuron kenkyū*, p. 87. This is a solo contest of 36 rounds in which Saigyō pitted his own poems against each other and asked for Shunzei's judgment.

13. *Mumyōshō* in *NKBT* 65: 87.

14. From *Jichin oshō jika'awase*, p. 472; also cited in Tanaka, *Chūsei bungakuron kenkyū*, p. 92.

15. Shunzei, *Korai fūteishō*, ed. Ariyoshi Tamotsu, in *Karonshū*, *NKBZ* 50: 276.

16. Roland Barthes imagines a "vocal writing" that will be carried by "the grain of the voice" and is less concerned with meaning than with "the whole carnal stereophony" of the contact between the voice organs and the aural properties of the words. What he has to say here is worth considering in relation to Shunzei's emphasis on the poem as an aural figuration, with the difference, however, that the Japanese poet's concept of the significance of aurality is inseparable from the symbolic operation of *yūgen*. Barthes, *The Pleasure of the Text*, trans. Richard Miller (New York: Farrar, Straus & Giroux, 1975), pp. 66–67.

Chapter Eleven

1. I mean that using "mind" to render *kokoro* is more appropriate in consideration of the close connection between medieval poetics and Buddhist philosophy, particularly in the view of poetic process as an intense mental concentration similar to Buddhist meditation. In other words, the rendering of *ushin* as "intense feeling" or "conviction of feeling" by Brower and Miner in *JCP*, 258–59, could be misinterpreted as valorizing the sincerity of a personal emotion, whereas what is at stake is the dissolution of the subject/object—or inner/outer—dichotomy through the discipline of meditation. This is not to say that "feeling" is irrelevant in poetics, but only that the feeling evoked by the poem is the impersonal manifestation of a state of mind in the meditation process and may or may not be a product of the poet's own personal circumstance. Ultimately, it may be said that the medieval poetic tradition evinces a conviction of feeling precisely because it has refused to separate subject from object, and has put what we call "feeling" through a process of philosophical analysis.

2. *Maigetsushō*, ed. Fujihira Haruo, in *Karonshū*, *NKBZ* 50: 515–16.

3. In the *Mumyōshō*, *NKBT* 65: 82.

4. In the *Shōtetsu monogatari*, *NKBT* 65: 221.

5. *Maigetsushō*, *NKBZ* 50: 519.

6. Ibid., 520–21.

7. In *Kindai shūka* 近代秀歌 (Superior Poems of Our Time), *NKBZ* 50: 471.

8. See the *Teika jittei* entry in *Waka bungaku jiten*, ed. Ariyoshi Tamotsu (Tokyo: Ōfūsha, 1991), p. 462. A complete translation of the fifty-eight poems classified as *yūgen* in the Teika anthology is available in Edwin Cranston, "'Mystery and Depth' in Japanese Court Poetry," in *The Distant Isle: Studies and Translations of Japanese Literature in Honor of Robert H. Brower*, ed. Thomas Hare, Robert Borgen, and Sharalyn Orbaugh (Ann Arbor, Mich.: Center for Japanese Studies, University of Michigan, 1996), pp. 86–100.

9. My reading of the two poems below differs somewhat from that of the editor of *Sasamegoto*, Kidō Saizō, as paraphrased in the headnotes. That is, I neither detect any sense of "gloom" (*monousa*) in the first poem nor feel that *mi zo aranu* in Shōtetsu's piece refers to the sense of transience as commonly understood. I note the difference to alert the reader to the fact that my aim is specific, and it is to construe the poems, within the context of their placement in the treatise, as manifestations of *ushin* as meditation process or state of mind.

10. In Teika's personal collection, *Shūi gusō* 拾遺愚草, the poem appears under the heading "A Hundred-poem Sequence on Dwelling in Tranquility, composed in Bunji 3 [1187] Winter, with Etchū-jijū [Fujiwara Ietaka]." *Fujiwara Teika zenkashu*, ed. Kubota Jun (Tokyo: Kawade Shobō Shinsha, 1985), 1: 52, no. 308. It also appears as *FGS* 106 under Spring; the headnote there (p. 71) reads the poem as expressing the unadulterated loneliness of things.

11. In Shōtetsu's personal collection, *Sōkonshū*, V: 3844, this appears under the topic "Morning Glory Flower." See *Shikashū taisei* 5: 647. The text of the poem lacks the last three lines in this compendium's base text, the Gosho-bon in the Imperial Archives; they are provided from the Sonkeikaku-bon in the "Kaidai" section, p. 924, and confirmed, of course, by the *Sasamegoto* text.

12. Jonathan Culler, "Changes in the Study of Lyric," in *Lyric Poetry: Beyond New Criticism*, ed. Chaviva Hosek and Patricia Parker (Ithaca, N.Y.: Cornell University Press, 1981), p. 50, passim. Culler seems particularly inspired in this new view of the apostrophe by Paul de Man's work on the subject.

Chapter Twelve

1. Here follows the Shunzei anecdote cited above.

2. See Taikō Yamasaki, *Shingon: Japanese Esoteric Buddhism*, trans, and adapted by Cynthia Peterson and Gregory Peterson (Boston: Shambhala, 1988), pp. 75–79. Significantly, in the Foreword (p. xi), Carmen Blacker describes the religious practice of identifying one's mind, body, and speech with the Vairocana Buddha as "symbolic mimesis."

Chapter Thirteen

1. These pairs and numerous others are listed in the *Renga shinshiki* rulebook under the heading *uchikoshi o kirau* (things that must be separated by more than one verse), a rule that implicitly recognizes their common occurrence in two contiguous

verses. The magnetic pull between the two items of a yoriai pair was strongly prohibited across one-verse intervals—that is, between verse 1 and 3 of any three-verse passage—because it signaled a "karmic" regression in the flow of the sequence. The standard modern source for such pairs is the one I have been citing earlier, Ichijō Kanera's "thesaurus," *Renju gappekishū*, in *Rengaronshū 1*, pp. 26-202.

2. M. M. Bakhtin, *Speech Genres and Other Late Essays*, trans. Vern W. McGee (Austin: University of Texas Press, 1986), p. 76; this is an eminently useful source for understanding the dialogical aspect of renga.

3. See *The Dialogic Imagination: Four Essays by M. M. Bakhtin*, trans. Caryl Emerson and Michael Holquist (Austin: University of Texas Press, 1981), pp. 275–300.

4. *Ichigon* (One word) is a brief, unpublished manuscript in the Osaka University Archives; the pagination is based on a handwritten copy kindly provided to the author by the late Kaneko Kinjirō, the foremost renga scholar of his time.

5. In translating this passage, I have supplied the last line, missing in the *Kodai chūsei geijutsuron* base text, from the Gosho-bon (Palace Text) of *Oi no kurigoto* in the Imperial Household Archives, the base text used in *Rengaronshū 3*, ed. Kidō Saizō, *Chūsei no bungaku* ser. (Tokyo: Miya'i Shoten, 1985); see p. 381 there.

6. See Itō Hiroyuki, "Shinkeiron," *Bungaku* 25, 3 (1957): 65–70.

7. For examples of "elitist" tone and opinions, see *Sasamegoto* §§ 18–19; 21–24.

8. For a closely argued critique of the possibility of recovering the author's intention in order to prove the validity of one's interpretation, see David Couzens Hoy, *The Critical Circle: Literature, History, and Philosophical Hermeneutics* (Berkeley: University of California Press, 1978).

9. "Implements," that is, what Shinkei calls *gusoku* 具足 in the advice to Kenzai, meaning objects of use and accessories like furniture or the armor of warriors.

10. Bakhtin, "From Notes Made in 1970–71," in id., *Speech Genres and Other Essays*, p. 142.

11. For the concept of iterability in conjunction with the issue of context, see Jacques Derrida, "Signature, Event, Context," in id., *Margins of Philosophy*, trans. Alan Bass (Chicago: University of Chicago Press, 1982), pp. 307–30.

Chapter Fourteen

1. Shinkei's hokku appears in *Shinsen Tsukubashū-shō* [excerpts from the second imperial renga anthology], ed. Ijichi Tetsuo, in *Rengashū*, NKBT 39 (Tokyo: Iwanami Shoten, 1960), p. 263, no. 227; also in the *Chikurinshō*, ed. Shimazu Tadao et al., SNKBT 49 (Tokyo: Iwanami Shoten, 1991), p. 370, no. 1825.

2. *Shinsen Tsukubashū-shō*, p. 256, no. 176; also *Chikurinshō*, p. 234, no. 1111. See *HF*, p. 252, for an exegesis.

3. Haga Kōshirō, *Higashiyama bunka* (Tokyo: Haniwa Shobo, 1962), p. 173. One of Haga's leading ideas in this book is that the old aristocratic aesthetics of courtly grace and splendor constituted the ground of Higashiyama culture, while the unadorned and withered beauty best represented by Shinkei and Zenchiku was its loftiest development.

4. *Kenzai zōdan, NKT* 5: 413.

5. Yoshimoto most likely means the gathas (verses) in the Buddhist sutras; the poems certifying enlightenment in the Zen records of a patriarch's sayings; and poetry expressing the sympathetic responsiveness between deities or deities and lay people in Japanese Buddhist narratives.

6. Bukkoku-zenji refers to Kennichi 顕日 (1241–1316), a high priest of the Rinshū Zen sect and a son of Emperor Gosaga. Musō Kokushi, or Soseki 疎石 (1275–1351), also of the Rinshū, was the founder of Tenryūji; he has thirteen verses appearing in the first official renga anthology *Tsukubashū* (1356–57), compiled by Yoshimoto himself.

7. *Tsukuba mondō* (Tsukuba Dialogues, 1372), *RH*, pp. 82–83.

8. See *Jūmon saihishō* (On Ten Most Secret Questions [1383]), *RH*, pp. 111–12.

9. Rudolf Arnheim makes a similar point about how the absence of color in black-and-white film enables more vivid and arresting symbolic effects precisely due to the formal restriction. Arnheim, *Film as Art* (Berkeley: University of California Press, 1957), pp. 65–73. Arnheim's discussion of montage, the joining together of scenes that have no inherent time-space continuity or, conversely, the separation of scenes that do, is also very suggestive of the affinity of linked poetry with filmic sequence.

10. Earl Miner, *Japanese Linked Poetry* (Princeton, N.J.: Princeton University Press, 1979), p. 136.

11. In Bashō's travel diary, *Oi no kobumi*, in *Teihon Bashō taisei*, ed. Ogata Tsutomu (Tokyo: Sanseidō, 1959), p. 301.

12. *Shinsen Tsukubashū-shō*, p. 253, no. 156.

13. From *Sōgi jisankachū* and *Kenzai jisankachū* as cited by Kubota Jun in *Shinkokinshū*, 2: 361.

14. *Makashikan* 1: 139.

15. *Makashikan* 1: 25–26; the translation of this passage is from Neil Donner and Daniel B. Stevenson, *The Great Calming and Contemplation: A Study and Annotated Translation of the First Chapter of Chih-i's Mo-ho-chi-kuan* (Honolulu: University of Hawaii Press, 1993), p. 115.

16. The Buddhist technical terms in this and other similarly encumbered passages are explained in the annotations to my translation of *Sasamegoto*, which is the *engi* of this whole study.

17. The first term of the Western classical triad, the "good" as a characteristic of the being of phenomena in their oneness with godhead, is interestingly absent in the terminology of classical Japanese criticism. However, phenomena seen and depicted poetically, with a pure heart and a contemplative gaze, might conceivably correspond to a concept of the "good." The question requires to be thought out further, complicated as it is by the absence of the one God, and by the principle of nondualism, in the Buddhist system.

Chapter Fifteen

1. I insert the Heideggerian word *auslegen* (to lay out) here to signal that my reading of this poem, as well as the next, is an interpretation (*Auslegung*). In addressing the concept of the hermeneutic circle in *Being and Time*, Heidegger theorizes that an interpretation is the explication or discursive laying out—in sum, the *external* articulation—of an initial implicit understanding. See Martin Heidegger, *Being and Time*, trans. John Macquarrie and Edward Robinson (New York: Harper & Row, 1962), pp. 188-95.

Glossary of Key Terms and Concepts

Alterity The double structure of signs: the signifier is itself only within a relation of difference from other signifiers in the system; similarly, the signified is governed by other signifieds; hence, any sign is both itself and other (alter) or, more radically, it is itself only by force of the other. In renga, the maeku may be seen as a signifier whose signified is revealed by the tsukeku; in this sense, each verse is inhabited, so to speak, by the other that precedes and follows it in the sequence, to which it is thus in a relation of alterity. Alterity recognizes the absence of self-identity and the mutual dependency of polar oppositions.

Ambiguity, The Mode of Refers to *fumyōtei*, the style of a poem whose logic and hence semantic content is deliberately unclear, ambiguous, or even self-contradictory on the level of diction, but evokes a sense of the ineffable depth of phenomena when actively interpreted by the reader. Shinkei states that it is a mode "constituted solely of nuance" and identifies it with the ultimate Dharma Body.

Aware あはれ In medieval aesthetics, the moving power of things when understood in their nature as lacking a substantial core and hence empty; as only provisionally real in being produced by temporally governed circumstance; and as ultimately indeterminate. This construction of the ineffable nature of things encourages a sense of the mystery of their existence, not a denial of it; similarly, the mundane understanding of their mutability encourages a sense of pathos, stoicism, and compassion. If there is, historically, a "Japanese" sense of basic human decency, of what it means to be a civilized human being in the world, then *aware* would be at its core.

Clashing *Uchikoshi o kirau*, clashing across one-verse intervals, a basic rule in renga that is designed to prevent the occurrence of coded pairs of associations beyond the two-verse linking nexus. Clashing was thought to produce a monotonous regression to an earlier association, and hence was also known as *rinne* (karmic return).

Darani (or *dharani*) Mystical words and phrases chanted by the Buddhist aspirant in order to concentrate his/her mind and empower it to fuse with the ultimate principle; the medieval view of poetry as *darani* is based on the understanding of the poem as the symbolic figuration of a mind in meditation on the principles of Suchness and of the Real.

Différance   A concept, philosophical observation, and neologism stemming from the work of the contemporary French philosopher Jacques Derrida. Based on the Saussurean analysis of language as a formal system of internal differences among the terms (phonemes, morphemes, statements, etc.) that constitute it, the concept of *différance* takes that analysis further by noting that as a consequence of this postulate of the mutually conditioning relation of the terms of a language, meaning, that which is signified by the sign, is never fully, simply, and positively present except as a trace or effect of the differences among the other signs that generate it, and that as an effect of this play of differences, meaning is constantly and ever *deferred* by the same system that solicits it. (Thus, a word is defined by other words, and those in turn by others ad infinitum, and there is no final determination of its meaning but only a provisional one governed by its relation to contexts that themselves are also provisional.) *Différance* is a productive concept for analyzing the renga link as a signifying relation of opposition, or difference, between maeku and tsukeku; the significance, moreover, is constantly revised and deferred until the sequence ends, as a matter of formal convention, with verse 100.

Duration   Also known as Seriation; the minimum and maximum number of verses through which a theme is allowed to continue once it is introduced at any point in a 100-verse sequence. For example, the seasonal themes of Spring or Autumn had a Duration value of three verses minimum and five maximum. This rule was designed to ensure sequential continuity and coherence. See also *Intermission*.

Emptiness   See *Kū*.

En 艶   Compelling grace or allure, the "seductive" quality of the evocative, the indirect and nuanced; Shinkei's term *kokoro no en* (spiritual radiance, compelling grace) refers to poetry that specifically evokes the charismatic quality of the hidden realm of principle by investing the sensual or material with the sheen of numinosity. See also *Yūgen*.

Engi 縁起   Dependent origination, the concept that phenomena lack self-identity or essential nature, as evidenced by the fact that they come into existence, change, and disappear through mutable circumstance or the workings of *innen* (cause and effect, causation). For this reason, *engi* is also another word for "history," particularly temple histories.

Existential Loneliness   See *Sabi*.

Fumyōtei 不明躰   See *Ambiguity, Mode of*.

Hen-jo-dai-kyoku-ryū 辺序題曲流   Literally, "prelude-beginning-topic-statement-dissolve," a technical term referring to the structural progression of the five-line waka poem; Shinkei uses the concept to explain the bipartite structure of the link between upper and lower verses (or maeku and tsukeku) in renga as a functional, codependent opposition between the apparently essential and its supplement.

Hermeneusis   The process of reading and interpreting a prior text, an activity understood in Japanese cultural history as the necessity of explicating the Chinese secular classics and Buddhist scriptures in such a way as to make them accessible to a Japanese understanding. The difficulty of reading renga led early on to the production of interpretive readings for the benefit of beginners and practitioners in various levels of training. In this book, the practice of linking as such is conceived, on the basis of Shinkei's analysis of it, as an instance of hermeneusis, in the sense that the tsukeu is an interpretive reading, or translation, of the maeku.

Hiesabi 冷え寂び   "Chill and still," an aesthetic-philosophical quality synonymous with the meditative state of mind of *shikan* (tranquility and insight) as registered in the impersonal stillness of phenomena in poetic figuration.

Hieyase 冷え痩せ   "Chill and reduced," "chill and meager"; also rendered as "cold and slender." Synonymous with *sabi*. As a description of formal poetic rhetoric, it refers to a precise and economic diction wherein a change in one single word would alter the effect of the whole verse or poem. This formal characteristic of tautness and tensility, however, is linked in Shinkei's poetics with the philosophical perspective of the Style of Meditation.

Hōben 方便   Skillful means, a Buddhist concept used by Shinkei to justify the value of mundane poetry based on words and form as a preliminary stage toward a higher realm. While he distinguishes a higher poetry that discards the conventional meanings and logic of language in order to evoke the ultimate principle, ultimately, he seems to hold that all poetry is itself but a means to enlightenment, an instrument and medium of meditation.

Hon'i 本意   Essential nature; apparently refers to the specific characteristics that make certain phenomena recognizably what they are, as rendered through centuries of unvarying poetic composition on the same traditional themes and images. However, the phrase *uta no hon'i* (the essential nature of poetry) as used by Shunzei refers to poetry specifically as a practice in the symbolic figuration of phenomena as apprehended in the Tendai three truths concept. Hence the critical history of *hon'i* usage must be rethought within this conceptual understanding, that is, as referring to the poetic-philosophical understanding of phenomena in all their mutability, their essential nature as appearance without substance, their coming-to-be and their disappearing within the context of a network of circumstance.

Horizon   Aspects of the intentional object that are not directly grasped by the subject at the specific moment of perception, but may be activated or recalled later in further acts of perception and reflection. These dormant aspects belong to the object as its "horizon." The phenomenal objects or images used in renga, such as plum blossoms or haze, may be understood as components or indices of a larger horizon, to which is given the thematic name, for example, of Spring. Hence a verse on haze implicitly includes, as a dormant, potential aspect, plum blossoms, melting snow, and the other "phenomenal" components of the Spring "horizon." In this sense, renga happens by the progressive actualization or expansion of horizons from one verse to the next. This description entails that the renga poets share common horizons through training in the language of the waka tradition; they exchange, as it were, a common phenomenal consciousness whose objects have been constituted by earlier poets. This fact does not, needless to say, wholly account for the wit or mental acuity by which each poet turns the maeku around to yield a new side of the object or even achieves a fusion of distinct horizons.

Hyakuin 百韻   Hundred-verse sequence; the standard length of a renga sequence composed by a group; can also be composed by a single poet as an exercise or solo performance.

Hyakushu 百首   Hundred-poem sequence, typically composed by a single poet as a small personal waka anthology arranged according to such conventional topics as the four seasons, love, and Buddhism.

Ineffable Depth   See *Yūgen*.

Innen 因縁   Cause and effect; causation, the principle that phenomena arise from the operation of internal cause (*in*) and external circumstance (*en*). The renga link may also be seen as the figurative and allegorical operation of *innen* when the maeku is taken as the internal cause and the tsukeku as the external circumstance, or vice versa. It must be noted that Buddhist philosophy gives equal value to *en* or external circumstance in the explanation or adjudication of effects, hence the importance of design, context, and milieu in Japanese aesthetic cognition and in Japanese social relations in general.

Intentionality   A term and concept in Husserlian phenomenology referring to the fact that consciousness is always consciousness of something; it is always "intended" toward an object. The concept aims to explain objects not simply as predetermined physical entities out there, but as products of the subject's "intentional" acts of consciousness, which constitutes them and endows them with meaning. For this reason, intentionality is a useful concept for theorizing the linking process as a phenomenological act of constituting the maeku as an object. See also *Horizon*.

Intermission   The number of verses on a different theme or themes that must intervene before the same theme is reintroduced at any point in the 100-verse sequence. For example, once a Spring passage has concluded, Spring may not recur until after a minimum of seven verses on a different theme have passed. The converse of the Duration rule, the Intermission rule was designed to ensure variation and change in the course of the sequence.

Ishin Denshin 以心伝心   "By mind transmit the mind," a Zen aphorism signifying that the ultimate principle, or wisdom, is achieved only through the personal experience of meditation; it cannot be taught through words alone. A master proposes a conundrum to a disciple and certifies whether he has arrived at the ultimate understanding by the quality of his response, whether manifested through words or gesture. The verbal logic and import of these cases, called kōan, are frequently obscure to the noninitiate who has not undergone the necessary mental transformation. Shinkei's foregrounding of *kokoro* implicitly compares the dialogical transaction of renga to the event of *ishin denshin*. A Buddhist-influenced medieval poetics tends to see it also as a paradigm for true poetic understanding and judgment, in accordance with the view that poetic composition is a meditational practice. The valorization of immediate perception (*jikkan*), an apparently intuitive acuity of response, in Japanese literary criticism until modern times manifests the historical importance of this enduring paradigm.

Iterability   The repeatability of discourse due to its inscription in a common language or in the general circulation of signs. Every iteration, however, occurs in a new and different context, hence it is necessarily different from—embodies a specific context-bound understanding of—the anterior discourse. Every text is a modified iteration of another text or texts; the same may be said of the renga verse when it achieves a link with its maeku.

Jo-Ha-Kyū 序破急   "Prelude-Break-Climax," the tripartite structural progression of a play or series of plays in Nō performance, also the progression of a 100-verse renga. A technical term originally from music, it describes the order of movement of a renga sequence as beginning from simplicity, developing through various orders of complexity, and returning to simplicity at the end. The Nō playwright and theorist Zeami, however, remarkably conceives the Break (or Development) section as a hermeneutic operation, a breaking-up and laying out in detail of the Prelude, and the Climax as a kind of crisis wherein dance and song rise to the most intense and violent pitch in the final act. *Jo-ha-kyū* is a complex concept with various applications in Nō and renga theory; ultimately, it is a principle of symbolic animation (of the physical and verbal gesture) that reflects the medieval understanding of process and motion or succession as embodied in a fully realized action on stage, in words that actually "speak" in poetry. It is important to note that both Zeami and Shinkei understand the process indicated by *jo-ha-kyū* as a signifying relationship among prior, present, and final moments.

Kehai けはひ   Aura, emanation, ambiance; see *Omokage*.

Kokoro 心   Heart-mind or, simply, mind, that which may be sensed in the diction, configuration, content, and aura of the poem or verse. While there is a tendency to set language against *kokoro* (as feeling or thought) in the history of waka poetics, there is also a recognition that the two are mutually dependent, like the wings of a bird in flight. Medieval poetics as expounded by its leading innovative poets like Shunzei and Teika, and later, Shōtetsu and Shinkei, is specifically distinguished by an overriding concern for the *kokoro* of the poem, for the poem as the figuration of a meditative state of mind (*ushin*), which is sensed as an aura or as such "aesthetic" qualities as ineffable depth.

Kotowari 理   Meaning, logic, or content of a poem; medieval symbolic poetry and poetics set less store by meaning or logic than by the wordless "aura" that emanates from the poem's words and configuration as sensed by the reader. Shunzei praised poetry whose meaning is neither clear nor determinate, yet evokes ineffable depth, and Shinkei saw poetry as "located" where there is no meaning (*kotowari naki tokoro ni*), that is, where the conventional semantic boundaries begin to merge and undergo slippage. However, in the phrase *en fukaki kotowari* (the profoundly compelling principle), *kotowari* is synonymous with *ri* (same graph) and refers to the ultimate truth.

Kū 空 (Skt. *śūnyatā*)   Emptiness, the absence of an eternal, unchanging core or essence in phenomena, since they come into existence through circumstance. One of the "three truths" in Tendai Buddhism, the concept should not be viewed negatively (except as a propaedeutic to discourage illusion), since the intrinsic emptiness of phenomena also signifies their character as a trace of other phenomena, hence emptiness is also a mark of fullness.

Maeku 前句   The immediately preceding verse to which the next verse must link in a renga sequence; in the sequence, each verse except the first verse, or hokku, functions as the maeku to the immediately following verse or tsukeku. In standard citations of a pair of verses from any renga sequence, the author of the maeku is not usually identified, since the point in such quotations is to show the skill of the tsukeku poet being cited.

Mae-maeku 前々句   The verse prior to the immediately preceding verse or maeku. While in renga, each verse need link only directly to the maeku, in practice, the poet must also attend to the mae-maeku in order to prevent the infraction of the rule against clashing.

Moto no Kokoro 基の心   The fundamental nature of things as understood in the Tendai "three truths" (*sandai*) concept; see also *Hon'i*.

Mujō 無常   Mutability or temporality, the coming into appearance and subsequent dissolution of things through the vicissitudes of time; epistemologically related to the absence of an eternal core, essence, or substance in things, hence their emptiness. *Mujō* may be said to be one of the principal registers of the Japanese traditional aesthetic sensibility, both in its privative and ecstatic modes. It is crucial to the experience of compassion, and a fundamental element in the awakening of religious faith.

Omokage 面影   The aura, ambiance, nuance, or phenomenal image suggested or given off by the diction and configuration of a poem. In medieval poetics, it is understood as the trace, shadow, or reflection cast by the poet's contemplative gaze on phenomena. In the history of classical poetics, the value placed on *omokage* is a distinctly medieval development. See also *Ambiguity*.

Real, The   In this book, renders *jissō*, the state of "ultimate" reality. May correspond to the truth of the Middle, which is that of the indeterminacy of phenomena conceived between the mundane polar oppositions of contingent reality and emptiness; synonymous with *shinnyo* (the true likeness) or Suchness, the way things really are as apprehended by a buddha or a person in a state of achieved meditation and enlightenment. The highest stage of poetry aims to evoke the Real, which is beyond words as such. It is a way of seeing or state of understanding, not an entity as such.

Renga 連歌   Linked poetry composed extemporaneously by a group ranging from two or three to ten or more poets at a single session lasting six hours or longer for the standard length of 100 verses. The main poetic vehicle of the medieval period, and also of the Edo period in the more colloquial version known as *haikai no renga* or, simply, *haikai.*

Sabi 寂 Existential or "metaphysical" loneliness; the impersonal stillness and serenity of phenomena perceived in a state of meditation, as evoked in poetry and other arts like calligraphy, black-ink painting, the landscape garden, or the cult of tea.

Sandai 三諦 (or *santai*) See *Three Truths.*

Shikan 止観 "Tranquility and insight," the name for the method and effect of Zen meditation in the Tendai tradition; a state of mental stillness, clarity, and serenity; characterized by absence of grasping and by nondualism; reflected in poetry by the absence of any categorical meaning and of narrativity.

Shina 品 Refinement, grace, and dignity of expression, as distinct from the vulgar or mundane.

Shinji 心地 Mind-ground, the nondualistic "deep mind" that is the originary source of all phenomena, hence also the mind involved in the process of poetic composition, when poetry is oriented toward the symbolic figuration of the essential nature of phenomena in the Buddhist understanding.

Shinku 親句 The Close Link; in renga, describes a link easily comprehensible through the verbal and semantic associations between the two verses; also used in waka criticism to indicate the phonological and semantic continuity between the first three and the last two lines of a poem.

Soku 疎句 The Distant Link; in renga, describes a link that seems disjunctive in not being easily comprehensible through the usual verbal or semantic associative clues, but accessible through creative analysis and imagination. In waka, also describes the apparent gap or discontinuity between the upper and lower parts of the poem, usually underscored by a caesura in line 3. In general, the Reizei school, including Shōtetsu and Shinkei, placed a higher value on *soku* than *shinku* because of its potential for producing novel, subtle, and marvelous effects.

Śūnyatā See *Kū.*

Take Takashi 長高し Sublime tensility, a sense of spatiotemporal extension, distance, and remoteness; a precise economy of diction and cogency of syntax that produce a single, integral effect; in renga, a way of linking that dovetails precisely with the maeku, while suggesting the supramundane realm of noumenon.

Temporality See *Mujō.*

Three Truths (*sandai, santai*) The Tendai Buddhist concept of the nature of phenomena understood on three levels of understanding as (1) empty in lacking an essential, unchanging core; (2) contingent or provisional in arising from changing circumstance and the cultural constructions of language, but no less real in the conventional or mundane sense; and (3) "middle" or ambiguous (indeterminate) in being beyond the dualism of the first two truths. Meditation aims to arrive at an apprehension of the third truth, and the highest stage of poetic training is also called the Middle Way of poetry by Shunzei and Teika.

Tsukeai 付合   Linking, the process of relating to the preceding verse or maeku, which is the fundamental method of renga, where a verse is judged not in isolation but always according to its success or failure in linking up to the maeku. Tsukeai is analyzed in this book as a poetic demonstration of the Buddhist concept of dependent origination, or *engi*, the arising of phenomena through contextual circumstance. It may also be described as the generation of meaning through the dynamic operation of différance.

Tsukeku 付句   The linking verse, the verse that links up to the immediately preceding verse or maeku; the second verse in any pair of verses in a renga or haikai sequence. Note that in renga, any verse except the first and last is both a tsukeku to the preceding verse and a maeku to the following.

Uchikoshi O Kirau 打越を嫌ふ   See *Clashing*.

Ushin 有心   The Style of Meditation; also called, variously, "the style of intense feeling" or "a conviction of feeling" in *Japanese Court Poetry*. Refers to poetry that renders a contemplative state of mind rather than transmitting a particular idea or feeling. Teika holds that among the various styles, it embodies the essential nature of poetry in reflecting the depth of the poet's mind, its utmost concentration, such that there occurs a felt fusion between mind and language, or subject and object, and words themselves are liberated from their finite semantic boundaries in ordinary linguistic usage. Shinkei describes *ushin* as a state in which the mind (the narrow, divisive mind bound by linguistic constructions and discriminations) has dissolved and finds its home ground. Hence the sublime tensility of *take takashi* is also the manifestation of the utmost concentration of *ushin*.

Waka 和歌   The classic five-line poem composed by a single poet; follows a 5-7-5-7-7-syllable count; the first three lines are conventionally called the "upper verse" (*kami no ku*) and the last two lines the "lower verse" (*shimo no ku*). The 100-verse renga sequence may be seen as a continuing alternation of these two parts.

Yojō 余情 (or *yosei*)   "Uncontained feeling," the overtones and ambience of a poem that cannot be wholly accounted for by the words but leak between the lines, as it were. The term manifests the classical skepticism about the ability of language as such to express the ineffable nature of phenomena and of existence. Synonymous with *Omokage*.

Yōon 幽遠 (or *yūen*)   "Ineffable remoteness," the specific effect of a poem or renga link that transports the mind to the realm of ultimate reality; synonymous with Yūgen in evoking what is otherwise inexpressible. Remoteness refers to the perceived inner distance of the realm just beyond the power of words to contain and directly express.

Yoriai 寄合   Verbal correspondences; conventional associations among words, usually pairs of words with a "magnetic" affinity with each other, such as the pair "orange blossoms = cuckoo," as an effect of their repeated co-occurrence in older poems, narratives, and other canonical sources. Yoriai are employed in renga to effect a link from one verse to the next; dictionaries of yoriai, with illustrative poems and verses, proliferated; they are similar to *engo* (associative words like "snow = melt") in waka.

Yūgen 幽玄   "Ineffable depth," the incalculable "depth" of phenomena when understood as produced by a network of circumstances whose origin and extent are beyond determination. Rendered as "mystery and depth" in earlier English critical works on Japanese poetry. Along with *Aware, Sabi, Take Takashi, Ushin*, and *Yōon*, one of the inflections of the Japanese sublime.

Bibliography

Primary texts and compendia are listed under their titles and/or authors. Abbreviations are as listed on p. xi. Unless otherwise noted, place of publication for Japanese-language sources is Tokyo.

Western Sources

Arnheim, Rudolf. *Film as Art*. Berkeley: University of California Press, 1957.
Bakhtin, M. M. *The Dialogic Imagination: Four Essays by M. M. Bakhtin*. Translated by Caryl Emerson and Michael Holquist. Austin: University of Texas Press, 1981.
———. *Speech Genres and Other Late Essays*. Translated by Vern W. McGee. Austin: University of Texas Press, 1986.
Barthes, Roland. *Empire of Signs*. Translated by Richard Howard. New York: Hill & Wang, 1982.
———. *The Pleasure of the Text*. Translated by Richard Miller. New York: Farrar, Straus & Giroux, 1975.
Bethe, Monica, and Karen Brazell. *Dance in the Noh Theater*. 3 vols. Ithaca, N.Y.: East Asia Program, Cornell University, 1982.
———. *Nō as Performance: An Analysis of the Kuse Scene of Yamamba*. Ithaca, N.Y.: East Asia Program, Cornell University, 1978.
Brower, Robert, and Earl Miner. *Japanese Court Poetry*. Stanford: Stanford University Press, 1961. Cited as *JCP*.
Caputo, John D. *Radical Hermeneutics: Repetition, Deconstruction, and the Hermeneutic Project*. Bloomington: Indiana University Press, 1987.
Carter, Steven D. *The Road to Komatsubara: A Classical Reading of the Renga Hyakuin*. Cambridge, Mass.: Harvard University Press, 1987.
Cranston, Edwin A. "'Mystery and Depth' in Japanese Court Poetry." In *The Distant Isle: Studies and Translations of Japanese Literature in Honor of Robert H. Brower*, ed. Thomas Hare, Robert Borgen, and Sharalyn Orbaugh, pp. 65–104. Ann Arbor, Mich.: Center for Japanese Studies, University of Michigan, 1996.
Culler, Jonathan. *On Deconstruction: Theory and Criticism After Structuralism*. Ithaca, N.Y.: Cornell University Press, 1982.

———. "Changes in the Study of Lyric." In *Lyric Poetry: Beyond New Criticism*, ed. Chaviva Hosek and Patricia Parker. Ithaca, N.Y.: Cornell University Press, 1981.

Derrida, Jacques. *Positions*. Translated and annotated by Alan Bass. Chicago: University of Chicago Press, 1981.

———. "Différance." In *Margins of Philosophy*, trans. Alan Bass, pp. 1–27. Chicago: University of Chicago Press, 1982.

———. "Signature, Event, Context." In *Margins of Philosophy*, trans. Alan Bass, pp. 307–30. Chicago: University of Chicago Press, 1982.

———. "Structure, Sign, and Play in the Discourse of the Human Sciences." In *Writing and Difference*, trans. Alan Bass, pp. 278–93. Chicago: University of Chicago Press, 1978.

Donner, Neal and Daniel B. Stevenson. *The Great Calming and Contemplation: A Study and Annotated Translation of the First Chapter of Chih-i's mo-ho chi-kuan*. Honolulu: University of Hawaii Press, 1993.

Frege, Gottlob. "On *Sinn* and *Bedeutung*." In *The Frege Reader*, ed. Michael Beaney, pp. 151–71. London: Blackwell, 1997.

Gadamer, Hans-Georg. *Philosophical Hermeneutics*. Translated and edited by David E. Linge. Berkeley: University of California Press, 1976.

———. *Truth and Method*. Translated by Joel Weinsheimer and Donald G. Marshall. New York: Crossroad, 1989.

Garfield, Jay L., trans. and commentary. *The Fundamental Wisdom of the Middle Way: Nagarjuna's Mulamadhyamakakarika*. New York: Oxford University Press, 1995.

Heidegger, Martin. *Being and Time*. Translated by John Macquarrie and Edward Robinson. New York: Harper & Row, 1962.

———. *On the Way to Language*. Translated by Peter D. Hertz. New York: Harper & Row, 1971.

Hoy, David Couzens. *The Critical Circle: Literature, History, and Philosophical Hermeneutics*. Berkeley: University of California Press, 1978.

Husserl, Edmund. *Cartesian Meditations*. Translated by Dorion Cairns. The Hague: Martinus Nijhoff, 1970.

———. "Essential Distinctions" and "Towards a Characterization of the Acts Which Confer Meaning." In *The Hermeneutics Reader*, ed. Kurt Mueller-Vollmer, pp. 166–86. New York: Continuum, 1985.

———. *The Shorter Logical Investigations*. Translated by J. N. Findlay. New York: Routledge, 2001.

Jacobson, Roman. "Linguistics and Poetics." In id., *Language in Literature*, ed. Krystyna Pomorska and Stephen Rudy. Cambridge, Mass.: Harvard University Press, Belknap Press, 1987.

Kalupahana, David J., trans. and annotation. *Nagarjuna: The Philosophy of the Middle Way*. Albany: State University of New York Press, 1986.

LaFleur, William R. *The Karma of Words: Buddhism and the Literary Arts in Medieval Japan*. Berkeley: University of California Press, 1983.

Loy, David. "The Clōture of Deconstruction: A Mahayana Critique of Derrida." *International Philosophical Quarterly* 27, 1 (March 1987): 59–88.

Miner, Earl. *Japanese Linked Poetry*. Princeton, N.J.: Princeton University Press, 1979.

Miyoshi Masao and H. D. Harootunian, eds. *Postmodernism and Japan*. Durham, N.C.: Duke University Press, 1989.

Moran, Dermot. *Introduction to Phenomenology*. New York: Routledge, 2000.

Murasaki Shikibu. *The Tale of Genji*. Translated by Edward Seidensticker. 2 vols. New York: Knopf, 1977.

Nietzsche, Friedrich. "On Truth and Lies in a Nonmoral Sense." In *Philosophy and Truth: Selections from Nietzsche's Notebooks from the Early 1870's*, ed. and trans. Daniel Breazeale. Atlantic Highlands, N.J.: Humanities Press International, 1979.

Ramirez-Christensen, Esperanza. *Heart's Flower: The Life and Poetry of Shinkei*. Stanford: Stanford University Press, 1994. Cited as *HF*.

Ricoeur, Paul. *The Rule of Metaphor: Multidisciplinary Studies of the Creation of Meaning in Language*. Translated by Robert Czerny with Kathleen McLaughlin and John Costello, SJ. Toronto: University of Toronto Press, 1977.

Saussure, Ferdinand de. *Course in General Linguistics*. Translated by Wade Baskin. Glasgow: Collins/Fontana, 1974.

Taylor, Mark C., ed. *Deconstruction in Context: Literature and Philosophy*. Chicago: University of Chicago Press, 1986.

Thornhill, Arthur H., III. *Six Circles, One Dewdrop: The Religio-Aesthetic World of Komparu Zenchiku*. Princeton, N.J.: Princeton University Press, 1993.

Wittgenstein, Ludwig. *Tractatus Logico-Philosophicus*. Translated by D. F. Pears and B. F. McGuiness. London: Routledge & Kegan Paul, 1961.

Yamasaki Taikō. *Shingon: Japanese Esoteric Buddhism*. Translated and adapted by Cynthia Peterson and Gregory Peterson. Boston: Shambhala, 1988.

Zeami Motokiyo. *On the Art of the Nō Drama: The Major Treatises of Zeami*. Translated by J. Thomas Rimer and Yamazaki Masakazu. Princeton, N.J.: Princeton University Press, 1984.

Japanese Sources

Amagasaki Akira. *Kachō no tsukai*. Keisō Shobō, 1983.

Bashō. *Oi no kobumi*. In *Teihon Bashō taisei*, ed. Ogata Tsutomu. Sanseidō, 1959.

Chikuenshō (ca. 1278). Attributed to Fujiwara Tameie's son Tameaki. *NKT* 3 (1963): 410–28.

Chikurinshō. Renga anthology compiled by Sōgi. In *Chikurinshō*, ed. Shimazu Tadao et al. *SNKBT* 49. Iwanami Shoten, 1991.

Chōtanshō (1390) by Bontō. In *Rengaronshū*, ed. Ijichi Tetsuo, 1: 144–202. Iwanami Shoten, 1953.

Chūgoku shijin senshū. Series edited by Yoshikawa Kōjirō and Ogawa Tamaki. 18 vols. Iwanami Shoten, 1958–61.

Fūgashū. Seventh imperial anthology, ca. 1348. In *Fūgawakashū*, ed. Tsugita Kōzumi and Iwasa Miyoko. Miya'i Shoten, 1974. Cited as *FGS*.

Fujiwara Teika. *Kindai shūka* [Superior Poems of Our Time]. Edited by Fujihira Haruo. In *Karonshū*, *NKBZ* 50: 467–90.

———. *Maigetsushō* [Monthly Notes, 1219?]. Edited by Fujihira Haruo. In *Karonshū*, *NKBZ* 50: 511–30.

Genji monogatari. In *Genji monogatari*, ed. Abe Akio et al. 6 vols. *NKBZ* 12–17. Shōgakkan, 1970–76.

Guhishō. Edited by Sasaki Nobutsuna. In *NKT* 4 (1958): 291–312.

Haga Kōshirō. *Higashiyama bunka*. Haniwa Shobo, 1962.

Ichijō Kanera. *Renju gappekishū* [before 1476]. Edited by Kidō Saizō and Shigematsu Hiromi. *In Rengaronshū 1*. Miya'i Shoten, 1972.

———. *Renga shogakushō* [Notes for Renga Beginners]. Edited by Ijichi Tetsuo. In *Rengaronshū*, 2: 287–310. Iwanami Shoten, 1956.

Itō Hiroyuki, "Shinkeiron." *Bungaku* 25, 3 (1957): 65–70.

Jichin oshō jikaawase [Priest Jichin's Solo Poem Contest]. Edited by Taniyama Shigeru. In *Utaawaseshū*. NKBT 74: 461–76. Iwanami Shoten, 1968.

[Retired Emperor] Juntoku. *Yakumo mishō* [The Sovereign's Eightfold Cloud Treatise]. Edited by Sasaki Nobutsuna. In *NKT* 3: 9–94. Kazama Shobō, 1956.

Kamo no Chōmei. *Mumyōshō*. Edited by Hisamatsu Sen'ichi. In *Karonshū Nōgakuronshū*. *NKBT* 65: 35–98. Iwanami Shoten, 1961.

Karonshū. Edited by Hashimoto Fumio, Ariyoshi Tamotsu, and Fujihira Haruo. *NKBZ* 50. Shōgakkan, 1975.

Karonshū Nōgakuronshū. Edited by Hisamatsu Sen'ichi and Nishio Minoru. *NKBT* 65. Iwanami Shoten, 1961.

Kenzai. *Kenzai zōdan* [A Miscellany of Kenzai's Lectures]. In *NKT* 5: 390–425. Kazama Shobō, 1977.

Kidō Saizō. *Renga shironkō*, 2 vols. Meiji Shoin, 1973.

———. *Sasamegoto no kenkyū*. Rinsen Shoten, 1990. First published as *Kōchū Sasamegoto kenkyū to kaisetsu*. Rokusan Shoin, 1952. Cited as *Kenkyū*.

Kodai chūsei geijutsuron. Edited by Hayashiya Tatsusaburō. Vol. 23 in the *Nihon shisō taikei* series. Iwanami Shoten, 1973.

Kokinshū. In *Kokinwakashū*, ed. Ozawa Masao. *NKBZ* 7. Shōgakkan, 1971. Cited as *KKS*.

Konishi Jin'ichi. "Shunzei no yūgenfū to shikan." *Bungaku* 20, 2 (1952): 12–20.

Korai fūteishō [Poetic Styles from Antiquity to the Present, 1197–1201]. *See under* Shunzei.

Kubota Jun, ed. *Fujiwara Teika zenkashu*. 2 vols. Kawade Shobō Shinsha, 1985–86.

———, ed. *Shinkokin wakashū zenhyōshaku*. 9 vols. Kōdansha, 1977.

Maigetsushō. *See under* Fujiwara Teika.

Makashikan. Translated by Sekiguchi Shindai. 2 vols. Iwanami Shoten, 1966.

Minase sangin hyakuin [Three Poets at Minase]. *See under* Sōgi, Shōhaku, and Sōchō.

Mumyōshō. *See under* Kamo no Chōmei.

Nihon kagaku taikei. Edited by Sasaki Nobutsuna. 10 vols. Kazama Shobō, 1956–63. Cited as *NKT.*

Nihon koten bungaku taikei, Edited by Takagi Ichinosuke et al. 102 vols. Iwanami Shoten, 1956–68. Cited as *NKBT.*

Nihon koten bungaku zenshū, Edited by Akiyama Ken et al. 51 vols. Shōgakkan, 1970–76. Cited as *NKBZ.*

Nijō Yoshimoto. *Jūmon saihishō.* [On Ten Most Secret Questions, 1383]. Edited by Kidō Saizō. In *Rengaronshū Haironshū,* 109–17.

———. *Tsukuba mondō* [Tsukuba Dialogues, 1372]. Edited by Kidō Saizō. In *Rengaronshū Haironshū,* pp. 69–106.

Rengaronshū. Edited by Ijichi Tetsuo. 2 vols. Iwanami Shoten, 1953, 1956. Cited as *RS.*

Rengaronshū. Chūsei no bungaku ser. 4 vols. to date. Vol. 1, ed. Kidō Saizō and Shigematsu Hiromi; vols. 2–4, ed. Kidō Saizō. Miya'i Shoten, 1972, 1982, 1985, 1990.

Rengaronshū Haironshū. Edited by Kidō Saizō and Imoto Nōichi. *NKBT* 66. Iwanami Shoten, 1961. Cited as *RH.*

Rengaronshū Nōgakuronshū Haironshū. Edited by Ijichi Tetsuo, Omote Akira, and Kuriyama Ri'ichi. *NKBZ* 51. Shōgakkan, 1973.

Rengashū. Edited by Ijichi Tetsuo. *NKBT* 39. Iwanami Shoten, 1960.

Renju gappekishū. See under Ichijō Kanera.

[*Shinkō*] *Roppyakuban utaawase.* Edited by Konishi Jin'ichi. Yūseidō, 1976.

Sangoki [Full Moon Record]. Attributed to Fujiwara Teika. Edited by Sasaki Nobutsuna. In *NKT* 4: 313–53. Kazama Shobō, 1956.

Sengohyakuban utaawase. Edited by Taniyama Shigeru. In *Utaawaseshū. NKBT* 74: 477–518.

Senjun. *Katahashi.* In *Rengaronshū 3,* ed. Kidō Saizō, pp. 139–48.

Shikashū taisei, Edited by Wakashi Kenkyūkai. 7 vols. Meiji Shoin, 1973–76.

Shinkei. *Hitorigoto.* Edited by Shimazu Tadao. In *Kodai chūsei geijutsuron,* ed.Hayashiya Tatsusaburō, pp. 464–78.

———. "Ichigon" [One Word]. MS in the Ōsaka University Archives.

———. *Iwahashi no jo, batsu.* In *Rengaronshū, 1,* ed. Ijichi Tetsuo, pp. 331–39. The Epilogue also appears as "Iwahashi batsubun" in *Rengaronshū 3,* ed. Kidō Saizō, pp. 321–29.

———. *Oi no kurigoto.* Edited by Shimazu Tadao. In *Kodai chūsei geijutsuron,* pp. 410–22. Iwanami Shoten, 1973. Also in *Rengaronshū 3,* ed. Kidō Saizō, pp. 369–85. Cited as *Oi.*

———. *Sasamegoto* [Murmured Conversations]. Edited by Kido Saizō. In *Rengaronshū Haironshū,* pp. 119–204. *NKBT* 66. Iwanami Shoten, 1961. Cited as *SSG.*

———. [Revised] *Sasamegoto* text. Edited by Ijichi Tetsuo. In *Rengaronshū Nōgakuronshū Haironshū. NKBZ* 51: 65–160.

———. *Tokoro-dokoro hentō* [Replies Here and There]. Three letters. Edited by Kidō Saizō. In *Rengaronshū 3:* 261–90. Also in Ijichi Tetsuo, ed., *Rengaronshū,* 1: 305–30. Cited as *Tokoro.*

Shinkokinshū. In *Shinkokin wakashū zenhyōshaku*, ed. Kubota Jun. 9 vols. Kōdansha, 1977. Cited as *SKKS*.

Shinsen Tsukubashū-shō. Excerpts from the second imperial renga anthology. Edited by Ijichi Tetsuo. In *Rengashū*. *NKBT* 39: 175–342. Iwanami Shoten, 1960.

Shogaku yōshashō [Do's and Don'ts for the Beginner]. A Muromachi-period renga manual attributed to Sōgi, but most likely by a Shinkei disciple, perhaps Kenzai. In *Rengaronshū 2*, ed. Kidō Saizō, pp. 423–55.

Shōtetsu. *Sōkonshū*. In *Chūsei III, Shikashū taisei* 5: 532–870. Meiji Shoin, 1976.

Shōtetsu monogatari. Edited by Hisamatsu Sen'ichi. In *Karonshū, Nōgakuronshū, NKBT* 65: 165–234.

Shūi gusō. Fujiwara Teika's individual poetic anthology. In *Fujiwara Teika zenkashū*, ed. Kubota Jun.

Shunzei. *Korai fūteishō*. Edited by Ariyoshi Tamotsu. In *Karonshū, NKBZ* 50: 271–466.

Sōgi. *Oi no susami* [1479]. Edited by Kidō Saizō. In *Rengaronshū 2*: 137–86. Miya'i Shoten, 1982.

————, comp. *Chikurinshō*. In *Chikurinshō*, ed. Shimazu Tadao et al. *SNKBT* 49. Iwanami Shoten, 1991.

Sōgi, Shōhaku, and Sōchō. *Minase sangin hyakuin*. In *Rengashū*, ed. Ijichi Tetsuo. *NKBT* 39: 345–66. Iwanami Shoten, 1960.

Taishō shinshū daizōkyō. Edited by Takakusu Junjirō and Watanabe Kaigyoku. 85 vols. Taishō Issaikyō Kankōkai, 1924-32. Cited as *T*.

Tanaka Yutaka. *Chūsei bungakuron kenkyū*. Hanawa Shobō, 1969.

Teika. *Maigetsushō*. Edited by Fujihira Haruo. In *Karonshū, NKBZ* 50: 511–30.

Utaawaseshū. Edited by Hagitani Boku and Taniyama Shigeru. *NKBT* 74. Iwanami Shoten, 1965.

Waka bungaku jiten, Edited by Ariyoshi Tamotsu. Ōfūsha, 1991.

Wakan rōeishū. Edited by Kawaguchi Hisao. *NKBT* 73. Iwanami Shoten, 1965.

Zeami Motokiyo. *Kakyō* [The Mirror of the Flower, 1424]. Edited by Nishio Minoru. In *Karonshū Nōgakuronshū, NKBT* 65: 410–38.

————. *Sandō* [The Three Elements, 1423], also called *Nōsakusho* [The Book of Composing Plays]. In *NKBT* 65: 470–81.

————. *Shūgyoku tokka* [Gathering Gems and Realizing the Flower, 1428]. In *NKBT* 65: 454–68.

Index